To Woody Woodson —

with appreciation

George Roche

Books by the Hillsdale College Press include: the *Champions of Freedom* series; *The Christian Vision* series; *Historic Hillsdale;* and other works.

Ronald L. Trowbridge, Executive Editor
Lissa Roche, Managing Editor

IN THE FIRST PLACE: 20 YEARS OF THE MOST CONSEQUENTIAL IDEAS FROM HILLSDALE COLLEGE'S MONTHLY JOURNAL *IMPRIMIS*

First Printing 1992
Library of Congress Catalog Card Number: 91-078024
ISBN 0-916308-77-4

William J. Koshelnyk, Project Designer

Production Coordinated by Myers & Associates, Bryan, Ohio
   • Tim Dreier, Graphic Designer
   • William Kuhlman, Illustrator

Printed and Bound by Edwards Brothers, Ann Arbor, Michigan

IN
THE FIRST
PLACE

20 YEARS OF THE
MOST CONSEQUENTIAL IDEAS
FROM HILLSDALE COLLEGE'S
MONTHLY JOURNAL

IMPRIMIS

To Warren Brookes,

a member of the Remnant who passed away

as this volume went to press.

TABLE OF CONTENTS

FOREWORD

Years ago, it was Nobel economist and long-time Hillsdale friend F.A. Hayek who said, "we must make the building of a free society once more an intellectual adventure." His words ring truer than ever in this "age of information." We are in constant danger, it seems, of acquiring too much knowledge and too little wisdom, defending too many political agendas and too few first principles, paying attention to too many 60-second news stories and too few good books.

In its own way, Hillsdale College has taken Hayek's message to heart. That is why *Imprimis* was created in 1972, to publish, in a lively and entertaining format, some of the lectures presented in the College's unique on- and off-campus forums. Meaning "in the first place," *Imprimis* was first sent to a little over a thousand friends with the message, "If you like this, share it. We'll give anyone interested a lifetime free subscription—no strings attached."

And how it has grown! As I write, our circulation is 335,000; by the time this book rolls off the press, that figure will be obsolete. We are growing at a phenomenal rate. In a few years, we hope to reach a half-million readers every month. For a journal of opinion like *Atlantic Monthly, Harper's, National Review* or the *New Republic,* that kind of circulation would be outstanding; *Imprimis* is, in fact, *already* far larger than all of these. For a rural liberal arts college with a mere 1,200 or so students, it would be, in short, a miracle. Anyone familiar with this little school's nearly 150-year past knows, however, that miracles are our specialty.

In the meantime, we have another achievement to celebrate: January 1992 marks the 20-year anniversary of *Imprimis.* From more than 240 issues, we have selected a few of the very best, by authors who have themselves lived the kind of intellectual adventure Hayek described.

Today, when conservatism, or at least conservative rhetoric, is almost commonplace, it is easy to forget how startling—indeed, how *risky*—it was for figures like Ronald Reagan, Russell Kirk, Malcolm Muggeridge and Aleksandr Solzhenitsyn to publicly champion the free society, with its commitment to individual liberty, the free market, anti-communism and the Judeo-Christian heritage. It is still risky, if one is uncompromising about it, as George Gilder, Warren Brookes, Jeane Kirkpatrick and others featured here know.

We honor their courage. And we pledge that we will continue to share their ideas with the hundreds of thousands of heartland Americans who are *Imprimis*.

Because ideas have consequences.

January 1992
Hillsdale, Michigan

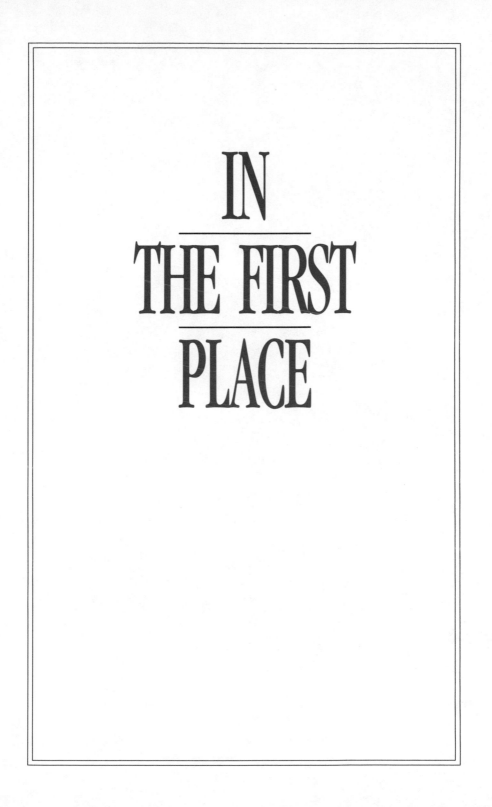

IN
THE FIRST
PLACE

EDUCATION
IN AMERICA

THE HILLSDALE IDEA

George Roche
October 1990

"WHAT HATH GOD WROUGHT?"

strange new device translated these pious words into impulses over an electrical wire. Another device at a distance received them instantly. History had changed. The barriers of time and space had fallen. Direct and immediate communication would henceforth be practical between anyone, in any land.

The words of Samuel F.B. Morse, farsighted yet humble, were a worthy message for a new era. For twelve years he had toiled to perfect his invention. He called it a telegraph, from Greek roots meaning "long distance" and "writing."

The year was 1844.

Please note the date. We will want to understand some perspectives from that long-ago time. This is difficult. More than twice man's "three score years and ten," two lifetimes, have passed. Indeed, from the view of 1844, five lifetimes have passed: for the average life expectancy then was less than thirty years. The changes since have been dizzying. In 1844, the Republic was young and robust. Within recent memory, two of its great Founders had died: Thomas Jefferson and John Adams, eerily, on the same day, July 4, 1826, the fiftieth anniversary of the Declaration of Independence. In little more than a half century, the population had grown about fourfold—from some 4,000,000 in 1790 to 17,069,453 in the 1840 census. The number of states had doubled, from the original thirteen to twenty-six. But in area, the country was only a quarter of the size it is today.

You would not recognize a map of America then. Its western reach extended no farther than the states along the Mississippi River: Louisiana, Arkansas and Missouri to the south, Illinois to the north. In part of Illinois, the Mississippi *was* the western frontier. Twenty-four of our present states were yet to join the Union: Florida in the south and all of the states to the west and north including the Great Plains, Hawaii and Alaska (the last two well over a century later). Only a few adventurers and trappers had penetrated the far West. The discovery of gold in California and the great westward migration it spurred still lay ahead.

Few of the great inventions we take for granted existed in 1844. The telephone was thirty years in the future, electric power forty, radio and the automobile fifty, the airplane sixty. Television, transistors, jet aircraft and computers were all a century away. Almost all transport was horse-drawn. The only powered conveyances were steamboats and the steam locomotive (introduced less than fifteen years earlier). Plumbing, where it existed, was crude, glass windows were a luxury, and household appliances as we know them did not exist. From our perspective, perhaps—but not from theirs—life, for most, was laborious, and amenities few. We would, however, be greatly mistaken in thinking our own life richer or more fulfilling. It was a time of great optimism, invention and energy, and of deep conviction in the "Great Experiment" that was America. Our country was secure in her faith, echoing St. Paul's famous declaration, "Where the spirit of the Lord is, there is liberty." It was not sodden as it is now with "problems" and guilt and self-doubts. America, born in a pilgrimage of unbelievable hardship from the Old World, was to be the "City on the Hill." A church was one of the first buildings at every crossroads settlement. The future looked grand.

In the realm of politics, America's watchword was liberty for all. Such phrases as "the land of the free" were by no means the exhausted political slogans they became later. They were the beacon and the reality. Do I exaggerate? You judge. In 1844, the spirit of the Revolution still animated America. Government was the implacable enemy of liberty, a potential tyrant, a barely necessary evil to be treated with suspicion and eternal vigilance and bound by the chains of the Constitution. Man was by nature free.

Accordingly, the power and reach of the federal government were duly and strictly limited. People usually lived their whole lives without encountering any federal presence other than the postman. And even the Post Office was under furious assault at the time from private entrepreneurs, who did the job faster and a lot cheaper. (The result was the Private Express Statutes giving the government a mail monopoly that still haunts us.)

There were no federal taxes. None. In fact, the income tax was a lifetime into the future. Federal spending was about $3 million per year. That is not a typo. It may seem so now that we are trying to "get used" to federal budgets in the trillions (a million millions), but it is correct: $3,000,000 – about fifteen cents per person per year. Needless to say, there was no bureaucracy worth mention, nor any welfarism, nor the ceaseless clamor by interest groups for handouts or privileges. The government had neither the power nor the money to buy votes.

Today the government spends more than a thousand times as much *every* day, and annually charges us something like $5,000 per person—man, woman and child—to do so. If there is any limit whatsoever on its power and grasp, I do not know it. The only constitutional rule I can think of that is still fully observed is electing two senators from each state. Since 1844, the smallest government in the world has become the largest. Does anybody in his right mind think we are better off because of this? And if not, where did we go astray, and what can we now do about it?

SESQUICENTENNIAL: HILLSDALE COLLEGE, 1844-1994

Never have we so needed to recall our roots. I do, of course, have a special reason for turning to the perspectives of 1844. In June of that year, a group of Free Will Baptists met in Michigan, newest of the twenty-six states. On the agenda was a resolution for the establishment of a denominational college. The motion was defeated. But a rump session refused to surrender the dream. They had "no endowment, no charter, no legal organization, no buildings, no library, no apparatus, no students."

So, in good American style, Michigan Central College was born within a few months. The new college began life on December 4, 1844, in Spring Arbor, Michigan. Its president and sole faculty member was Daniel McBride Graham, a June graduate of Oberlin College. School convened in a two-room deserted store so decrepit that snow came in through the chinks in the walls. In a few years, the school moved to the little town of Hillsdale and became Hillsdale College, of which I am privileged to be president.

The first class had five students. I feel as if I know them all. Let me tell you about two of them. One was Clinton Bowen Fisk, a "particularly lively pupil." These were abolitionist times, and Fisk meant to have a full say in ending slavery. He was an early Civil War volunteer, rose quickly in rank, and was a brevetted major general by the war's end. A year later, in 1866, he founded a school for Negroes in an army barracks in Nashville. Whether this was the first such school for freed slaves is unclear, but it was certainly among the first. A year later it was chartered as Fisk University. Before many years, freshmen at Fisk received a classical education, including readings in original Latin and Greek, and Bible studies in Hebrew. Harvard, today, does not even come close. Anyone who now sees limited educability among minorities or among any group is going to hear from me and from Clinton Bowen Fisk.

The other in that first class of five I'd like to mention was Livonia Benedict. She was the first woman in the state to be admitted to a degree program by a Michigan college on a par with men, and went on to be the first woman in Michigan and the second in the nation to earn the coveted Bachelor of Arts degree in 1852, and the second to earn a degree of any kind. (Her classmate, Elizabeth D. Camp of Palmyra, New York, was the first in the state to win a Bachelor of Science degree the year before.) Miss Benedict married the Reverend William Perrine, another Hillsdale graduate. She was a founder of the first auxiliary of the Women's Foreign Missionary Society of Michigan and a leader of the Women's Christian Temperance Union. After her husband died, she endowed a scholarship in the Bareilly Theological Seminary in North India in his name.

Nondiscrimination and true academic freedom were principles carved in stone at Hillsdale from its inception so long ago. We were graduating women and blacks more than a century before the federal government decided to get into the "equal opportunity" business. In the period 1868 to 1907, we also graduated foreign students (including women) from India, Prussia, England, Persia and

Japan, and a full-blooded Cherokee Indian from the Oklahoma Territory (he played guard on the 1893 championship football team). Women have been serving on the Hillsdale Board of Trustees continuously since 1893. Hillsdale was the first college in Michigan, and one of the first in the nation, to elect a female trustee and to employ women as faculty members.

The College had a showdown with federal officiousness as early as World War I. An army lieutenant (a Southerner) ruled that a black student, though otherwise qualified, could not serve in the regular Hillsdale R.O.T.C., but would have to be inducted into a Negro unit. This "touched off a flurry of telegrams between [Hillsdale] President Mauck and a War Department committee, resulting in final instructions to [the lieutenant] to follow the age-old Hillsdale practice of treating individuals without regard to color or creed."

But the real crunch came almost sixty years later, in 1975. Sticking to our first principles, we had a ferocious encounter with a federal bureaucratic machine that, in effect, ordered us to practice discrimination by admitting students and hiring faculty on the basis of race and gender. Little Hillsdale said no. We stood alone. We fought. We gave it everything we had. And, after many years of litigation, we lost to sheer federal power. That story follows. It is an eye-opener, especially as to the real purposes of some so-called "civil rights" laws.

Today, legislation to "correct" Hillsdale's insistence on its freedom has become law. What the legislation really attacks is *your* freedom, and in an unprecedented way. It will put you under the federal bureaucrat's thumb in your farm or factory, your school board or your city council, your corner store or your church. Its reach is without limit.

Hillsdale will fight again. But this time, if we must fight alone, you and all America will lose.

STANDING FIRM:
A TRUE STORY–WITH A WARNING FOR US ALL

The letter came as a shock.

I remember well that summer day in 1975 when it arrived. After fifteen years of litigation, legal fees and public discussion, I can say with feeling that nothing has been quite the same since at Hillsdale College. But I am proud of our stand, and can also say that Hillsdale has emerged the stronger for it, and more determined than ever to maintain its independence.

This is the story of what happened when a small private liberal arts college, standing alone, resisted regulation by the vast federal bureaucracy: regulation that would have compromised its academic integrity and freedom. It is a story that ought to alert every American that we each and all must be ready to fight again for our independence. The reach of overweening government power has been extended into every store, office and farm, every school and church, in every corner of America. This is a new, meddlesome, officious use of force, far beyond any governmental powers that our Founding Fathers contemplated. The Founders, indeed, fought and died to free us from just such arbitrary power, and tried to prevent it from ever occurring again, in Jefferson's words, with "the chains of the Constitution." Now our fundamental liberty is, again, very much at stake. The battle Hillsdale has been fighting concerns all Americans.

Our story: The letter was from the federal government. To be specific, it was from the Office of Civil Rights of the then Department of Health, Education and Welfare (HEW). It said Hillsdale College, as a "recipient institution," must sign a compliance form agreeing to submit information to HEW listing the sexual and ethnic makeup of our school.

This is obnoxious. The student's race and gender are of no concern to the educator. To the contrary, one function of a liberal arts education is to overcome such invidious distinctions and to promote a civilized, color-blind, harmonious order. This ideal was very widely shared until recent times and has always been the rule at Hillsdale. At its founding in 1844, Hillsdale threw open its doors to anyone of any race, creed or nationality. It was established by men and women "grateful to God for the inestimable blessings" of religious and civil liberty and "believing that the diffusion of learning is essential to the perpetuity of these blessings." It was their goal "to furnish all persons who wish, irrespective of nation, color, or sex a literary and scientific education," and to combine with this such moral "and social instructions as will best develop the mind and improve the hearts of its pupils." Hillsdale was educating women and freed slaves on an equal basis with others before the Civil War—more than a century before there were any federal bureaucrats to tell us what the "right" ethnic or gender composition of a school should be. In those days this was quite a radical stance. But we meant it then and we mean it just as much today when the civilized ideal is again under attack from bureaucracy. Genuine education focuses on the individual and does not admit of any such quotas. It is open to all—and it always has been at Hillsdale.

And Hillsdale a *"recipient institution"*? Absurd. Since its founding, Hillsdale has *never* accepted a penny of federal funding—which makes it all but unique among colleges these days. (Don't even ask about the big universities.) From the beginning our trustees have always been aware that nothing comes dearer than "free" money. The school has felt all along that we would surrender our academic freedom by taking any such funding, and we have always refused even to consider it. Whatever did these bureaucrats mean, we were a "recipient" of federal funds? Naturally, I thought at first it must be a mistake. Bureaucracies, especially very big ones, *have* been known to make mistakes. (HEW at the time ranked as the third largest "government" in the world, behind only the Soviet state and the U.S. government as a whole.)

It was not a mistake. The bureaucratic reasoning was that, although Hillsdale did not take any federal funds, some of its students had government loans or grants. The students spent some of this money paying for their education. That made Hillsdale a "recipient" too. If you think this reasoning is cockeyed, that makes two of us. By the same logic, every fast food franchise, laundry and bookstore in Hillsdale, Michigan, would be equally a "recipient institution," and thus be put under the bureaucratic thumb. It goes a lot further than this. Think of the countless millions who receive Social Security checks, food stamps, Medicare, grants and other federal benefits. Every place they spend anything becomes, equally, a "recipient institution." In effect, every place of business in America, down to the last lemonade stand, would be subject to bureaucratic control. So ran my thoughts and fears. A dozen years later it is all the law of the land. How we came to this appalling situation is part of our story.

The form, said HEW, was required under Title IX of the Education Act Amendments of 1972, which barred discrimination based on sex. HEW would then determine in bureaucratic fashion if we were meeting the gender requirements for this particular act. I remind you, it was never shown or even alleged that we were discriminating against anyone or violating any laws. We were not defendants. The only point of this maneuver was to put us under federal regulation.

The same form, or something of the sort, went out to every institution of higher education in the country. Almost all of them dutifully complied, because almost all of them are avid diners at the federal trough, or, more politely, "recipient institutions." Does anyone remember that, when federal aid to education was being debated in the 1960s, its opponents were jeered out of the arena for arguing that federal aid meant federal control? That academic freedom was at stake? The loudest jeering was precisely from those institutions most eager for the money: the ones now snarled in government red tape.

There were at least a few schools left, however, that cared more about education than about federal slops. A bare handful of these, we learned later, did not fill out the HEW compliance form. But neither did they announce their noncompliance to HEW. They hoped matters would fall through a crack in our Byzantine bureaucracy and never be noticed. (And for a time they were right about that.)

So it was that Hillsdale was the only college in America to notify the government in the fall of 1975 that it would not sign the compliance form. Hillsdale alone took a stand, stood up to HEW, and said "No. And we are prepared to make a legal issue of it." We stood alone for several years. Ours was the lone voice raised to insist that the government's definition of a recipient institution was wrong. It had changed the definition to one that defied all sense. The old definition was simply an institution that received federal funds. The new one was radically different: any institution having on its campus any *individual* who received a federal grant or loan. This would extend bureaucratic power into countless areas it had no business. It was wrong.

Our position was clear: We had never accepted funds from the government, so we were under no obligation to divulge proprietary information. In this we were by no means objecting to government civil rights policy per se. For us, the issue had nothing to do with civil rights or affirmative action. Nor was our record on civil rights ever in question. Rather, we were convinced that if we complied with the HEW order we would be unjustly liable to future regulation. This would mean abandoning Hillsdale's long-standing and cherished independence from government support and interference.

The agency countered that because some Hillsdale students received student loans and scholarships, the college was an "indirect" recipient of federal funds, and, therefore, obligated to comply. This was exactly why we were objecting. There was no point in discussing it any further.

We took it to court.

Several years later Grove City College, which is affiliated with the Presbyterian Church, came under similar bureaucratic pressure. It was enjoined by the government to submit the compliance form. Grove City, like Hillsdale, had never taken any federal funds. They approached us for information and help in their defense and we were able to provide substantial documentation to aid them in preparing their case. From that point the two cases wound through different paths in the federal appeals court circuits. Hillsdale eventually won a partial victory in the Sixth Circuit. The Court of Appeals ruled that, while federal loans and grants did make Hillsdale an indirect recipient of federal funds, the federal regulation was too broad and could not cover the whole institution.

Meanwhile, Grove City suffered defeat in the Second Circuit. In a way this set the stage for the resolution of both cases. The government chose not to appeal the Hillsdale decision. Instead, it concentrated on Grove City. The path was thus cleared for Grove City's case to be heard by the Supreme Court. Ironically, the legal battle Hillsdale had undertaken almost a decade earlier finally came to national attention as the case of *Grove City* v. *Bell* (named for then-Secretary of Education Terrel H. Bell).

In February 1984, the Supreme Court ruled that any American college or university was the recipient of federal funds if loans and grants were received by a *single* student on its campus. The government, however, could withhold funds only from specific departments or programs which were not in compliance with federal regulations. In other words, the statutory powers were again found to be too broad. This was essentially the same decision Hillsdale had received earlier in the Sixth Circuit Court of Appeals.

The Supreme Court ruling was a blow to academic freedom. It gave the government an enormous amount of economic leverage with which to control the internal affairs of educational institutions—even those not receiving funds directly. This was intolerable to a school that had fiercely guarded its independence for 140 years. The decision had a profound effect on Hillsdale. We met and discussed and agonized. There was only one way out left to us. We seized it, grateful that we still had the freedom to do so, however painful the price. The trustees resoundingly reaffirmed our private status and our stand against government intervention. They vowed to resist any such intrusions to the full extent of Hillsdale's resources.

In June 1985, Hillsdale announced that it would no longer accept students who intended to pay for any part of their college education with federal grants and loans. We informed the government that no student listing Hillsdale as the school of matriculation should be given a federal grant or loan, because we could not accept that student. We then notified our parents and students that if they needed financial assistance for education, we would do what we could to find private dollars to make it possible for them to attend Hillsdale.

Most colleges at the time were relying more and more on government aid to their students, for tuition and other expenses. And as federal grants and loans to students were rising sharply, tuitions were also rising sharply. Supply and demand works in the groves of academe as well as it works everywhere else. We were painfully aware of these trends and what they would cost us, but that only made us the more resolved to resist. When we said no, we meant it for once and for all. Hillsdale's stand did not go unnoticed.

The *Wall Street Journal* commended us, noting that "President Roche has in effect replied to HEW's quota overtures the same as General McAuliffe replied to German demands that he surrender at Bastogne ('Nuts!')." Nobel economist Milton Friedman commented in *Newsweek,* "...they have with clear conscience regarded themselves as not subject to HEW control." Writing in *Fortune,* Irving Kristol observed, "Hillsdale, a small, traditional and generally excellent liberal arts college, refused on principle to accept any government funds. Roche is therefore free to speak up, as most other college presidents are not—and he does." (I'm afraid Irving has my number.) The *Indianapolis Star* concluded: "So hurrah for

Hillsdale! If the ever-expanding grasp of federal intervention in the lives of private citizens and institutions is to be turned back, it will be by just such determination to stand and fight."

Needless to say, we were much cheered by this enthusiastic response. It was welcome proof that Hillsdale would no longer stand alone, that many share our concern about the lengthening reach of bureaucratic coercion in the field of education and in our private lives. But, of course, Hillsdale's immediate problem required more than moral support. Now we had to find the funds to back up our pledge to aid our students. To this vital need the response was all the more gratifying, and translated into tangible support for our Freedom Fund. Over $30 million in contributions came from individuals and organizations who endorsed and aided Hillsdale's determination to remain private. That support proved all the more that a national leadership community is committed, as we are, to the traditional, private ways to get things done.

DAVID VS. 100 GOLIATHS

Despite this impressive outpouring of public generosity, the problems we face have only been blunted, not solved. The reason is easy to find. In providing financial aid for our students, we are forced to compete with the biggest money machine in all human history: the U.S. government. This is like David versus one hundred Goliaths. Federal aid to students is skyrocketing. You have been hearing otherwise from the media since 1980 and the story you have heard is simply not true. If you have heard college and university presidents whining about how the administration has gutted higher education, you heard no more than the usual pleadings of panhandlers. All this is nonsense. The federal government is pouring money—your money, I might add—into student aid. Today, three out of every four dollars of need-based student aid come from federal programs. Tuitions soar to soak up all this nice "free" money, creating new pressures to raise student aid to even higher levels. But the level of education does not rise at all. Somehow, all those billions drift away into urgent "administrative" budgets and are lost to education. Bureaucracy breeds bureaucracy.

What this means for us is trying to match that torrent of tax monies, dollar for dollar, for the students who need financial aid to attend Hillsdale. In the first three years of our program, our outlays nearly *tripled*. Does that tell you something about federal spending? And the burden is growing almost daily.

If this seems too abstract, let me give you a down-to-earth human example of what it means. Not long ago I had to report to the trustees about 27 students whom we had accepted and who were committed to come to Hillsdale. The gist of my report was that these were all quality students, the very sort we like to see. They all had good academic credentials. They wanted to attend Hillsdale. We offered them the best aid package we could afford—and lost them. Other schools, with the help of tax dollars, could offer far more aid than we could. It isn't that other schools could offer more of their own resources. They couldn't. The fact is, they are committing a very small amount of their own resources, compared to our commitment. The other schools, however, had the advantage of being able to pick the pockets of taxpayers for their package. *That we will not do.* It does put us at a disadvantage, and we did lose some promising students. But we sleep nights.

The problem is only going to get worse—for everyone, not just for Hillsdale—until we all say "no." As things stand, enormous amounts of money flow to the "higher education" factories that are losing all sense of what an education is. In this, the students are the first and hardest-hit victims. Not only are they cheated out of a real education, they are stuck with an ever-increasing bill for all that nice, easy grant and loan money they were given in order to attend. For the last few private schools that struggle to survive and preserve the liberal arts tradition, the invasion of federal funds is nothing but trouble. How are we to compete with the power of taxation? We try, but with increasingly demanding measures. Yet we few who fight the battle alone keep alive and uphold the proud tradition of private education.

Think about this. *All* higher education in America was once private. All of it was established by groups with religious affiliations who freely gave their energies and resources so that education might be open to anyone. The trend has long been in the other direction, of course: toward huge, secular, tax-supported, bureaucratically approved universities. Think about this, too, as you contemplate what everybody knows to be true: Bureaucratic ("public") management of education goes up and up; the quality of education goes down and down. But did anyone ever really expect bureaucrats to be educators, or even to know why such a thing as a liberal arts education should exist? Would you buy your bread from a bakery that had never handled flour? That is precisely the kind of thinking that turns education over to bureaucrats.

There are more than a thousand birds, beasts and bugs on the endangered species list. None is remotely as close to extinction as traditional private education. If and when the last vestiges of private purpose and charity and skills in education are shot down, education itself must fall. For education is a continuing process, a transmission of knowledge and values from generation to generation. When the last real schools are gone, who will educate the next generation of educators? The U.S. Department of Education? Forget it.

In a word, Hillsdale is fighting for its life. Don't take me amiss; we are not going to fold up the day after tomorrow for lack of funds. Money, as I have said, is an increasing problem in competition with tax funding, but it will be a good while before we have to move to the intensive care unit. No, the real question is whether this country is going to offer educational opportunity to all. To do this, we have to go on providing the real item in the only setting that still can sustain it: the private college.

What I, and the trustees, and all of us at Hillsdale fear is the next invasion of bureaucratic power. The one that will say in effect: "Never mind that you are a private institution, we are taking over now." There is no legal way for this to happen yet. But what new legislation will be written? Thanks to its stand, Hillsdale is a prime target. Already discussed in bureaucratic memoranda is the idea that tax exemption is really a loss of government revenue: as if the government already *owned* all of our earnings, and merely lets us keep some at its own pleasure. This is a complete inversion of property rights and due process. It may also be argued that deductions for religion, charity, education or other high-minded activities are no longer valid, because the government itself provides all such services. (Insane, but power-wielders and their friends are not very fussy about how they reduce private life to subjection.) Finally, I suspect the argument will be raised that private education has religious overtones and is therefore in violation of the famous "wall of separation" between church and state that doesn't happen to exist in the Constitution. When arguments sink this low, there will be no further point in referring to the Constitution or to the law at all. We will be ruled by naked power.

It is foolish to shelve these concerns, thinking "we'll cross that bridge when we come to it." I believe it is only a matter of time until another assault is mounted against Hillsdale and private education in general. We must be ready for it. At Hillsdale, we are already building our defenses. It is grating to have to do so. What harm has one small college done to the Republic that it should be subject to such attack? We have done no wrong except in the eyes of those who demand that government control every detail of life. To them, Hillsdale's independence is insolent defiance of their power and designs. And they have a point. We will remain defiant.

If you think my concerns are exaggerated or overblown, read on. The story isn't over. The Supreme Court's decision in *Grove City* v. *Bell* did not, as one might expect, please liberal legislators. In truth, they were furious that they had not quite reduced private colleges to unconditional surrender. There was that one last small loophole, that an entire institution could not be brought to account for some violation in one of its departments or programs. Bullying one department would not do; the point is to bully the whole school.

They promptly whipped up the Civil Rights Restoration Act, a bill to "correct the defects" in the enforcement of Title IX of the Education Amendments of 1972. The principal sponsor was Senator Ted Kennedy. What the bill provides is that the government may cut all funds to any institution that fails to comply fully with a regulation—in even one department. It applies to any direct or indirect recipient of federal funds. This certainly "corrects" the loophole. It is also, in my opinion, one of the most sweeping impositions of federal power over free Americans that has ever been seriously proposed. Note well its means of enforcement: "Toe our line or we'll take away your funds." It is scarcely possible to pose a more naked threat. They might as well announce, "You take our money, we own you." With this, America's great experiment in self-government has lost its last battle. This kind of absolutism is cut from the cloth of the tyrannies of the Old World, whose peoples were not citizens but subjects with no basic rights. What is especially galling about this is that "federal" money was forcibly extracted from us in the first place. When they "give" some of it back, it comes not with strings attached but with chains.

Things get very much worse. The law targets all indirect recipients of federal funds. That means corner stores that take food stamps. That means churches that feed the poor in programs with even minimal federal connection. That means every American in any economic activity whatever. There is no way to prevent "federal" dollars from entering the operation somehow. It was argued: "Oh, no, the law wasn't meant to go this far; we will always use a 'narrow' interpretation." But the law *does* go this far. And the power will be used. I don't think there is a case in history when government, given such power, has not ultimately used it.

The false definition of "recipient institution" that we at Hillsdale tried so hard to fight in 1975 now comes back to haunt all of America. Even in a "narrow" application, the law is an affront to even-handed justice. Where the blind goddess of justice was once supposed to view all who appeared before her with impartiality, now she peeks. "Tell me your race, your creed and your sex," she says, "and I will tell you how I will treat you." This is not justice. It *is* racism, it *is* sexism.

The Civil Rights Restoration Act floated around Congress for four years. I wrote a number of articles warning about it, from Hillsdale's firsthand experience in the case. These were heard in some circles, but rejected with scorn in Congress. The magic words, "Civil Rights," have a dazzling effect. Legislators hardly dare vote against anything labeled "Civil Rights." But the label was utterly false. The bill had nothing to do with restoring civil rights. Remember that the two schools involved, Hillsdale and Grove City College, had never been accused of any civil rights violations in the first place. The issue was the reach of federal power, plain and simple—and on an unprecedented scale.

The Act was passed in 1988. President Reagan vetoed it, infuriating its liberal sponsors even more. Both houses of Congress provided the large majorities necessary to override the veto. The Civil Rights Restoration Act is now law. How bad is this law? Let me give you the barest taste of its potential. Due to a recent court ruling, alcoholics, drug addicts and transvestites are categorized as "handicapped" and are thus protected under the Civil Rights Act. Ponder this all-too-possible scenario: A drug addict applies for a job at a pharmacy. The pharmacy, which accepts Medicare and Medicaid payments via its clientele, cannot turn down this "handicapped" applicant. It is required to comply with the federal regulations, even if it is aghast at turning a junkie loose in its supplies of drugs. Moreover, every other pharmacy in the same "geographic area" (also defined by government) is then obliged to submit to regulations also. There is quite literally no limit to the number or scope of similar cases that may affect us (and probably will). The law is wide open. About anything you can imagine may be a future civil rights case.

The power and responsibility to enforce civil rights regulations by withholding funds from violators is now the law. By all the canons of justice, the law must be equitably and fully enforced. Moreover, the status of civil rights enforcement is so loose and capricious that almost any slight (whether real or unintended) to a member of a legally protected group can be construed a violation of federal law.

What began (let us allow) with the best of intentions, the decent impulse to protect the weak, the needy, the handicapped, has evolved into a federal bulldozer to flatten the rights of all Americans. No business or organization, profit-making or not-for-profit; no school or church; no local government is safe from vague federal fishing expeditions—or outright threats—to "enforce civil rights." Where it will all end, no one knows. I do know this is the price we invariably pay when we allow government coercion to replace all the bonds of reason and sympathy that join us together in civilized society. Will we ever learn, with Lord Acton, that power corrupts, and absolute power corrupts absolutely?

Hillsdale has taken its stand. If need be, we will fight again. We will defend ourselves, as best we can, by distancing ourselves from governmental reach, whether that is intended to harm or (God forbid) help us. As best we can, we will build our resources in hopes of surviving the next assault and carrying on our work: liberal arts education. It may be that we will be swept away in the flood; but we do not, as Canon Bell reminded us, have to sing Hosannahs to the river gods.

What will *you* do? I said earlier that if little Hillsdale has to go it alone this time, all America will lose. Perhaps at first reading that claim sounded a bit self-inflated. Do you see now what I mean?

ABOUT THE AUTHOR

George Roche has served as president of Hillsdale College since 1971. "Firing Line," the "MacNeil-Lehrer News Hour," "Today," *Newsweek, Time, Reader's Digest* and the *Wall Street Journal* have chronicled his efforts to keep the College free from federal intrusion. Formerly the presidentially appointed chairman of the National Council on Educational Research, the director of seminars at the Foundation for Economic Education, a professor of history at the Colorado School of Mines, and a U.S. Marine, Dr. Roche is the author of ten books, including five Conservative Book Club selections, among them: *America by the Throat: The Stranglehold of Federal Bureaucracy* (Devin-Adair, 1985), *A World Without Heroes: The Modern Tragedy* (Hillsdale College Press, 1987), *Going Home* (Jameson Books, 1986), and *A Reason for Living* (Hillsdale College Press, 1989). His most recent book is *One by One: Preserving Freedom and Values in Heartland America* (Hillsdale College Press, 1990).

WHO KILLED EXCELLENCE?

Samuel L. Blumenfeld
September 1985

he history of American education can be roughly divided into three distinct periods, each representing a particular and powerful world view. The first period—from colonial times to the 1840s—saw the dominance of the Calvinist ethic: God's omnipotent sovereignty was the central reality of man's existence. In the Calvinist scheme the purpose of man's life was to glorify God, and the attainment of Biblical literacy was considered the overriding spiritual and moral function of education. Latin, Greek and Hebrew were studied because they were the original languages of the Bible and of theological literature. Thus, this period in American education was characterized by a very high standard of literacy.

The second period, lasting from the 1840s until about World War I, reflects the Hegelian mindset. G.F. Hegel's statist-idealist philosophy spread throughout the Western world like a malignant spiritual disease, destroying Calvinism. In this pantheistic scheme, the purpose of life was to glorify man and the instrument through which man's collective power could be exercised—the state. Hegel dethroned the Jehovah of the Old Testament and the Christ of the New Testament, and offered a view of the universe in which everything was a somewhat formless "God" in the process of perfecting himself or itself through a dynamic, endless struggle called the dialectic. Yet even the Hegelian period was one of high literacy, for Hegel had stressed intellectual development, since he considered man's mind to be the highest manifestation of God in the universe. Latin and Greek were studied because they were the languages of the pagan classics.

During this Hegelian period the public school movement developed, promoting a secular form of education which gradually eliminated the Bible from the classrooms of America. Discipline, punctuality, high academic standards and achievement were the hallmarks of the public schools.

The third period, from World War I to the present, was the "Progressive" era. It came into being mainly as a result of the new behavioral psychology developed in the experimental laboratories of Wilhelm Wundt at the University of Leipzig in Germany. The major American figures who studied under Wundt—James McKeen Cattell, G. Stanley Hall, Charles H. Judd and James Earl Russell—came back to the United States to revolutionize American education. In this scheme, the purpose of man's life is to deny and reject the supernatural and to sacrifice oneself to the collective, often referred to as "humanity." Science and evolution replace religion as the focus of faith, and dialectical materialism supersedes Hegel's dialectical idealism as the process by which man's moral progress is made. The word "progressive," in fact, comes from this dialectical concept of progress.

G. Stanley Hall beat the first path to Wundt's laboratory in Leipzig. Hall had already spent the years 1868-70 studying in Germany and had returned home seething with hatred for his Puritan New England heritage. He wrote in his autobiography:

"I fairly loathed and hated so much that I saw about me that I now realize more clearly than ever how possible it would have been for me to have drifted into some, perhaps almost any, camp of radicals and to have come into such open rupture with the scheme of things as they were that I should have been stigmatized as dangerous, at least for any academic career, where the motto was 'Safety First.'

And as this was the only way left open, the alternative being the dread one of going back to the farm, it was most fortunate that these deeply stirred instincts of revolt were never openly expressed and my rank heresies and socialistic leanings unknown."

Hall returned from his Wundtian experience in 1878, and in 1882, he created America's first psychology laboratory at Johns Hopkins University. Two of Hall's students were James McKeen Cattell and John Dewey. Cattell journeyed to Leipzig in 1884 where he spent two years studying under Professor Wundt. He returned to the U.S. and created the world's first psychology department at the University of Pennsylvania in 1887. One biographical account of Cattell's life states: "Cattell's student years in Baltimore, Germany and England—the period of his greatest originality and productivity in psychology—were laced with inner complaint. Cattell confided only in his private journal his recurrent feelings of depression, his frequent need of hallucinogenic drugs, and his underlying philosophic stance as a 'sceptic and mystic.' "

Is it not interesting that hallucinogenic drugs were already being used by students of psychology as far back as the 1880s? In 1891, Cattell established Columbia University's department of psychology. During his years at Columbia, Cattell trained more future members of the American Psychological Association than any other institution. Indeed, Cattell was one of the founders of the American Psychological Association and the *Psychological Review*. Under his direction, psychology at Columbia became one of the strongest departments of research and advanced teaching.

No doubt Cattell's most celebrated pupil was Edward L. Thorndike, who had gotten his master's degree under William James at Harvard, where he had also conducted experiments in animal learning. Under Cattell, Thorndike continued his experiments which were to have a devastating impact on American education. He reduced psychology to the study of observable, measurable human behavior—with the complexity and mystery of mind and soul left out. In summing up his theory of learning, Thorndike wrote: "The best way with children may often be, in the pompous words of an animal trainer, 'to arrange everything in connection with the trick so that the animal will be compelled by the laws of its own nature to perform it.' ''

In 1904, Cattell invited his old friend John Dewey to join the faculty at Columbia. From Johns Hopkins, Dewey had not gone to Leipzig like Cattell and others. Instead he taught philosophy at the University of Michigan for about nine years. He had left Johns Hopkins a Hegelian idealist but became a materialist at Michigan. In 1894, he became professor of philosophy and education at the University of Chicago where he created his famous Laboratory School.

The purpose of the school was to see what kind of curriculum was needed to produce socialists instead of capitalists, collectivists instead of individualists. Dewey, along with the other adherents of the new psychology, was convinced that socialism was the wave of the future and that individualism was passé. But the individualist system would not fade away on its own as long as it was sustained by the education American children were getting in their schools. According to Dewey, "...education is growth under favorable conditions; the school is the place where those conditions should be regulated scientifically." In other words, if we apply psychology to education, which we have done now for over fifty years, then the ideal classroom is a psych lab and the pupils within it are laboratory animals.

Dewey's joining Cattell and Thorndike at Columbia brought together the lethal trio who were literally to wipe out traditional education and kill academic excellence in America. It would not be accomplished overnight, for an army of new teachers and superintendents had to be trained and an army of old teachers and superintendents had to retire or die off.

By 1908, the trio had produced three books of paramount importance to the progressive movement. Thorndike published *Animal Intelligence* in 1898; Dewey published *School and Society* in 1899; and in 1908 Cattell produced, through a surrogate by the name of Edmund Burke Huey, *The Psychology and Pedagogy of Reading.*

Dewey provided the social philosophy of the movement, Thorndike the teaching theories and techniques, and Cattell the organizing energy. There was among all of them, disciples and colleagues, a missionary zeal to rebuild American education on a foundation of science, evolution, humanism, and behaviorism. But it was Dewey who identified high literacy as the culprit in traditional education, the sustaining force behind individualism. He wrote in 1898:

> "My proposition is, that conditions–social, industrial, and intellectual–have undergone such a radical change, that the time has come for a thoroughgoing examination of the emphasis put upon linguistic work in elementary instruction....The plea for the predominance of learning to

read in early school-life because of the great importance attaching to literature seems to me a perversion."

But in order to reform the system, the mind had to be seen in a different way. Dewey wrote:

"The idea of heredity has made familiar the notion that the equipment of the individual, mental as well as physical, is an inheritance from the race; a capital inherited by the individual from the past and held in trust by him for the future. The idea of evolution has made familiar the notion that mind cannot be regarded as an individual, monopolistic possession, but represents the outworkings of the endeavor and thought of humanity."

To Dewey the one part of our identity that is the most private, the mind, is really not the property of the individual at all, but of humanity, which is merely a euphemism for the collective or the state. That concept is at the very heart of the Orwellian nightmare, and yet the same concept is the very basis of our progressive-humanist-behaviorist education system. He realized that such radical reform was not exactly what the American people wanted: "Change must come gradually. To force it unduly would compromise its final success by favoring a violent reaction."

The most important of the reforms to be instituted was changing the way children were taught to read. Since it had been ordained by Dewey and his colleagues that literacy skills were to be drastically de-emphasized in favor of the development of social skills, a new teaching method that deliberately reduced literacy skills was needed. The traditional school used the phonics or phonetic method. That is, children were first taught the alphabet, then the sounds the letters stand for, and in a short time they became independent readers. The new method—look-say or the word method—taught children to read English as if it were Chinese or Egyptian hieroglyphics.

The new method had been invented in the 1830s by Rev. Thomas H. Gallaudet, the famous teacher of the deaf and dumb. Since deaf-mutes have no conception of a spoken language, they could not learn a phonetic—or sound-symbol—system of reading. Instead, they were taught to read by a purely sight method consisting of pictures juxtaposed with whole words. Thus, the whole word was seen to represent an idea or image, not the sounds of language. The written word itself was regarded as a little picture, much like a Chinese ideograph. Gallaudet thought that the method could be adapted for use by normal children and he wrote a little primer on that concept.

In 1837, the Boston Primary School Committee decided to adopt the primer.

By 1844, the results were so disastrous that a group of Boston schoolmasters published a blistering attack on the whole-word method and it was thrown out of the schools. But look-say was kept alive in the new state normal schools where it was taught as a legitimate alternative to the alphabetic-phonics method. When the Progressives decided to revive look-say, they realized that an authoritative book would be necessary to give the method the seal of approval of the new psychology. In Wundt's laboratory, Cattell had observed that adults could read whole words just as fast as they could read individual letters. From that he concluded that a child could be taught to read simply by showing him whole words and telling him what they said.

For some reason Cattell did not want to write a book himself. So he got one of G. Stanley Hall's students, Edmund Burke Huey, to write a book arguing that look-say was the superior way to teach reading. The book, which I mentioned earlier, *The Psychology and Pedagogy of Reading,* was published in 1908. What is astounding is that by 1908 Cattell and his colleagues were very well aware that the look-say method produced inaccurate readers. In fact, Huey argued in favor of inaccuracy as a virtue! The book was immediately adopted by the Progressives as the authoritative work on the subject despite the fact that it was written by an obscure student who had had no experience whatever in the teaching of reading, who wrote nothing further on the subject, and about whom virtually nothing is known.

When a nation's leading educational reformers start arguing in favor of illiteracy and inaccurate reading, and damning early emphasis on learning to read as a perversion, then we can expect some strange results to come from our education process. In fact, by the 1950s, the Progressives had done such a good job that Rudolf Flesch could write a book in 1955 entitled, *Why Johnny Can't Read.* Why indeed! Flesch minced no words: "The teaching of reading—all over the United States, in all the schools, in all the textbooks—is totally wrong and flies in the face of all logic and common sense." How did this happen? Flesch explained:

> "It's a foolproof system all right. Every grade-school teacher in the country has to go to a teachers' college or school of education; every teachers' college gives at least one course on how to teach reading; every course on how to teach reading is based on a textbook; every one of those textbooks is written by one of the high priests of the word method. In the old days it was impossible to keep a good teacher from following her own common sense and practical knowledge; today the phonetic system of teaching reading is kept out of our schools as effectively as if we had a dictatorship with an all-powerful Ministry of Education."

The educators were furious with Flesch. He had made them appear stupid and incompetent. They knew they were not stupid. They had pulled off the greatest conspiracy against intelligence in history. Although Dewey, Thorndike and Cattell were dead, their disciples, Arthur I. Gates at Columbia and William Scott Gray at the University of Chicago, were determined to carry on the work of their mentors. In 1955, the professors of reading organized the International Reading Association to maintain the dominance of look-say in primary reading instruction. Today, look-say permeates the educational marketplace so thoroughly, and in so many guises, and is so widely and uncritically accepted, that it takes expert knowledge by a teacher or parent to know the good from the bad, the useful from the harmful.

Even the best students have fallen victim to this "dumbing-down" process. In a speech given to the California Library Association in 1970, Karl Shapiro, the eminent poet-professor who had taught creative writing for over 20 years told his audience: "What is really distressing is that this generation cannot and does not read. I am speaking of university students in what are supposed to be our best universities. Their illiteracy is staggering....We are experiencing a literacy breakdown which is unlike anything I know of in the history of letters."

This literacy breakdown is no accident. It is not the result of ignorance or incompetence. It has been, in fact, deliberately created by our progressive-humanist-behaviorist educators whose social agenda is far more important to them than anything connected with academic excellence. Perhaps their mindset was best expressed by psychologist Arthur W. Combs in an essay entitled, "Humanistic Goals of Education," published in 1975. Dr. Combs writes: "Modern education must produce far more than persons with cognitive skills. It must produce humane individuals....The humane qualities are absolutely essential to our way of life–far more important even, than the learning of reading, for example. We can live with a bad reader; a bigot is a danger to everyone."

The inference, of course, is that you can't have both good readers and humane persons, that one must be sacrificed for the other. Note also the very subtle suggestion that high literacy may even produce bigotry. If this is what the humanists believe, then how can we expect them to promote high literacy? In 1935, Dewey argued that: "The last stand of oligarchical and anti-social seclusion is perpetuation of this purely individualistic notion of intelligence." To kill this individualistic intelligence, which is the source of excellence, Dewey and his behaviorist colleagues proceeded to strip education of mind, soul, and literacy. In 1930, the percentage of illiteracy among white persons of native birth was 1.5 percent. Among foreign-born whites it was 9.9 percent, and among blacks it was 16.3. Among urban blacks the illiteracy rate was 9.2 percent.

In 1935, a survey was made of Civilian Conservation Corp (CCC) enrollees. Of the 375,000 men studied, 7,369, or 1.9 percent, were found to be illiterate, that is, they could not read a newspaper or write a letter. That's a remarkably low rate of illiteracy considering that most of the men who joined the CCC were in the lowest socio-economic group in the nation.

Today the illiteracy rate among urban blacks is probably about 40 percent, while the illiteracy rate among whites has been estimated to be from 7 to 30 percent. No one really knows the exact figure, including the Department of Education, which has guessed that there are about 27 million functional illiterates in America. In fact, Dr. Flesch wrote another book in 1981, *Why Johnny Still Can't Read*, in which he noted with some sadness, "Twenty-five years ago I studied American methods of teaching reading and warned against educational catastrophe. Now it has happened."

At the moment every state legislature in the nation is grappling with an education reform bill. Not one of them has addressed this basic problem of primary reading instruction. The trouble is that most would-be reformers are convinced that merit pay, longer school days, smaller class size, more homework, career ladders, competency tests, higher pay for teachers, compulsory kindergarten and more preschool facilities will give us excellence. But they won't for one very significant reason. The academic substance of public education today is controlled lock, stock and barrel by behavioral psychologists, and they don't believe in excellence. The American classroom has been transformed into a psych lab and the function of psych lab is not academic excellence.

If education consists of the interaction between an effective teacher and a willing learner, then you can't have it in a psych lab which has neither. In the lab you have the trainer and the trainee, the controller and the controlled, the experimenter and the subject, the therapist and the patient. What should go on in a classroom is teaching and learning. What goes on in the psych lab is stimulus and response, diagnosis and treatment. Many people think that behaviorism is simply the study of behavior. But, according to B.F. Skinner, behaviorism is a theory of knowledge, in which knowing and thinking are regarded merely as forms of behavior. Although psychology was supposed to be the study of the life of the psyche—the mind—behaviorists, starting with Thorndike, reduced the functions of the mind to where today the mind ceases to be a factor in education. Behavioral objectives are the goals of today's teachers.

Who killed excellence? Behavioral psychology did. Why? Because it is based on a lie; that man is an animal without mind or soul, and can be taught as an animal. And that concept is based on an even greater lie; that there is no God, no Creator. And so the future of American education rests on the resolution of profoundly philosophical questions. Apparently no compromise between the ruling behaviorists and the rebellious fundamentalists is possible. As long as the progressive-humanist-behaviorists control the graduate schools of education and psychology, the professional organizations and journals, and the processes whereby curricula are developed and textbooks written and published, there is little possibility that public education can achieve academic excellence.

It is the better part of wisdom to admit that the government schools are the permanent captives of the behaviorists who also seem to control the sources of public and private funding that sustain them. They seem to be impervious to the pressures of excellence. There is a growing belief that the solution lies in abandoning government education and transferring our energies and resources to the private sector, thereby expanding educational freedom, opportunity and entrepreneurship. The American people want better education. They ought to be able to get it. But to do so they will have to sweep away whatever obstacles to excellence the educators have erected. In fact, that is the problem—how to break down, overcome or circumvent the obstacles to excellence.

The exodus of children from the public schools is an indication that this is already happening. But the millions of children who remain in the government schools are at risk, in danger of becoming the functional illiterates, the underclass of tomorrow. Can we save them? We have the knowledge to do so. But do we have the will? The next few years will provide the answer.

ABOUT THE AUTHOR

S amuel Blumenfeld is the author of many books on education: *How to Start Your Own Private School and Why You Need One* (Arlington House, 1972), *The New Illiterates* (Arlington House, 1973), *How to Tutor* (Arlington House, 1973), *Is Public Education Necessary?* (Devin-Adair, 1981), *Alpha-Phonics: A Primer for Beginning Readers* (Paradigm Company, 1983), and *NEA: Trojan Horse in American Education* (Paradigm Company, 1984). His writings have appeared frequently in major journals as well. He has taught in both public and private schools, including a private school for children with learning and behavioral problems.

PUBLIC EDUCATION AND THE GLOBAL FAILURE OF SOCIALISM

Warren Brookes
April 1990

n the last few months, Americans, especially those of Eastern European national descent, watched with both awe and elation as democracy and freedom reared their hesitant heads above the ebbing tides of Marxist socialism in the Warsaw Pact nations. It is hard to imagine that just ten years ago, the Soviets invaded Afghanistan and those socialist tides were running strongly in the opposite direction, and the waves of communism were lapping at the beachheads of the West.

But, today we can say with some confidence that the decade of the 1980s will be remembered as the period when Marxism finally admitted it was wearing no clothes, and market capitalism swept the global economy with the sheer momentum of its high technological development and telecommunications revolution. Sadly, though, the 1990s could well be the decade when that global information revolution leaves the U.S. market economy in the dust, falling far behind the Pacific Rim nations and Europe.

PUBLIC EDUCATION: SOCIALISM'S LAST REFUGE

And the ironic cause of that demise could very well be our own reluctance either to privatize or radically restructure the most socialist enterprise in the Western world, that $180 billion near-monopoly known as U.S. public education.

Some years ago I asked Nobel economist Milton Friedman why it was, given the appalling and obvious failures of socialism everywhere in the world contrasted with the stunning successes of market capitalism, that most American students still graduated from high school with such a surprisingly socialist perspective. His answer was characteristically clear: "Because they are products of a socialist system—namely public education. How can you expect such a system to inculcate the values of free enterprise and individual entrepreneurship and competition when it is based on monopoly state ownership, abhors competition, and survives only through compulsion and taxation?"

How indeed. Yet, how can a nation expect to compete in an increasingly dynamic and competitive global market when its most important economic capital, its people and their ideas and talents and energies, are the product of such an obviously failed monopoly enterprise? In spite of one of the highest levels of spending (per capita) in the industrial world, the American public school system is generating students who rank 13th out of 13 advanced nations in science and math, and 11th out of 13 in social studies and language. If we want to be genuinely candid about it, the American public education system today is not that much more effective than the Polish economic system that Lech

Walesa reluctantly inherited, and the challenge facing would-be education reformers in the U.S. is no less daunting. Unless they, like Walesa, first understand why the system has been failing, they cannot hope to succeed. If they follow his example and merely tinker at the margins, and "reform" within the present system, their efforts could well be as Myron Lieberman warned in his new book on education privatization, entirely "futilitarian."

Marxist socialism has failed primarily because of its total failure to comprehend the true nature of wealth and of man, seeing both as primarily physical and finite. If such a view were correct, it would be both fair and just to have a system that collectively ensured equitable distribution of a limited resource base. Instead, of course, both reason and revelation, not to mention history and experience, have taught us that wealth is primarily metaphysical, the product more of mind than of matter, and that man himself is primarily mental and spiritual, and not merely a physical component of a collective mass. This alone explains why individual freedom combined with market capitalism has invariably produced greater economic growth, wealth and prosperity than collectivist planning and redistribution. Spirituality and freedom will always triumph over materialism and totalitarian tyranny.

THE QUANTUM ECONOMY

If the economic pie is, as we have learned, primarily the result of imagination, ideas, intelligence and human creative energy, the freer the sources of those mental and spiritual qualities are, the fewer the limits to the potential size of that pie, and the development of individual human beings. Although this was the fundamental hypothesis of Adam Smith some two centuries ago, namely that turning loose the creative, God-given energies of the human spirit would enrich all nations, it is infinitely more true today in what George Gilder calls the "quantum economy." In his new book, *Microcosm,* he writes:

"Quantum physics is a complex and elaborate theory....But it can be summed in a simple proposition: the overthrow of matter. In quantum theory, the materialist superstition—the belief that all reality can be explained by the interplay among material particles (or as Marx would describe it, the struggle among classes) has collapsed at the heart of matter itself. The most important intellectual event of our century, this development is now transforming global economics and geopolitics."

In a world where information is now capital, and capital is now synonymous with information, wealth becomes virtually unlimited, universally accessible, and totally decentralized. In the 24-hour-a-day rolling referendum that is now the global financial marketplace, national borders disappear, interventionist governments and politicians become dangerously irrelevant and costly, and power is moving inexorably back to the individual from whom (in this country at least) it sprang. As Gilder notes, "unlike the industrial revolution which imposed economies of scale (and which so preoccupied Karl Marx), the information revolution imposes economies of microscale. Computer power continually devolves into the hands and onto the laps of individuals."

A single five-cent plastic disc can contain millions of dollars' worth of programs and access codes that put the world economy within reach of the individual and beyond the reach of government. In this new global marketplace, mercantilism is as obsolete as fascism and Marxism, conglomeration as foolish as state central planning—or, I might add, totally state-run public schools. Instead of man as a helpless pawn in a huge mechanistic economy, the economy is increasingly within the mind of man, and within each one of us. Indeed, an economy in mind is by definition an economy in us, and not the other way around. This vast technological revolution has reversed the inexorable 19th- and 20th-century flow of power to central governments and corporate headquarters—and is once again re-establishing individual man as the center of his own economic universe and the key to collective national wealth.

But at the same time it has made the individual and his nation more dependent than ever for economic well being on knowledge, understanding, intelligence, information. And this in turn means that more than ever before the key to competitive survival lies in extending, not limiting, liberty and improving our education. As Thomas Jefferson wisely put it, "If a nation expects to be ignorant and free...it expects what never was and never will be."

It is this reality that is driving the revolution in Warsaw and perestroika in Moscow. Gorbachev is pursuing glasnost not because he is a secular saint, but because he is wise enough to understand that Russia is being buried by the information revolution in global markets, and, unless he can open the Soviet system up, it will suffocate, buried under the mounting global sea of intelligence-laden microchips, or else explode from the unleashing of frustrated human aspirations. But perestroika is doomed to failure unless Gorbachev is prepared to tear down Russia's massive, leaden central bureaucracy, arm his people with access to information, and thus free up and turn loose the creative energies of his people.

ECONOMIC DECLINE LINKED TO EDUCATION

What can be said about Gorbachev can also be said about the tragedy of American public education, a kind of collectivist millstone around the neck of our nation which is now in the battle of its life for survival in a world where, as Gilder notes, "Knowledge is not merely *a* source of power. It is supremely *the* source of power." The fact that since the 1970s economic power has been shifting rapidly to the Pacific, and to Europe, and away from the U.S. is a clear demonstration that there is something basically wrong with our knowledge machinery. One of the economic mysteries of the 1970s and 1980s is why the nation's productivity growth suddenly fell from nearly three percent a year to one percent and even less. Among the nation's leading students of productivity and national income, John Kendrick, economist emeritus from George Washington University, has maintained for some time now that, contrary to traditional capitalist notions, investment in business equipment explains less than a third of the nation's productivity trends. The leading element, accounting for perhaps 70 percent, is what Kendrick calls "the knowledge factor." To put it simply, as knowledge advances, so does output. That means that knowledge and understanding are now our most basic form of capital.

The brilliant social philosopher Michael Novak argues that it is no accident that the word "capital" derives from the Latin "capitalis," which stands for head, or mind, suggesting that all real wealth has always been seen as ideas and thought. This knowledge=wealth equation is becoming more demonstrable each year. An increasing share of our capital is not even in the form of hardware (machinery and plants) but in software, logical mental programs that determine everything from product design to the conversion of ideas into goods and services. Indeed, as Gilder shows, with the emergence of the silicon compilers, customized chips or computer hardware is now being "manufactured" entirely at the keyboard by programmers.

If Kendrick is right, the primary reason productivity began to fade in the U.S. can only be explained by a rapid fall-off in the trend of the "knowledge factor" beginning in the early 1970s just as the information revolution was dawning. That just happens to coincide (with some lag) with the sudden decline in U.S. education performance.

Last March, a scholarly study in the *American Economic Review* by Cornell University economist John H. Bishop ("Is the Test Score Decline Responsible for the Productivity Growth Decline?") suggested Kendrick's thesis is on target. While Bishop was able to ascribe only 10 percent of the "unexplained" productivity slowdown from 1973 to 1980 to the significant achievement test score decline that began in 1967, "its major impact on [productivity] growth has come in the 1980s," and has "explained" about 20 percent of that decline. And this factor is now accelerating as the better educated workers retire, replaced by less and less well educated ones. By the 1990s, it will account for as much as 40 percent of our productivity gap, given earlier trends.

These numbers may not sound like much, but the economic costs both to the nation and to workers are enormous. Bishop estimates that as a result of the test score decline, "the labor quality shortfall was 1.3 percent in 1980 and 2.9 percent in 1987...is projected to be 3.6 percent in 1990, 5.5 percent in 2000 and 6.7 percent in 2010." This means, Bishop concludes in a scholarly understatement, that "the effect of general intellectual achievement (GIA) on wage rates and productivity is larger than heretofore believed." He also notes that "Productivity growth and test scores declined almost simultaneously," and he points out that students graduating in 1980 "had learned about 1.25 grade-level equivalents less than those who graduated in 1967."

In the middle 1960s Bishop found that GIA was rising about five percent a year and productivity was rising about three percent. By 1980 it was falling at nearly six percent a year and productivity growth was down to less than one half of one percent a year. The direct economic costs of that lower knowledge (in 1987 dollars) was $34 billion in 1980, $86 billion in 1988, and will be $334 billion in the year 2010. And, "If the forecasted shortfalls in output up to the year 2010 are cumulated, assuming a three percent rate of growth of GNP...the total present discounted costs of the test score decline is $3.2 trillion...."

SPENDING NOT THE ANSWER

Now, I can just hear the National Education Association licking its chops and saying, "You see? This is why we should make much bigger investments in education spending!" Aside from the fact that education spending *has* risen over 25 percent in real terms since 1981, the trouble with that hypothesis is, as Bishop notes, "prior to 1967 student test scores had been *rising* steadily for more than 50 years," and had they continued to rise at that rate, "labor quality would now be 2.9 percent higher."

Yet, the constant dollar growth in education spending per student rose substantially *faster* in the 20 years *since* 1967 (4.0 percent a year in real terms) than it did the 20 years *before* 1967 (3.3 percent). Small wonder education economist Eric Hanushek of the University of Rochester was recently able to demonstrate the weak statistical relationship between student performance and various traditional education inputs—from teacher/pupil ratios to spending per student—all of which are far stronger today amidst declining academic performance than they were when performance was rising. In his May 1989 paper in *Educational Researcher,* Hanushek analyzed 187 separate qualified studies of public schools across the country. His findings were a devastating annihilation of the educationists' agenda. On spending per student, he found that of 65 studies on this subject only 20 percent showed a statistically significant positive connection, and even those correlations were not robust. In 152 studies of variations in student-to-teacher ratios only nine percent showed a "positive" correlation between lower class size and better performance, and eight percent showed a "negative" correlation.

He also found few positive correlations between education performance and teacher education (seven percent), teacher salaries (16 percent), administrative support (11 percent), and facilities (nine percent). Only teacher experience seemed to count somewhat, but even that correlation was amazingly weak. As a result, Hanushek warned, "Expenditures' increases if undertaken *within the current institutional structure* are likely to be dissipated on reduced class sizes or indiscriminate raises in teacher salaries with a result that growth in costs will almost surely exceed growth in student performance."

Within weeks of the publication of this controversial study, the *Detroit News* conducted a study of its own that completely confirmed Hanushek's findings in "Schools Can't Buy Success." That was the banner headline of a major article on June 11, 1989 by *News* reporter Mark Hornbeck which concluded that "equalizing how much money was spent by school districts would do little to equalize education opportunity." The *News* analyzed the relative performance and spending levels of Michigan's schools and found that "there is little relationship between spending for instruction and scores on the Michigan Educational Assessment Program (MEAP) tests in the 1986-1987 school year...." Hornbeck confirmed that "home life has far more impact on test scores than high teacher salaries, or small class size, and that student dropout rates, a much publicized problem in Michigan (which has the third worst such rate in the nation), generally were highest in school districts with a high percentage of adults who had dropped out of high school years ago." Like parent, like child.

The *News* also found in town after town where high spending coincided with low performance, and vice versa, and that "only weak links exist between a district's average teacher salary and student performance on the MEAP." One article stated that "This finding would seem to shoot holes in the argument that higher salaries lure better teachers leading to better pupil performance. Little relationship can be determined between class size and MEAP scores. Teacher-pupil ratios also played little role." One school on Mackinac Island had only 10 students per teacher but "the lowest scores in the state on the MEAP exams."

ACCOUNTABILITY AND CONTROL

The most important observation was that "intense parental involvement in their children's schooling was the most frequently recurring theme in high scoring districts." Parental involvement, of course, raises the whole issue of accountability and control. The performance of any system, of any institution, of any business is a function of its accountability to its constituents or customers.

Socialist systems fail not only because they fail to energize the most productive asset of all, the individual human mind, but because as entrenched monopolies they are so totally unaccountable to the individual consumer—because they provide no market in which competing ideas and products can be tested, priced, approved or rejected, modified or abandoned. As Ray Eppert, the one-time chairman of Burroughs and a Detroit stalwart, once said in effect, "the freedom to succeed is the flip side of the freedom to fail." Abolish the freedom to fail, as socialists both abroad and here have been so eager to do, and you kill or punish the freedom to succeed. (That, incidentally, was the $166 billion lesson of the U.S. thrift industry.)

One reason why Gorbachev has such an economic mess on his hands is that the Soviet Union has no marketplace in which success or failure can be judged or priced. Its currency isn't convertible because there is no domestic market to determine or confirm its buying power. Without a market, without accountabilty, without individual power and control, you have a vast stagnant swamp. And that may explain precisely why, after so many years of early relative success, American public education suddenly went into such a tailspin in the middle 1960s. That tailspin coincided with the rapid centralization of public education away from parental control and local accountability, and into the hands of state and federal bureaucracies.

The genius of the American federal system is that it is the only system on earth that promotes competition among government entities, among cities, towns, counties, and states. That competition, that ability to generate better economic and social performance through better policies, keeps governments from abusing their monopoly powers.

I don't think it is any accident that in the early 1960s when we hit our all-time peak test score levels, about 60 percent of the funding of and therefore the control over public education was still at a local level—and therefore more directly accountable to the local taxpayers. We owned our schools, we paid for them, and we demanded performance from them and our children. But over the next 20 years, that control rapidly shifted away from local taxpayers and local school boards and parents, to the state and federal level, and with it went the performance levels of education. By 1980, when test scores bottomed out at 890 on the SAT's, that local control had fallen to its lowest level in history, 43 percent:

FALLING LOCAL CONTROL = FALLING PERFORMANCE?

Local Funding	%	SAT Scores
1960	60.0	978
1963	59.4	983
1966	55.5	967
1970	52.9	948
1976	46.4	903
1980	43.0	890
1983	44.6	893
1986	43.9	906
1987	43.9	904

Source: U.S. Department of Education

In short, precisely as the public education system centralized itself into more and more of a classic socialist monopoly model with greater and greater union domination under the two million-member National Education Association, the less accountable it became to the education consumer, and the poorer the result. This was precisely the finding of a lengthy and well documented Brookings Institution study of education by John Chubb and Terry Moe which asked the question why private schools, especially parochial schools, performed so much better even with similar lower income and minority students than public schools. The 1985 study concluded that parental choice and direct school accountability is what makes "Catholic schools and to a lesser extent other private schools produce significantly greater gains in achievement than public schools... equivalent to as much as a full year of learning...."

Chubb and Moe looked at the longitudinal studies of some 60,000 students in public and private schools, and concluded that apart from basic socio-economic conditions the one thing that mattered most to school performance was "the differences in the organization of public and private schools." The biggest difference: "Public schools have their resources allocated to them by authorities who do not directly consume their services, while private schools receive their resources in direct exchange for services rendered." One has no marketplace, the other is in the education marketing business. "Perform or perish," said the Brookings analyst, "brings considerable certitude to the relationship between private schools and their environments," and "only by increasing school autonomy, and "relying more on the signals from the market" do we have any chance to "offer the public the means to improve their schools...."

HOW LOCAL CONTROL PRODUCES BETTER EDUCATION

The best way to prove that they are right is to look at the relative performance of the school systems in this country that are most locally controlled and therefore the least like the socialist model versus those that are most state and federally controlled:

	% Local Funding	% SAT/ACT Scores	Grad. Rate
National Average	43.9	100.0	71.5
10 Most Locally Funded	60.1	109.4	75.4
10 Least Locally Funded	21.2	95.3	66.4
New Hampshire	90.7	103.5	73.3
Vermont	60.6	101.0	78.0
10 Most – NH, NB, OR, VT, SD, MI, WY, WI, IL, CO			
10 Least – HI, NM, WA, AK, AL, DE, MS, KY, WV, NC			

Source: U.S. Department of Education

The contrast is striking. The 10 most locally controlled states have 15 percent higher achievement levels than the 10 least accountable and nearly a 10 percentage point advantage in graduation rates. What's more, the locally-controlled systems actually tend to spend more on their students than the state-controlled, and to provide much higher teacher pay levels, and lower pupil-to-classroom ratios. While this is clearly not a scientific analysis, it does hint strongly at the correctness of the theory that when you pay for schools, you tend to demand more of them, and to get more from them, and in return you are willing to pay more for them.

Perhaps the most clear-cut example of this thesis in action is New Hampshire which, to the dismay of the educationists and unions, funds 90 percent of its public schools out of one of the highest local property tax rates in the nation. Its SAT scores are also consistently the highest in the nation, most recently at 938. What is intriguing is to contrast its performance with Vermont which funds only 60 percent of its education locally and has a large state education bureaucracy. A recent study by Colin and Rosemary Campbell of Dartmouth shows that while Vermont spends 39 percent per capita and 14 percent per student more than New Hampshire, it pays its teachers almost the identical average salaries and has about the same low teacher-to-student ratios. This means all of Vermont's extra spending goes into administrative bureaucracy. New Hampshire's SAT scores are 24 points higher than Vermont's, suggesting that not only has centralization weakened education accountability, it has added nothing of real instructional value, only higher costs.

THE CHOICE MOVEMENT AND EDUCATION PERESTROIKA

It is precisely this notion of accountability and local control that is driving the education "choice" movement which is so essential to education perestroika. As Bill Bennett told us back in 1988 when he still wore the less daunting hat of Education Secretary: "Until parents are given more choice in their children's education—and thus force more competititon and accountability on the education bureacracy, nothing fundamental will change, no mattter how much money we spend." He added: "Take the disaster in the Chicago school system where parents are literally begging us to help them get a voucher system started. You're talking about a system that spends $6,000 a kid in education costs with a 50 percent drop-out rate. These kids either get educated or they become criminals or get on drugs. For $6,000, parents have a right to expect something good, something positive." Indeed they do. I might add that in Boston they are now spending over $9,000 per attending student, per year, on a system where nearly 46 percent of the graduating class of 1990 were found unable to read or write at the 8th grade level when they were tested in the fall of 1989.

That would have forced nearly half the class to be held back under a new state regulation. What was the response of the state education bureaucracy? Repeal the regulation, or exempt the students from it! This is precisely why Bennett argued that an "education president" has to promote "a voucher system of some kind to empower parents to find better teaching, especially in low-income urban areas where it is obvious the system has broken down. Chicago, for example, can't make the case that parents, making their own choices, could do worse. How can they do any worse than they are doing now?"

John Chubb and Terry Moe reached the same conclusion, namely that "full or partial voucher systems" may be essential to force real education reform, in addition to magnet schools and other forms of public school choice. But Chubb admitted then that neither vouchers nor really wide open choice and accountability systems were likely to go anywhere. In a *Public Interest* article under the glum title of "Why the Current Wave of Education Reform Will Fail," he warned, "As long as public education is governed and administered as it is, politicians and administrators will not grant schools substantial autonomy." That's because, as he said, "reforms [like vouchers] that would transform the controls over schools from political and administrative arrangements to those of the market would shift much of the power over public education from elected and appointed government officials to...the professionals within the schools and to their essential clientele, students and their parents. That is where they run into trouble."

That is precisely why we need an "education president" with the courage to buck the entrenched education establishment and the politicians they now control. Unfortunately, so far, President Bush and Education Secretary Cavazos, while expressing strong support for choice within the public education monopoly, have been unwilling to support either serious privatization or vouchers. This is, I fear, somewhat analogous to Mikhail Gorbachev trying to get agricultural collectives to compete in the marketplace without extending the right to own private property to individual farmers, thus leaving consumers no private market option.

As much as we should welcome the rise of the educational choice movement now sweeping the various states, it is foolish to think that this alone will effect the kind of serious reform we need. The Boston school system has, after all, pioneered magnet schools for more than a decade, and has seen virtually no improvement in its dismal academic performance. The best proof that choice represents no serious threat to the monopoly is that even the quintessentially establishmentarian Carnegie Foundation, in its 1988 report on "The Imperiled Generation," endorsed the notion of choice within the public system. The whole theme of that report was the need for "more accountability" and more "market discipline." Yet the underlying premise of that report was that choice should not be allowed to kill off bad schools or punish teachers.

As Bill Bennett despairingly told us at the time, "the trouble is their approach has no teeth. No one gets fired in the Carnegie report. What you need in some systems like Chicago is a real house-cleaning, especially of the bureaucracy. You need somebody to take it over and just clean it out and start over." And what if this kind of voucherized private market approach kills off some schools? "So,"

Bennett told the Yale Political Union students who raised this question, "give them a funeral. No one gives a funeral to the kids who are now dropping out of those bad schools, and maybe out of life itself." But that is why he is now drug czar, and the education presidency has faded to an idle campaign promise—all rhetoric but little real reform. Sadly, we have seen somewhat the same dilution of the reformist zeal at the state and local level where a number of school committee candidates have won on the idea of parental empowerment, but which have since accommodated their agenda to the realities of an entrenched education and political bureaucracy.

This is why I now tend to agree with Myron Lieberman, Milton Friedman, George Roche, and others, that education choice without the private market-place option is doomed to fail, because it is merely tinkering at the margins and from within a basically bankrupt system. As Lieberman puts it in *Privatization and Educational Choice,* "Contrary to conventional reform proposals, the only ways to improve American education are (1) to foster private schools that compete with public schools and among themselves and/or (2) foster for-profit competition among service providers within the public school system. Both require privatization...transferring activities conducted by public employees to the private sector." Lieberman is precisely right when he says that too many of today's "educational reformers show a pervasive bias in favor of the status quo." Just as none of Eastern Europe's new leaders will change their nation's dismal economic performance until they break the grip of the central bureaucracies of *apparatchiks,* it is unlikely that we are going to fundamentally alter the results of the American public schools unless we either move their funding and control back to the local level, or break their monopoly position with aggressive private sector competition.

EDUCATION REFORM,
NOT TINKERING, KEY TO U.S. FUTURE

Yet, unless we do alter those results dramatically, the U.S. economy cannot survive the reckoning that is coming now in the global marketplace, and which will accelerate after 1992. Xerox Chairman David Kearns has argued, "the new agenda for school reform must be driven by competition and market discipline...the objective should be clear from the outset: complete restructuring. The public schools must change if we are to survive." Unfortunately, last June the delegates to the National Education Association (NEA) voted overwhelmingly to oppose all significant parental choice programs, or any competition between schools. It said "federal or state mandated parental option plans compromise the NEA's commitment to free, equitable, universal and quality public education for every student...."

It remains to be seen whether there is enough political will and courage to stand up to this education monopoly, particularly in the inner cities and among minorities, from which 40 percent of our future workforce entrants will come over the balance of this century. Our productive and competitive future as a nation clearly depends on it. Not only are we facing a steady decline in the rate of growth of entry-level workers, but at the very moment when their education performance continues to falter, the demands on those workers are growing geometrically.

In the 1970s less than 25 percent of the new jobs created were in what are classified as managerial or professional occupations—the highest Labor Department classification.

By the mid 1980s, contrary to the spurious disinformation of organized labor, over half the new jobs are in these higher paying and more demanding skills. As one expert, Janet Norwood, told the Joint Economic Committee of Congress in August 1988, "We are seeing a very large shift in occupational mix. Many of the jobs that used to require very little training are not growing as fast as those that require a lot of training." The Labor Department concluded in a 1987 study of long-term job trends: "Between now and the year 2000, a majority of all new jobs will require post-secondary education...and even the least skilled jobs will require a command of reading, computing and thinking that was once necessary only for the professions."

In the information revolution, our economy is increasingly dependent on each one of us. It is in our minds, and wholly the result of our individual abilities and understanding. Yet with a nearly 30 percent average drop out rate (up to 50 percent in inner cities in the nation's high schools), and with test scores stalled 74 points below their 1963 levels, there is no way the American education system can keep up with this developing demand upon us.

Thus, serious education reform is not merely a public policy issue—it is essential to our economic future survival. We cannot expect to compete in a world which is decentralizing power and freeing up economic wealth, with an education system that is still choking on its past centralization, and chained to a stagnating bureaucracy.

That system is still too deeply involved, both organizationally and ideologically in the old macro-view of socializing "little people" to become physical cogs in a big mechanistic, material machine, instead of opening up the unlimited individual mental horizons that exist in the quantum age. We are still teaching them instead how to adjust to an allegedly limited physical environment, rather than mentally embracing, shaping, and expanding it.

As I listened last June to President Mary Louise Hatfield Futrell's farewell address to the National Education Association, with its applauded litany of social, ecological, and economic limitation and disaster, I realized how far removed our present school bureaucracy and teaching profession are from grasping the emerging and exciting metaphysical reality of the information age, the cosmic potential of the economy in mind. To paraphrase the Preacher in Ecclesiastes, "Where there is no vision, the children perish."

ABOUT THE AUTHOR

Warren Brookes was an award-winning syndicated columnist for the *Detroit News* whose articles appeared regularly in the *Wall Street Journal*, *Reader's Digest, Policy Review* and approximately 50 daily newspapers nationwide. The author of *The Economy in Mind,* (Universal Books, 1982), he specialized in looking at the economic side of political and social issues. The well-known annual *Media Guide* gave him four stars every year, making him one of only two journalists to earn that distinction.

HOW COLLEGES ARE
FAILING OUR STUDENTS

Charles J. Sykes
July 1990

he banner that hung across the stage read simply, "Thank You, Alan Brinkley! We'll Miss You." As the young professor ended his last lecture, more than 500 students who filled the seats and aisles of Harvard's Sanders Theater rose in a standing ovation. By all accounts, Brinkley was one of Harvard's most gifted teachers. At 37, he taught the largest course in Harvard's history department and had won an American Book Award for his study of the Depression era. He further stood out from many of his Harvard colleagues because of his open-door policy and willingness to meet with students one-on-one, even though by some estimates, he taught one-third of all Harvard undergraduates in his various classes.

"Professor Brinkley was the first teacher who took an interest in me as a person," one student said afterward. "He advised me when I was choosing a concentration, helped me with my term paper for his class...." One of his colleagues, Professor David H. Donald, himself a leading authority on 18th-century American history, called Brinkley "a splendid young scholar and a superb teacher."

In 1985, Harvard denied Alan Brinkley tenure and effectively fired him. A slim majority of the tenured faculty members in the history department (13 of 23) had voted to recommend tenure, but the favorable recommendation was overturned by the dean of arts and sciences. Brinkley's case dramatically highlighted the fate of professors who emphasize teaching. It was particularly notable because of the contrast between Brinkley and his colleagues at the nation's most prestige-encrusted university. Harvard's history professors were notorious for the frequency of their absences from campus and the rarity with which many of them entered a classroom.

WHO'S LOOKING OUT FOR THE STUDENTS?

But even if Alan Brinkley were the exception because of his teaching ability, the way his case was handled was hardly exceptional. Shortly before Brinkley's dismissal, another popular professor, Bradford A. Lee, an expert in modern history and, like Brinkley, a winner of the teaching prize, had also been dismissed. With Brinkley's departure, three of the last four recipients of Harvard's teaching award had been denied tenure. Harvard is not the only school where the teaching award is a jinx. At Stanford, Yale and other schools, the pattern is the same and it goes beyond denying tenure: "There is little direction, little contact with professors, and so few courses offered each year," the Harvard student guide says, "that you'll swear they left half the course catalog on the floor of the registrar's office."

This is not much of an exaggeration. The course catalog denotes courses that are not being offered that year by putting them in brackets. So many Harvard history courses were bracketed one year that students printed up T-shirts reading simply: [History]. One recent year, almost all of the professors of American history were gone at the same time, gutting the curriculum and leaving undergraduates interested in American history at America's leading university to fend for themselves. "No one is looking out for the students," complained one major.

The academic culture is not merely indifferent to teaching, it is actively hostile to it. In the modern large university, no act of good teaching goes unpunished. Many academics try to justify themselves by blaming their students who are, they insist, often poorly prepared and uninterested in the subject matter. University professors are often loud in their criticism of the public elementary and secondary schools. Frequently they attempt to shift the debate on the failures of higher education to the failures at the lower levels.

But when the Holmes Group issued its report on the reform of teacher education in 1986, it reversed field on the professors. Part of the reason for the widespread ineptness of America's schoolteachers, the Holmes Group concluded, lies in the universities themselves. "They strive to hire highly qualified academic specialists, who know their subjects well and do distinguished research," the Holmes Group said. "But few of these specialists know how to teach well, and many seem not to care. The undergraduate education that intending teachers—and everyone else—receives is full of the same bad teaching that litters American high schools."

HOW TENURE REALLY WORKS

At the heart of the system are the academic departments and their power over the system of tenure. The process by which a young professor wins tenure—in effect, a lifetime job at a university—is widely misunderstood outside the academy itself. Although university administrators often have the final say, the tenure system is controlled by the professors themselves. Because a professor once granted tenure is virtually immovable for life and ties up a spot in the department's budget for decades, the decision to grant tenure is the most important made in academia.

Almost every school claims that tenure candidates' teaching abilities are weighed along with their published scholarship. The evidence to the contrary, however, is overwhelming. "Chancellors and vice chancellors say teaching is important," one professor at the University of Illinois says, "but no one believes it." Only a tiny percentage of schools ever sends faculty observers into a junior professor's classroom to evaluate his teaching. The treatment of teachers indicates academia's indifference to teaching, but it only hints at how deeply the contempt for it is ingrained within the academic culture. "It's the kiss of death," Associate Professor David Helfand, winner of one of Columbia University's General Studies Distinguished Teachers Awards, told *Newsweek on Campus*, "if you volunteer to teach two classes instead of one before tenure. They will say, 'This guy is a teacher.' "

CHANGING ATTITUDES TOWARDS TEACHING

The message is a common one in the university. Discussing one of his professors in "American Culture," a University of Michigan senior says: "He didn't even want to deal with students, it seemed like. He would just give a lecture and say, 'No, just deal with my T.A.' He didn't want to deal with us when we weren't in class."

My own experience may serve to underscore his point. Several years ago, I sat in on a meeting of the chairs of the various departments of sociology at the annual convention of the American Sociology Association. Much of the meeting was spent discussing the various lures the chairmen used to attract top students for their graduate schools, including packaging grants with what they called "honorific distinctions" and even giving academic stars "signing bonuses" to get them to attend their schools. "The graduate applicants expect this, and you better give it to them," one chair warned. The discussion of grants and perks and honorific distinctions had gone on for the better part of an hour before Eric Wagner spoke up.

Wagner, the chairman of Ohio University's sociology department, had a simpler recommendation. His department had sent students to some of the top graduate schools, but they had come away unimpressed and in some cases disgusted by what they found. The professors in the elite departments, he said, "are so busy with their own research they don't have time to spend with our students." He told the group that students he sent to Stanford were so upset by the arrogance and apparent indifference of the professors there that "they wouldn't touch your fellowships." His advise was simple: "Just pay attention to them," he pleaded. "That may be more important than just throwing money at them." The department chairs listened politely and went on to another subject.

TRIVIALIZATION OF THE CURRICULUM

The university curriculum is the flip side of the academic culture's attitude toward teaching. "In an environment that is serious about the quality of teaching," the Association of American Colleges said in its 1985 report, *Integrity in the College Curriculum*, "the grand design of the curriculum will receive the attention it deserves." But the actual environment of the university is anything but serious about the quality of teaching. And its attention to the design of the curriculum is reflected in the intellectual confusion, nonexistent standards, junk courses, so-called "guts," and blow-offs that are (or should be) the shame of American education.

But the curriculum is not completely without its rationale. Indeed, it bears the unmistakable mark of the professorial touch. As absurd as it is, the curriculum keeps the universities well-stocked and the students reasonably pacified, while demanding as little as possible from either students or professors. No other explanation can account for the melange of incoherence that confronts students at the modern university. Roaming freely through the trackless wastes of registration, a liberal arts sophomore at the University of Illinois bitterly laments his disappointment: "It seems like preregistration is a joke," he says. He had signed up for "Human Sexuality," but there were no available places. "I don't feel like taking bowling," he says. "I was looking forward to it. I guess there are a lot of undersexed people on this campus."

Not so at Middlebury College in Vermont, where students filled a class that discussed the issues of "popular culture, eroticism, esthetics, voyeurism, and misogyny" as they are reflected in the films of Brigitte Bardot. There are, in fact, few interests to which higher education does not cater. Auburn University offered a course in "Recreation Interpretive Services," which was described as "principles and techniques used to communicate natural, historical, and cultural features of outdoor recreation to park visitors." The school also listed in-depth courses in "Principles of Recreation," "Park and Recreation Maintenance," and "Recreation Leadership." At Kent State, students have been offered a smorgasbord of intellectual offerings, including "Camp Leadership," a course that covers "the role of the camper and counselor," and "Records Management," in which students "set up, explain, and maintain alphabetic, geographic, numerical, and subject filing systems." For the scholarly inclined, there is "Socio-Psychological Aspects of Clothing"; for the less rigorous minded, "Basic Roller Skating"; and for the adventurous, "Dance Roller Skating."

At the University of Illinois, students have been able to work toward their B.A. by taking "Pocket Billiards," or the "Anthropology of Play," which is described as "the study of play with emphasis on origin, diffusion, spontaneity, emergence, and diversity." The University of Massachusetts at Amherst has listed courses for credit in "Slimnastics" and "Ultimate Frisbee." Students at the University of Michigan who have taken "Sports Marketing and Management" have been given exams with such questions as: "Athletic administrators should be primarily concerned with two (2) groups: Name them." (Answer: players and coaches.) "True or false: At the Michigan Stadium a spectator can be readmitted to the game if he has a hand stamp visible." (Answer: False.) And for students fortunate enough to gain admission to "Music Video 454," the only textbook was the *Rolling Stone Book of Rock Video,* and one class project was a field trip to Hollywood where the students acted as extras in rock videos–for credit. On slower days, they analyzed videotapes of Weird Al Yankovic singing, "Dare to Be Stupid."

"CENTRAL TO THE TROUBLES . . ."

When the Association of American Colleges issued its report on the state of the curriculum in 1985, its conclusions were not surprising. "[W]hat passes as a college curriculum," the report said, had degenerated into "almost anything goes." But what distinguished the AAC report from its counterparts–and indeed from most analyses issued over the last 50 years–was the directness of its indictment. "Central to the troubles and to the solution are the professors...," the report charged.

"Adept at looking out for themselves–department staffing, student enrollments, courses reflecting narrow scholarly interests, attendance at professional meetings–professors unquestionably offer in their courses exquisite examples of specialized learning. *But who looks after the shop? Who takes responsibility, not for the needs of the history or English or biology department, but for the curriculum as a whole? Who thinks about the course of study as it is experienced by students? Who reviews and justifies and rationalizes the academic program for which a college awards the coveted credential: a bachelor's degree?* [Emphasis added.]"

The answer, of course, was nobody. Even the major, the AAC concluded, had become "little more than a gathering of courses taken in one department, lacking structure and depth...." The nature of the majors also "varies widely and irrationally" from one institution to another. The chair of the Committee for Economic Education of the American Economic Association confirmed that, confessing: "We know preciously little about what the economics major is or does for students."

The problem of the university curriculum is no longer merely that there is no central body of shared knowledge at the heart of the university education—certain books that all educated men and women presumably would read. In the last several decades—a period that corresponds exactly to the professoriate's rise to unchallenged power—the bachelor's degree has been so completely stripped of meaning that employers cannot even be sure if its holder has minimum skills that were once taken for granted among college graduates. Somewhere in the professoriate's endless curricular shell game, the universities lost track of the need to teach critical thinking, writing skills, or even basic knowledge about the world.

ILL-PREPARED GRADUATES

Even as academia's claims of success—and pleas for money—grew ever more insistent, stories about the ignorance of college students became nearly cliches. Typical is the story of the Harvard senior who thanked his history professor for explaining World War I, saying, "I've always wondered why people kept talking about a *Second* World War." When a literature professor asked a class of 200 students at a Midwestern school how many of them had heard of Don Quixote, only two students raised their hands. How many, she asked, were familiar with the "The Man of La Mancha?" Not a single hand went up. When historian Diane Ravitch visited one urban Minnesota university, she found that not one of 30 students in a course on "ethnic relations" had ever heard of the Supreme Court's landmark *Brown* v. *Board of Education* case.

The capacity of American higher education to turn out graduates utterly ignorant of international affairs and foreign languages continues to be the wonder of the world. Less than 15 percent of the seniors who were tested on their knowledge of world affairs in 1981 could answer even two-thirds of the questions correctly. Another survey found that 75 percent of college students had studied a foreign language at one time or another, but only seven percent thought they could understand a native speaker. Occasional surveys of college students' knowledge of geography have yielded horrific results.

What does a college degree mean in 1990? There once was a time when employers could be reasonably certain that the holders of a bachelor's degree from prestigious universities had a certain set of skills associated with educated men and women; that they could write a reasonably coherent business letter, that they could find Hong Kong on a map. That's unfortunately no longer the case.

THE NUMBERS GAME

The curriculum is a direct product of a fundamental paradox of life in academia. Even the most esoteric researcher scaling the highest peaks of scholastic sorcery ultimately relies on the undergraduates huddled in the foothills because they support his endeavors. This is particularly true in state universities where budget priorities are often closely tied to statistical measurements of enrollment. Because students are essentially hostages held by the universities to ensure society's continued good will (how long would universities survive if they dropped the pretense of educating undergraduates?), an elaborate numbers game colors the entire academic landscape.

The politics of this game, particularly when money is tight, virtually dictates the destruction of traditional standards of performance and intellectual integrity. "Guts"–undemanding, unchallenging courses of notoriously low standards–are a symbol of the process. But the gut is not an aberration in the modern university: It is the inevitable by-product of the professoriate's desire to expend as little time and energy on teaching combined with the imperative of keeping classrooms stocked with warm tuition-paying bodies. Nor is this limited merely to the lower end of the academic spectrum.

The numbers game also leads to the collapse of standards within the classroom itself. "If two-thirds of the students do not possess the skills necessary for professional success," wrote Professor David Berkman, a former chairman of a journalism department at an urban university, "there is no way you can flunk out a number anywhere near that percentage. There is simply too much intimidation in the academic environment. This is especially true for junior–meaning untenured–faculty members who teach many of the lower division courses where the bulk of the weeding out should take place....No junior instructor who wishes to gain tenure will flunk out 67 percent in an introductory course." The result, charges Berkman, is rampant pandering.

Perhaps the clearest evidence of the extent to which the bargain came to dominate undergraduate education was the inflation of grades that accompanied the rise of the new professoriate. At Harvard in 1978, 78 percent of the student body made it onto the dean's list, compared with 20 percent in the 1920s and 26 percent in the 1930s. The University of Michigan's 1974-75 freshman class had the weakest SAT scores in decades but was given the highest grade-point average ever. In 1975, 70 percent of the grades at Princeton were A's or B's. At Stanford, the average grade was A minus. "A lenient grader," observed author Lansing Lamont, "could draw students to his course like sparrows to a feeder."

The same pressures of the numbers game corrupted even the attempts to reform the badly rusting system. The most popular response to complaints about the incoherence of the curriculum was the introduction of new "core curriculums." But even the reforms were drawn into the professors' curricular numbers game.

In practice, observers argue, the latent function of the core curriculum at most state universities "is to allocate student credit hours across colleges and departments." The fact is that curricular coherence is the archenemy of the academic culture. If the undergraduate were ever to be placed at the center of the university and the curriculum molded around the kind of education he or she should receive, the entire focus of the university would be disrupted, and the power of the "academic villages" badly shaken.

The academy would be forced to revoke its carte blanche to the professors; and the villages would not only have to begin communicating within one another, they would have to make concessions to one another based on priorities other than their own. Some might even have to wither away. And the professors are not going to let that happen, at least not without an epic struggle in which they will use their entire arsenal of academic double-think.

A FAILURE TO SET STANDARDS

In the mid-1970s, the Carter administration summoned academic leaders to Washington to discuss the possibility of holding a White House conference called "Liberal Learning in the 1980s and Beyond." Harvard had just introduced its core curriculum, and the administration had noted with interest the apparent enthusiasm for reform among the nation's academic leaders.

But when confronted with specifics, they found that the academics were less forthcoming. Many professors bitterly opposed any effort to develop even a minimum curriculum, because they saw it as a reactionary infringement on their own prerogatives. Some were concerned over simple turf issues. But in public they took a different and by now predictable tack: They expressed lugubrious concern over the problems of defining any curriculum in light of the diversity of the student body, particularly the so-called new learners, who would not be in schools if they were forced to conform to traditional standards. After two days of wrangling, the organizers dropped the goal of defining liberal learning and in a burst of inspired profspeak changed it to "legitimizing diversity in the solving of common problems." Plans for a full-dress White House parley were quietly scrapped.

As if to prove that this was not a fluke, a 1983 conference sponsored by the National Endowment for the Humanities came to a similar "conclusion." At the NEH conference, representatives from 11 institutions of higher learning could agree only that "the curriculum should reflect the particular goals and character of the institution. There is no single effective education, and what works well at one institution may be a disaster at another...." In other words, they punted. But deciding not to decide was itself a powerful ratification of curricular disintegration because it left the academic culture untouched.

A slightly different variant of the new ideology can be seen in Brown University's hot "New Curriculum." More aptly, it is a non-curriculum. When it was introduced in the late 1960s, it abolished all course requirements and most of the other traditional standards of academia as well. The grade "D" was summarily dropped. But that hardly mattered because Brown students could take any number of courses pass/fail. And if by chance they did fail, that also did not really matter. Under the new dispensation, failures were not recorded on transcripts. ("I regard recording [failures] for the external world both superfluous and intimidating, or punishing," a Brown dean explained.) A Brown student could also fail as many as four courses and still graduate—with the equivalent of seven semesters of work at most schools.

Not coincidentally, after the New Curriculum was installed, Brown quickly became the hottest school in the Ivy League, if not the country. It has become, in fact, one of the nation's first "designer colleges." At one time or another in the 1980s, it boasted such luminaries in its student body as Amy Carter and the daughters of Jane Fonda, Geraldine Ferraro, Barbara Bach, Claus von Bulow, and Prince Michael of Greece. For a few years, it was the trendiest school in the country, even topping Harvard in the number of applications. It is also a museum piece of the academic mind in its purest state.

MORE HILLSDALES, FEWER HARVARDS NEEDED

What begins in the upper reaches of the academy inevitably works its way down into the classrooms of elementary schools where the basic issues of literacy are at stake. Ultimately, the legacy of the "guts" culture is a generation of kids with self-esteems well intact, but unable to read, write, or do even basic math—in other words, self-satisfied illiterates. It is hard to avoid the conclusion that despite its thinly veiled contempt for the lower level schools, the university is, in fact, the home office of educational mediocrity in America. Moreover, higher education simply is failing to educate students properly. That failure is not incidental nor is it the result of occasional lapses; it is built into the large-scale modern university system. In order to recover, schools need to go back to the fundamental question: What are the values and goals of a liberal education? They also need to return to educating undergraduates, and to a coherent curriculum, rather than pursuing grants. Professors need to be reminded that students and classroom teaching are their first priorities.

It is no accident that the handful of schools which haven't forgotten what education is all about are small private liberal arts colleges, or that these institutions are neglected by their larger and more "mainstream" counterparts, the Big Ten and state universities. Hillsdale College is a sterling example, however, of a place where professors and administrators acknowledge that teaching is more than the mere transmittal of dead facts and that teachers are molders of human beings who can, in the act of communicating, convey passion and excitement about learning while fostering new skills in students. This is why we ought to hope for more Hillsdales and fewer Harvards in the future of American education.

ABOUT THE AUTHOR

*C*harles J. Sykes is the author of *Profscam: Professors and the Demise of Higher Education* (Regnery Gateway, 1988), and *The Hollow Men: Politics and Corruption in Higher Education* (Regnery Gateway, 1990). He is also co-editor of *The National Review College Guide* (National Review Books, 1991) From 1983-87, he served as editor-in-chief of the nation's top award-winning metropolitan journal, *Milwaukee Magazine*.

Portions of this essay originally appeared in *Profscam* and are reprinted with the permission of Regnery Gateway.

FREE MARKETS
AND FREE MEN

WHATEVER HAPPENED TO
FREE ENTERPRISE?

Ronald Reagan
January 1978

uring the presidential campaign last year, there was a great deal of talk about the seeming inability of our economic system to solve the problems of unemployment and inflation. Issues such as taxes and government power and costs were discussed, but always these things were discussed in the context of what government intended to do about it. May I suggest for your consideration that *government* has already done too much about it? That indeed, government, by going outside its proper province, has caused many if not most of the problems that vex us?

How much are we to blame for what has happened? Beginning with the traumatic experience of the Great Depression, "We the People" have turned more and more to government for answers that government has neither the right nor the capacity to provide. Unfortunately, government as an institution always tends to increase in size and power, and so government attempted to provide the answers.

The result is a fourth branch of government added to the traditional three of executive, legislative and judicial: a vast federal bureaucracy that's now being imitated in too many states and too many cities, a bureaucracy of enormous power which determines policy to a greater extent than any of us realize, very possibly to a greater extent than our own elected representatives. And it can't be removed from office by our votes.

To give you an illustration of how bureaucracy works in another country, England in 1803 created a new civil service position. It called for a man to stand on the cliffs of Dover with a spyglass and ring a bell if he saw Napoleon coming. They didn't eliminate that job until 1945. In our own country, there are only two government programs that have been abolished. The government stopped making rum on the Virgin Islands, and we've stopped breeding horses for the cavalry.

We bear a greater tax burden to support that permanent bureaucratic structure than any of us would have believed possible just a few decades ago. When I was in college, governments, federal, state and local, were taking a dime out of every dollar earned and less than a third of that paid for the federal establishment. Today, governments, federal, state, and local, are taking 44 cents out of every dollar earned, and two-thirds of that supports Washington, D.C. It is the fastest growing item in the average family budget, and yet it is not one of the factors used in computing the cost of living index. It is the biggest single cost item in the family budget, bigger than food, shelter and clothing all put together.

When government tells us that in the last year Americans have increased their earnings nine percent, and since the inflation is six percent, we're still three percentage points better off, or richer than we were the year before, the government is being deceitful. That was *before* taxes. After taxes, the people of America are three percentage points worse off, poorer than they were before they got the nine percent raise. Government profits by inflation.

At an economic conference in London several months ago, one of our American representatives was talking to the press. He said you have to recognize that inflation doesn't have any single cause and therefore has no single answer. Well, if he believed that, he had no business being at an economic conference. Inflation is caused by one thing, and it has one answer. It is caused by government spending more than government takes in, and it will go away when government stops doing that, and not before.

Government has been trying to make all of us believe that somehow inflation is like plague, or drought, or locusts, trying to make us believe that no one has any control over it and we just have to bear it when it comes along and hope it will go away. The truth is simpler than that. From 1933 until the present, our country has doubled the amount of goods and services that are available for purchase. In that same period we have multiplied the money supply by 23 times. So $11.50 is chasing what one dollar used to chase. And that is all that inflation is: a depreciation of the value of money.

Ludwig von Mises once said, "Government is the only agency that can take a perfectly useful commodity like paper, smear it with some ink, and render it absolutely useless."

There are 73 million of us working and earning, by means of private enterprise, to support ourselves and our dependents. We support, in addition, 81 million other Americans totally dependent on tax dollars for their year-round living. Now it is true that 15 million of those are public employees and they also pay taxes, but their taxes are simply a return to government of dollars that first had to be taken from 73 million. I say this to emphasize that the people working and earning in private business and industry are the only resource that government has.

IN DEFENSE OF FREE ENTERPRISE

More than anything else, a new political and economic mythology, widely believed by too many people, has increased government's ability to interfere as it does in the marketplace. "Profit" is a dirty word, blamed for most of our social ills. In the interest of something called consumerism, free enterprise is becoming far less free. Property rights are being reduced, and even eliminated, in the name of environmental protection. It is time that a voice be raised on behalf of the 73 million independent wage earners in this country, pointing out that profit, property rights and freedom are inseparable, and that you cannot have the third unless you continue to be entitled to the first two.

Even many of us who believe in free enterprise have fallen into the habit of saying, when something goes wrong, "There ought to be a law." Sometimes I think there ought to be a law against saying: "There ought to be a law." The German statesman Bismark said, "If you like sausages and laws you should never watch either one of them being made." It is difficult to understand the ever-increasing number of intellectuals in the groves of academe (Hillsdale College excepted) who contend that our system could be improved by the adoption of some of the features of socialism.

In any comparison between the free market system and socialism, nowhere is the miracle of capitalism more evident than in the production and distribution of food. We eat better, for a lower percentage of earnings, than any other people on earth. We spend about 17 percent of the average family's after-tax income for food. The American farmer is producing two and one-half times as much as he did 60 years ago with one-third of the man-hours on one-half of the land. If his counterparts worldwide could reach his level of skill we could feed the entire world population on one-tenth of the land that is now being farmed worldwide.

The most striking example is a comparison between the two superpowers. Some years ago the Soviet Union had such a morale problem with the workers on the collective farms that they finally gave each worker a little plot of ground and told him he could farm it for himself and sell in the open market what he raised. Today, less than four percent of Russia's agricultural land is privately farmed in that way, yet that four percent produces 40 percent of all of Russia's vegetables, and 60 percent of all its meat.

A number of American scholars did some research on comparative food prices recently. They had to take the prices in the Russian stores and our own stores and translate them into minutes and hours of labor at the average income of each country. With one exception, they found that the Russians have to work two to ten times as long to buy various food items than do their American counterparts. The one exception was potatoes. There the price on their potato bins equalled less work time for them than it did for us. There was one hitch though—they didn't have any potatoes!

In spite of all the evidence that points to the free market as the most efficient economic system in the world, we continue down a road that is bearing out the prophecy of Alexis de Tocqueville, a Frenchman who came here 130 years ago. He was attracted by the miracle that was America. Think of it: our country was only 70 years old and already we had achieved such a miraculous living standard, such productivity and prosperity, that the rest of the world was amazed. So he came here and he looked at everything he could see in our country, trying to find the secret of our success, and then he went back and wrote a book about it. Even then, 130 years ago, he saw signs prompting him to warn us that if we weren't constantly on guard, we would find ourselves covered by a network of regulation controlling every activity. He said if that came to pass we would one day find ourselves a nation of timid animals with government the shepherd.

Was Tocqueville right? Well, today we are covered by tens of thousands of regulations to which we add about 25,000 new ones each year.

THE COST OF GOVERNMENT REGULATION

A study of 700 of the largest corporations has found that if we could eliminate unnecessary regulation of business and industry, we would instantly reduce the inflation rate by half. Other economists have found that overregulation of business and industry amounts to a hidden five-cent sales tax for every consumer. The misdirection of capital investment costs us a quarter of a million jobs. That is half as many as the President wants to create by spending $32 billion over the next two years. And with all of this comes the burden of government-required paperwork.

It affects education—look, for example, at the problems of financing, particularly at private educational institutions. I had the president of a university tell me the other day that government-required paperwork on his campus alone has raised the administrative costs from $65,000 to $600,000. That would underwrite a pretty good faculty chair. Now the president of the Eli Lilly drug company says his firm spends more man-hours on government-required paperwork than they do on heart and cancer research combined. He told of submitting one ton of paper, 120,000 pages of scientific data, most of which he said were absolutely worthless for FDA's purposes, in triplicate, in order to get a license to market an arthritis medicine. So, the United States is no longer first in the development of new health-giving drugs and medicines. We are producing 60 percent fewer than we were 15 years ago.

And it is not just the drug industry which is overregulated. How about the independent men and women of this country who spend $50 billion a year sending 10 billion pieces of paper to Washington where it costs $20 billion each year in tax money to shuffle and store that paper away? We are so used to talking billions—does anyone realize how much a single billion is? A billion minutes ago, Christ was walking on this earth. A billion hours ago, our ancestors lived in caves, and it is questionable as to whether they had discovered the use of fire. A billion dollars ago was 19 hours in Washington, D.C. And it will be another billion in the next 19 hours, and every 19 hours until they adopt a new budget at which time it will be almost a billion and a half.

It all comes down to this basic premise: if you lose your economic freedom, you lose your political freedom and, in fact, all freedom. Freedom is something that cannot be passed on genetically. It is never more than one generation away from extinction. Every generation has to learn how to protect and defend it. Once freedom is gone, it is gone for a long, long time. Already, too many of us, particularly those in business and industry, have chosen to switch rather than fight.

We should take inventory and see how many things we can do ourselves that we have come to believe only government can do. Let me take one that I'm sure everyone thinks is a government monopoly and properly so. Do you know that in Scottsdale, Arizona, there is no city fire department? There, the per capita cost for fire protection and the per capita fire loss are both one-third of what they are in cities of similar size. And the insurance rates reflect this. Scottsdale employs a private, profit-making, firefighting company, which now has about a dozen clients out in the western states.

Sometimes I worry if the great corporations have abdicated their responsibility to preserve the freedom of the marketplace out of a fear of retaliation or a reluctance to rock the boat. If they have, they are feeding the crocodile hoping he'll eat them last. You *can* fight city hall, and you don't have to be a giant to do it. In New Mexico, there is a little company owned by a husband and wife. The other day two OSHA inspectors arrived at the door. They demanded entrance in order to go on a hunting expedition to see if there were any violations of their safety rules. The wife, who happens to be company president, said "Where's your warrant?" They said, "We don't need one." She said, "You do to come in here," and she shut the door. Well, they went out and got a warrant, and they came back, but this time she had her lawyer with her. He looked at the warrant and argued that it did not show probable cause. A federal court has since upheld her right to refuse OSHA entrance.

Why don't more of us challenge what Cicero called the "arrogance of officialdom?" Why don't we set up communications between organizations and trade associations? This would rally others to come to the aid of an individual like that, or to an industry or profession when they're threatened by the barons of bureaucracy, who have forgotten that we are their employers. Government by the people works when the people work at it. We can begin by turning the spotlight of truth on the widespread political and economic mythology that I mentioned.

A recent poll of college and university students (they must have skipped this campus) found that the students estimated that business profits in America average 45 percent. That is nine times the actual average of business profits in this country. It was understandable that the students made that mistake, because the professors in the same poll guessed that the profits were even higher.

Then there is the fairy tale born of political demagoguery that the tax structure imposes unfairly on the low earner with loopholes designed for the more affluent. The truth is that at $23,000 of earnings you become one of that exclusive band of 10 percent of the wage-earners in America paying 50 percent of the income tax but only taking five percent of all the deductions. The other 95 percent of the deductions are taken by the 90 percent of the wage-earners below $23,000 who pay the other half of the tax.

The most dangerous myth is that business can be made to pay a larger share of taxes, thus relieving the individual. Politicians preaching this are either deliberately dishonest, or economically illiterate, and either one should scare us. Business doesn't pay taxes, and who better than business could make this message known? Only people pay taxes, and people pay as consumers every tax that is assessed against a business. Passing along their tax costs is the only way businesses can make a profit and stay in operation.

The federal government has used its taxing power to redistribute earnings to achieve a variety of social reforms. Politicians love those indirect business taxes, because it hides the cost of government. During the New Deal days, an undersecretary of the Treasury wrote a book in which he said that taxes can serve a "higher purpose" than just raising revenue. He claimed they could be an instrument of social and economic control to redistribute wealth and income and to penalize particular industries and economic groups.

We need to put an end to that kind of thinking. We need a simplification of the tax structure. We need an indexing of the surtax brackets, a halt to government's illicit profiteering through inflation. It is as simple as this: every time the cost-of-living index goes up one percent, the government's revenue goes up one and one-half percent. Above all, we need an overall cut in the cost of government. Government spending is not a stimulant to the economy; it is a drag on the economy. Only a decade ago, about 15 percent of corporate gross income was required to pay the interest on corporate debt; now it is 40 percent. Individuals and families once spent about eight percent of their disposable income on interest on consumer debt, installment buying, mortgages, and so forth. Today, it is almost one-fourth of their total earnings. In the last 15 years state and local government costs have gone from $70 billion to $220 billion. The total private and public debt is growing four times as fast as the output of goods and services.

Again, there is something we can do. Congressman Jack Kemp (R-NY) has a bill before the Congress designed to increase productivity and to create jobs for people. Over a three-year period, it calls for reducing the income tax for all of us by a full one-third. It would also reduce the corporate tax from 48 to 45 percent. The base income tax would no longer be 20 percent but 14 percent and the ceiling would be 50 percent instead of 70 percent. Finally, it would double the exemption for smaller businesses before they get into the surtax bracket. It would do all of the things that we need in order to provide investment capital, increase productivity, and create jobs.

We can say this with assurance, because it has been done twice before: in the 1920s under Harding and Coolidge and again in the 1960s under John F. Kennedy. In the 1960s the stimulant to the economy was so immediate that even government's revenues increased because of the broadening base of the economy. Kemp's bill is gaining support but unfortunately the majority in Congress is concerned with further restrictions on our freedom.

To win this battle against big government, we must communicate with each other. We must support the doctor in his fight against socialized medicine, the oil industry in its fight against crippling controls and repressive taxes, and the farmer, who hurts more than most because of government harrassment and rule-changing in the middle of the game. All of these issues concern each one of us, regardless of what our trade or profession may be. Corporate America must begin to realize that it has allies in the independent business community, the shopkeepers, the craftsmen, the farmers, and the professions. All these men and women are organized in a great variety of ways, but right now we only talk in our own organizations about our own problems. What we need is a liaison between these organizations to realize how much strength we as a people still have if we will only use that strength.

In regard to the oil industry, is there anyone who isn't concerned with the energy problem? Government caused that problem while we all stood by unaware that we were involved. Unnecessary regulations and prices and imposed price limits back in the 1950s are the direct cause of today's crisis. Our crisis is not due to a shortage of fuel; it is due to a surplus of government. Now we have a new agency of enormous power, with 20,000 employees and a $10.5 billion budget. That is more than the gross earnings of the top seven oil companies in the United States. The creation of the Department of Energy is nothing more than a first step towards nationalization of the oil industry.

While I believe no one should waste a natural resource, the conservationists act as if we have found all the oil and gas there is to be found in this continent, if not the world. Do you know that 57 years ago our government told us we only had enough for 15 years? Nineteen years went by, and they told us we only had enough left for 13 more years. We have done a lot of driving since then, and we'll do a lot more if government will do one simple thing: get out of the way and let the incentives of the marketplace urge the industry to find the sources of energy this country needs.

We've had enough of sideline kibitzers telling us the system they themselves have disrupted with their social tinkering can be improved or saved if we'll only have more of that tinkering or government planning and management. They play fast and loose with a system that for 200 years made us the light of the world, the refuge for people everywhere who just yearn to breathe free. It is time we recognized that the system, no matter what our problems are, has never failed us once. Every time *we* have failed the system, usually by lacking faith in it, usually by saying we have to change and do something else. A Supreme Court Justice has said the time has come, is indeed long overdue, for the wisdom, ingenuity, and resources of American business to be marshalled against those who would destroy it.

What specifically should be done? The first essential for the businessman is to confront the problem as a primary responsibility of corporate management. It has been said that history is the patter of silken slippers descending the stairs and the thunder of hobnail boots coming up. Through the years, we have seen millions of people fleeing the thunder of those boots to seek refuge in this land. Now too many of them have seen the signs, signs that were ignored in their homeland before the end came, appearing here. They wonder if they will have to flee again, but they know there is no place to run. Before it is too late, will we use the vitality and magic of the marketplace to save this way of life, or will we one day face our children, and our children's children, when they ask us where we were and what we were doing on the day that freedom was lost?

ABOUT THE AUTHOR

Ronald Reagan served two terms as President of the United States (1980-1988), and inspired the "Reagan Revolution," which called for lower taxes, less government intervention, a strong defense, and a return to traditional values. Elected governor of California in 1966 and reelected through 1970, he relinquished a career as an actor; his move into the world of politics has led him to become one of the world's most popular statesmen.

COPING WITH IGNORANCE

F.A. Hayek
July 1978

I t is to me not only a great honor but also the discharge of an intellectual duty and a real pleasure to discuss here Ludwig von Mises. There is no single man to whom I owe more intellectually, even though he was never my teacher in the institutional sense of the word.

I came originally from the other of the two original branches of the Austrian school. Mises had been an inspired pupil of Eugen Böehm von Bawerk, who died comparatively early and whom I knew only as a friend of my grandfather before I knew what the word "economics" meant. I was personally a pupil of his contemporary, friend and brother-in-law, Friedrich von Wieser. I was attracted to Wieser because, unlike most of the other members of the Austrian school, he had a good deal of sympathy with a mild Fabian socialism to which I was inclined as a young man. He prided himself that his theory of marginal utility had provided the basis of progressive taxation, which then seemed to me one of the ideals of social justice.

It was he who, just retiring as I graduated, sent me with a letter of introduction to Ludwig von Mises. Mises was one of the directors of a new temporary government office concerned with settling certain problems arising out of the treaty of St. Germain, and he was looking for young lawyers with some understanding of economics and knowledge of foreign languages. I remember vividly how, almost exactly fifty-six years ago, after presenting to Mises my letter of introduction by Wieser, in which I was described as a promising young economist, Mises said, "Well, I've never seen you at my lectures."

That was nearly true. I had looked in at one of his lectures and found that a man so conspicuously antipathetic to the kind of Fabian views which I then held was not the sort of person to whom I wanted to go. But of course things changed.

The meeting was the beginning. After a short conversation, Mises asked, "When can you start work?" This led to a long, close collaboration. First, for five years, he was my official chief in that government office and then vice president of an institute of business cycle research which we had created together. During these ten years he certainly had more influence regarding my outlook on economics than any other man. It was essentially his second great work, *Die Gemein Wirtscaft* of 1922, which appeared in English translation later as *Socialism*, that completely won me over to his views. And then in his private seminar, as we called the little discussion group which met at his office, I became gradually and intimately familiar with his thinking.

I do not wish, however, to claim to be an authoritative interpreter of Mises' views. Although I do owe him a decisive stimulus at a crucial point of my intellectual development, and continuous inspiration through a decade, I have perhaps most profited from his teaching because I was not initially his student at the university, an innocent young man who took his word for gospel, but came to him as a trained economist, versed in a parallel branch of Austrian economics from which he gradually, but never completely, won me over. Though I learned that he usually was right in his conclusions, I wasn't always satisfied by his arguments, and retained to the end a certain critical attitude that sometimes forced me to build different constructions. To my great pleasure these usually led to the same conclusions. I am to the present moment pursuing the questions that he made me see, and that, I believe, is the greatest benefit a scientist can confer on one of the next generation.

I do not know whether my making our incurable ignorance of most of the particular circumstances which determine the course of this great society the central point of the scientific approach would have Mises' approval. It is probably a development that goes somewhat beyond his views, because Mises himself was still much more a child of the rationalist age of Enlightenment and of continental rather than of English liberalism, in the European sense of the word, than I am myself. But I do flatter myself that he sympathized with my departure in this direction, which I like to describe briefly as a movement back from Voltaire to Montesquieu.

I've come to believe that both the aim of the market order, and therefore the object of explanation of the theory of it, is to cope with *the inevitable ignorance of everybody regarding most of the particular facts which determine this order.* By a process which men do not understand, their activities have produced an order much more extensive and comprehensive than anything they can comprehend, but on the functioning of which they have become utterly dependent.

Even two hundred years after Adam Smith's *Wealth of Nations,* it is not yet fully understood that it is the great achievement of the market to have made a far-ranging division of labor possible, that it brings about a continuous adaptation of economic effect to millions of particular facts or events which in their totality are not known and cannot be known to anybody. A real understanding of the process which brings this about was long blocked by post-Smithian classical economics which adopted a labor or cost theory of value.

For a long time, the misconception that costs determined prices prevented economists from recognizing that it was prices that operated as the indispensable signals telling producers what costs it was worth expending on the production of the various commodities and services, and not the other way around. It was this crucial insight which finally broke through and established itself about a hundred years ago through the so-called marginal revolution in economics.

The chief insight gained by modern economists is that the market is essentially an ordering mechanism, growing up without anybody wholly understanding it, that enables us to utilize widely dispersed information about the significance of circumstances of which we are mostly ignorant. However, the various planners (and not only the planners in the socialist camp) and dirigists have still not yet grasped this. I do not believe that it is merely present ignorance, that we expect the future advance of knowledge will partly remove, that makes a rational effort at central planning wholly impossible. I believe such a central utilization of necessarily widely dispersed knowledge of particular and temporary circumstances must forever remain impossible. We can have a far-ranging division of labor only by relying on the impersonal signals of prices. That, here and now, we economists do not know enough to be justified to undertake such a task as the planning of the whole economic system seems to me so obvious that I find it increasingly difficult to treat the contrary belief with any respect.

It is a basic fact that we as scientists have to explain the results of the actions of men, that produces a sort of order by following signals inducing them to adapt to facts that they do not know. It creates a comparable or similar problem of coping with ignorance such as the people in economics encounter even more than the people who undertake to explain this process. It is a difficulty that all attempts at a theoretical explanation of the market process face, though it appears that not many economists have been clearly aware of the source of the difficulties that they encounter.

If the chief problem of economic decisions is one of coping with inevitable ignorance, the task of a science of economics trying to explain the joint effects of hundreds of thousands of such decisions on men in many different positions has to deal with an ignorance as it were, of a second order of magnitude, because the explaining economist does not even know what all the acting people know; he has to provide an explanation without knowing the determining facts, not even knowing what the individual members in the economic system know about these facts.

We are not in the happy position in which the theorists of a relatively simple phenomena find themselves. When they have formed a hypothesis about how two or three variables are interrelated, they can test such a hypothesis by inserting into their abstract formula, observing values replacing the blanks, and then see whether the conclusions are correct. Our problem is that even if we have thought out a beautiful and possibly correct theory of the complex phenomema with which we have to deal, we can never ascertain all the concrete specific data of a particular position, simply because we do not know all that which the acting people know. But it is the joint results of those actions which we want to predict.

If the market really achieves a utilization of more information than any participant in this market process possesses, the outcome must depend on more particular facts than the scientific observer can insert into his tentative hypothesis that is intended to explain the whole process.

There are two possible ways in which economists have endeavored at least partly to overcome this difficulty.

The first, represented by what today we call microeconomics, resignedly accepts the fact that because of this difficulty we can never achieve a *full* explanation, or an exact prediction of the particular outcome of a given situation, but must instead be content with what I have occasionally called a "pattern prediction" or, earlier a "prediction of the principle." All we can achieve is to say what kinds of things will not happen and what sort of pattern the resulting situation will show, without being able to predict a particular outcome.

This kind of microeconomics attempts, by the construction of simplified models in which all the kinds of attitudes and circumstances we meet in the real life are represented, to simulate the kind of movements and changes which we observe in the real world. Such a theory can tell us what sort of changes we can expect in the real world, the general character of which our model indicates, that reduces (not so much in scale as in the number of distinct elements), the facts with which we have to deal, to make its workings still comprehensible or surveyable.

I still believe that this is the only approach that is entitled to regard itself as scientific. Being scientific involves in this connection a frank admission of how limited our powers of prediction really are. It still does lead to some falsifiable predictions, namely what sorts of events are possible in a given situation and which are not.

It is, in this sense, an empirical theory even though it consists largely, but not entirely, of propositions that are self-evident once they are stated. Indeed, I doubt whether microeconomic theory has ever discovered any new facts. Decreasing returns, decreasing marginal productivity or marginal utility, decreasing marginal rates of substitution were of course all phenomena familiar to ordinary people even if these did not call them by those names. In fact, it is only because ordinary people knew these facts, long before economists discovered their importance, that they have always been among the determinants of how the market actually functions. What the economic theorists found out was merely the relevance of these particular facts for the decision of individuals in their interactions with other persons.

It is the obscuring of the empirical fact of people learning what others do by a process of communication of knowledge that has always made me reluctant to accept Mises' claim of an *a priori* character of the whole of economic theory, although I agree with him that much of it consists merely in working out the logical implications of certain initial facts.

I recognize with him microeconomic theory as the only legitimate economic theory because, and in so far as, it recognizes the inevitable limitation of our possible knowledge of the objective facts that determine any given situation; and we need claim no more than we are entitled to claim.

I will not deny that we find also in the microeconomic literature a good deal of indefensible pretense of a great deal more. There is, of course, in the first instance, the frequent abuse of the convenient conception of "equilibrium" toward which the market process is said to tend. I will not say that there are not forces at work that can usefully be described as equilibrating tendencies.

But equilibrating forces are of course at work in any stream of a liquid and must be taken into account in any attempt to analyze the flow of such a stream. Such a stream in the physical sense of the word will never reach a state of equilibrium. And the same is true of the economic efforts of the production and use of goods and services where every part may all the time tend toward a partial or local equilibrium, but long before that is reached the circumstances to which the local efforts adapt themselves will have changed themselves as a result of similar processes. All we can claim for the achievement of microeconomic theory is that the signals which the prices constitute will always make the individuals change their plans in the direction made necessary by actual changes of which they have no direct knowledge—not that this process will ever lead to what some economists call an equilibrium.

Not content with this limited insight, which economics can in fact supply, economists ambitious to make it more precise have often spoiled microeconomics by a tendency, which we shall encounter in a more systematic form when I pass on to the second type of approach, macroeconomics. They tried to deal with our inescapable ignorance of the data required for a full explanation, the macroeconomic one, by trying measurements I shall discuss later.

I will at this stage make only two further comments on this. The first is that it is an erroneous belief, characteristic of bad mathematicians, that mathematics is essentially quantitative and that, therefore, to build on the great achievements of the founders of mathematical economics, men like Jevons, Walras and Pareto, one has to introduce quantitative data obtained by measurements. That was certainly not the intention of the founders of mathematical economics. They understood much better than their successors that algebraic mathematical formulae are the preeminent method for describing abstract patterns without assuming or possessing particular information about the specific magnitudes involved. One great mathematician has indeed described a mathematician as a maker of patterns. In this sense mathematics can be very helpful to us.

The second point that I want to make is that a particular reason that in the physical sciences makes measurements of concrete magnitudes the hallmark of scientific procedure do not apply to the explanation of human action. The true reason why the physical sciences must rely on measurements is that it has been recognized that things that appear alike to our senses frequently do not behave in the same manner, and that sometimes things that appear alike to us behave very differently if examined.

The physicist, to arrive at valid theories, is often compelled to substitute for the classification of different objects that our senses provide to us a different classification that is based solely on the relations of objective things toward each other.

Now this is really what measurement amounts to: a classification of objects according to the manner in which they act on other objects. But to explain human action all that is relevant is how the things appear to human beings, to acting men. This depends on whether men regard two things as the same or different kinds of things, not what they really are, unknown to them. For our purposes the results of measurements (at least so far as these are not performed by the people whose actions we want to explain) are wholly uninteresting.

The belief derived from physics that measurement is an essential foundation of all sciences is very old. More than 300 years ago, there was a German philosopher, Erhard Weigel, who strove to construct a universal science which he proposed to call "Pantometria," based, as the name says, on measuring everything. Much of economics (and much of contemporary psychology) has indeed become "Pantometria" in the sense that if you don't know what measurements mean, you should measure anyhow because *that* is what science does. The social sciences building at the University of Chicago, since it was built 40 years ago, still bears on its outside an inscription taken from the famous physicist Lord Kelvin: "When you cannot measure, your knowledge is meager and unsatisfactory." I will admit that that may be true, but it is certainly not scientific to insist on measurement when you don't know what your measurements mean. There are cases in which measurements are not relevant. What has done much damage to microeconomics is striving for a pseudo-exactness by imitating methods of the physical sciences which have to deal with what are fundamentally much more simple phenomena. And the assumption that it is possible to ascertain all the relevant particular facts still completely dominates the alternative methods of dealing with our constitutional ignorance, which economists have tried to overcome. This of course, is what has come to be called macroeconomics, as distinct from microeconomics.

The basic idea on which this approach proceeds is fairly simple and obvious.

If we cannot know all the individual facts that determine individual action and thereby the economic process, we must start from the most comprehensive information that we can obtain about them, and that is the statistical figures about aggregates and averages. Again, the model that is followed is provided by the physical sciences which, where they have to deal with true mass phenomena such as the movement of millions of molecules with which thermodynamics has to deal (where we admittedly know nothing about the movement of any individual molecule), the law of large numbers enables us to discover statistical regularities or probabilities that indeed, in this way, provide an adequate foundation for reliable predictions.

The trouble is that in the disciplines which endeavor to explain the structure of society, we do not have to deal with true mass phenomena. The events which we must take into account in any attempt to predict the outcome of particular social processes are never so numerous as to enable us to substitute ascertained probabilities for information about the individual events. As a distinguished thinker, the late Warren Weaver of the Rockefeller Foundation, has pointed out, both in the biological and in the social sciences frequently we cannot rely on probabilities, or the law of large numbers, because, unlike the positions that exist in the physical sciences, where statistical evidence of probabilities can be substituted for information on particular facts, we have to deal with what he calls "organized complexity," where we cannot expect to find permanent constant relations between aggregates or averages.

Indeed, this intermediate field between the simple phenomena of the physical sciences, where everything can be explained by theoretical formulae that contain no more than two or three unknowns, and the instance where a large enough number of events to be able to deal with true mass phenomena to rely on probability is our subject. In the social sciences, moreover, phenomena are not made up of sufficiently large numbers of similar events to enable us to ascertain the probabilities for their occurrence.

In order to provide a full explanation we would have to have information about every single event that, of course is impossible to obtain. But while microtheorists have resigned themselves to the consequent limitations of our powers and admit that we must be content with what I've called mere pattern predictions, many of the more ambitious and impatient students of these problems refuse to recognize these limitations to our possible knowledge and possible power of prediction, and therefore also of our possible power of control.

What drives people to the pursuit of statistical research is usually the hope of discovering in this way new facts of general and not merely historical importance. But this hope is inevitably disappointed. I certainly do not wish to underrate the importance of historical information about the particular situation. I doubt, however, whether the observation and measurement of true mass phenomena has significantly improved our understanding of the market process. What we can find by this procedure, as by all observation of particular circumstances, may possibly be special relations, determined by the particular circumstances of the moment and the place, which indeed perhaps for some time may enable us to make correct predictions. But with general laws that help to explain how at different places the course of economic affairs is determined, these quantitative relations between measurable magnitudes have precious little to do. Indeed, even the very moderate hopes that I myself had at one time concerning the usefulness of such economic forecast based on observed statistical regularities has mostly been disappointed. The concrete course of the process of adaptation to unknown circumstances cannot be predicted. All we can predict is certain abstract features of the process, not its concrete manifestations.

It is now frequently assumed that at least the theory of money, in the nature of that subject, must be macro theory. I can see no reason whatever for this. The cause for this belief is apparently the fact that the value of money is usually conceived as corresponding to an average of prices. But that is no more true than it is of the value of any other commodity. I do not see, for instance, that our habitual use of index numbers of prices, although undoubtedly very convenient for many purposes, has in any way assisted our understanding of the effect of monetary changes, or to draw relevant conclusions except, perhaps about the behavior of index numbers.

The interesting problems are those of the effect of monetary changes on particular prices, and, about these, index numbers or changes of general price levels, tell us nothing.

More and more it seems to me that the immense efforts that during the great popularity of macroeconomics over the last thirty or forty years have been devoted to it were largely misspent, and that if we want to be useful in the future we shall have to be content to improve and spread the admittedly limited insights which microeconomics conveys. I believe it is only microeconomics that enables us to understand the crucial functions of the market process; that it enables us to make effective use of information about thousands of facts of which nobody can have full knowledge.

ABOUT THE AUTHOR

F A. Hayek, a native of Vienna born in 1889, was awarded the Nobel Prize in Economic Science in 1974. The author of more than 20 books, including *The Road to Serfdom* (University of Chicago, 1944), *Individualism and Economic Order* (University of Chicago, 1948), *The Counter-Revolution of Science* (Free Press, 1952), *Law, Legislation and Liberty* (University of Chicago, 1981), and *The Fatal Conceit* (University of Chicago, 1988), he is a prominent founder of the "Austrian school" of free market economics. During his career, he has taught at numerous institutions, including the University of Vienna, the University of Chicago and the London School of Economics.

THE PROBLEM
OF BIG GOVERNMENT

J. Peter Grace
January 1988

here are 2.7 million federal employees in the United States, occupying 2.61 billion square feet of office space—the equivalent of all of the office space in our ten largest cities multiplied by four. These are astonishing statistics for a country that claims to be guided by the principle that government ought to play an extremely limited role in men's lives. It is even more surprising that we tolerate such an enormously bloated bureaucracy when everywhere in America it is recognized that the public sector simply does not work as well as the private sector, and furthermore, it is small private organizations that work better than big ones.

With all the serious problems we must face today, the problem of big government is among the most critical. Yet solutions are not lacking; most of them are readily understandable and of a practical rather than an ideological nature. For instance, at least 600,000 civil service jobs are completely unnecessary, and the President's Private Sector Survey on Cost Control recommended in 1984 that they be privatized immediately. The survey recommended a few other reforms, too—2,478 of them to be precise. But only a small number of these have been implemented. Why? One of the reasons lies in the fact that the federal government is controlled by Congress. Rarely do people realize how many day-to-day actions of the government are affected by the 535 elected members of Congress who micromanage each agency and thus exert a powerful influence beyond their legislative function.

Let me illustrate. Several years ago, John Shad, head of the Securities and Exchange Commission, was able to streamline the time-consuming and labor-intensive registration process for the corporations it regulates. Consequently, he was also able to cut his staff, or RIF (reduction-in-force, as it is commonly called), 230 employees. Two days later, he was summoned before the congressional subcommittee responsible for overseeing the SEC.

"Why are you RIFing 230 people?" he was asked. He gave them a reasonable explanation.

"Come back to the chairman's office, and we'll talk about this for a few minutes." He was presented with a list of items he had included in his agency's operating budget for the next year. "Do you want cooperation on this budget?"

"Yeah, I have to have this budget."

"All right, then cancel the RIFs."

"Okay, I'm learning."

So it goes in Washington, D.C. Look at the exorbitant freight rates for the Defense Department's operations in Alaska and Hawaii: $68 million was spent over a recent three-year period. Why? Congress does not permit competitive bidding for shipping military freight to and from the mainland for these two states.

The average middle-American family pays $2,218 in taxes, so it is fair to assume that 34,000 families are working all year long to pay that $68 million.

NASA puts out a highly successful magazine which is oversubscribed (General Electric, alone, requests 5,000 copies each month), but the Office of Management and Budget (OMB) insists upon limiting production. Some time ago, the editors declared their intent to solicit advertising in order to print the magazine privately. Going private would also mean a great savings—proofreaders from the Government Printing Office are paid $32,000 a year and can look forward to retiring on 82 percent of their final salary. Ordinary proofreaders, in comparison, make about $15,000 and have little or no pension benefits outside of Social Security. But another subcommittee reared its head and prevented NASA from going ahead. Coincidentally, most of the subcommittee members who decided against privatizing the magazine were senators whose constituents included a disproportionate share of civil service employees, many of whom worked for the Government Printing Office.

The head of the Veterans Administration is also under the thumb of Congress. Changing the jobs of three employees requires that a written request be submitted by February 1, and Congress has until October 1 to respond. Micromanagement is perhaps too mild a term to describe what Congress is doing to our government.

The Defense Department has certified that the United States needs 326 military bases: We have 4,000. These include Fort Collins, built to protect Salt Lake City from the Indians, and another installation in Virginia which still has a moat around it. A move to turn it into a museum was blocked by the congressional delegation from...need I tell you? Virginia. Typically, the congressmen who complain loudest about the defense budget are the same ones who cavil at such sensible ideas as reducing the number of active military bases. Absurdity leads to absurdity. You have undoubtedly heard of two-cent screws bought for $91.00, $7.50 hammers for $435.00, and toilet seat covers for $678.00—all due to the specifications which Congress has imposed. The Defense Department makes roughly 1.5 million purchase decisions each year. It hardly needs the kind of help Congress has to offer.

PERPETUAL DEBT AND DECEPTION

Pertinent today is Thomas Jefferson's warning, "To preserve our independence, we must not let our rulers load us with perpetual debt." He added, "We must make our election between economy and liberty...or profusion and servitude." We are spending $220 billion more than we accumulate in revenues each year. We face a debt of $2.2 trillion. Now, you cannot really conceive of a trillion dollars and neither can I. We can figure out the calculations, of course—a million million, a thousand billion—but that is not really going to help us to understand; as Ronald Reagan, among others, has observed, if someone started ticking off the seconds since the time of Christ's birth, today the count would be at a little over 65 billion, with less than seven percent of the task finished. It takes 31,700 years to count to a trillion, or 317 centuries, and we are only in the 20th. But in Washington, D.C., "trillions" is a commonly used term and some of our civil servants don't even bother with that; they casually refer to "trills."

I've been a businessman long enough to have experienced the horrors of unbridled government indirectly for years, but since 1982, when President Reagan approached me about heading up the Private Sector Survey on Cost Control, I have been able to relate many incidents firsthand. At the outset, he asked me to discover the answers to a series of questions. One of the primary ones was prompted by his former governorship of California. During his own tenure, he knew that federal employees outnumbered state employees but was unable to discover anything more concrete. As president, he felt that it was important to pursue the issue and find out not only how many federal employees there were but where they were located and what they were doing. The day after our conversation, I went to the OMB and asked those three simple questions.

"We don't know," was the answer, and I could not get any specific data. So I changed my tactics.

"If I can't present the White House with a complete report by next week, I will hold a press conference and tell the American people that there are 2.7 million federal employees in the United States and that the OMB hasn't got the slightest idea of where they are or what they're doing."

The bureaucracy relented, and I received a massive computerized listing of the number of federal employees in each state, but that was all. I went to Edwin Meese, then the Counselor to the President for Domestic Affairs, who earnestly tried to help, but more than three years later, I am still waiting for the answer to the other questions President Reagan asked.

I made other sallies at the OMB in the meantime, asking logical questions like, "How many social programs does the government sponsor?"

The answer was "110 to 130."

One of our staff visited a bookstore soon after that and came across a revealing volume called *How to Get Yours In Fat City*. In the appendix, 300 government social programs were featured. We took this interesting information back to our OMB sources, but they were unimpressed. We conducted our own research and dug up a total of 963 social programs. They are all formularized in Congress and many of them are called "entitlements." Keep that word "entitlement" in mind because, if you're not getting anything, you're a sucker—you're "entitled" to a lot of these programs. You can enroll in 17 of them simultaneously and draw 160 percent of the minimum wage. Now, W. R. Grace & Co. owns, among other things, 740 restaurants. One waitress I visited with in New Orleans makes $130 a day just in tips. Not everyone who waits tables makes this much, but say they make $50 per day, three days a week. That amounts to $150 a week in tax-free income, and if they are making 160 percent of the minimum wage from government social programs to boot, they are enjoying a very tidy setup. For those of us who declare our incomes, the underground economy is an affront, not only because it means a loss of over $100 billion in tax revenues a year, but because these people are on the dole at the same time they are evading taxes.

Student loan programs are also a haven for fraud. Our Commission decided to investigate and found that there are three separate student loan programs. "Why have three?" we said. "How much is their overhead? Is it possible for them to merge into one program?" Aside from the usual recalcitrance displayed by federal agencies, we came up against another obstacle, one which we had encountered in every one of our investigations: the federal government's 332 incompatible accounting systems and 319 payroll systems, all handled by 17,500 computers, 12,000 of which were obsolete. When I found that out, my reaction was "Let's get Frank Cary down here"—the chief executive officer of IBM at the time, a businessman known for his expertise and his integrity.

I called Frank up and he said, "Sure, I'll be there."

Congress cried, "Conflict of interest! He knows too much!" and Frank Cary, along with many other committed, expert volunteers like him, was denied the chance to help our Commission. But eventually we were able to determine that approximately $2.5 billion in defaulted student loans had not been collected. Who owed the money? People like a Mets pitcher and a Honolulu land developer and, among others, 46,000 federal employees. Now maybe $2.5 billion does seem like a small percentage of the $850 billion in outstanding loans owed to the government at the time, but it is certainly not outrageous to suggest that these folks ought to make good on their legal obligations.

Earlier, I noted that the debt stands at $2.2 trillion, but I was lying to you, just as Congress always does. Another trillion dollars in the Social Security system and $1.1 trillion in military and civil service pensions account for past liabilities that have not been recognized or provided for. Social Security is a nightmare you probably already know a lot about, but did you know that the military retirement program is exactly six times as generous as comparable private programs? A man or woman entering at age 17 can retire in 20 years with 50 percent of his or her salary indexed, of course, to inflation. During President Carter's term, we endured annual inflation averaging almost 10 percent, with the peak year at 13.5 percent. Let us estimate that over an extended period inflation levels out to about seven percent. In ten years, a pension settlement will double. At age 47, a military retiree will receive 100 percent of his or her final salary each month; at age 57, it becomes 200 percent, at age 67, doubling to reach 400 percent, and so on. This is not a pension plan; it is a bonanza.

Federal civil service employees may retire with very similar benefits, so it is no wonder that unfunded pension liabilities exceed $1 trillion. Added to all the other hidden debts Congress refuses to tell its citizens about, the real debt is between $4 and $5 trillion. When President Lyndon Johnson launched the Great Society he was already committed to a war in Vietnam. His administration spent $158 billion. Now, that sum is only the *interest* on the national debt. That is some "legacy" for our children. I saw a cartoon recently which featured a bunch of politicians having a meal in a restaurant. The headwaiter brought the bill and they replied, "Stick it on the kids' tab." And that's what we are doing. We are just sticking it on the kids' tab. What right do we have to live this way? How can we go on spending so much ($400 billion more than we took in last year, including all the off-budget expenditures) when we know where our folly will lead?

THE REAL JOB OF GOVERNMENT

The Grace Commission effectively demonstrated that $424.4 billion could be saved over a three-year period by following its 2,478 specific recommendations. Moreover, the Commission showed its own commitment to cost-cutting by raising $76 million from private organizations to underwrite all of its own expenses. It did not cost the government a nickel, unless, of course, you agree with Ralph Nader. He claims that a least half of the study was paid for by the government because the donors were able to deduct their contributions, costing millions in lost tax revenue. Tax evasion does account for lost revenue as I indicated in the case of the underground economy, but Ralph Nader is unsafe at any speed when he suggests that your pre-tax income belongs to the government and that by giving any of it away to a commission, a church, or any other charity you are bilking the government out of its rightful due. That is socialism, plain and simple.

Unfortunately, socialism has far too great a hold on us already, and anybody who disagrees ought to look at those 963 social programs the government has burdened us with. When Kennedy was president, he was our King Arthur and he reigned over Camelot, but Camelot's social programs, $28.9 billion worth, were only 5.2 percent of the Gross National Product (GNP). Reagan, who has been called Scrooge, presides over a $500 billion social agenda which swallows up 10.5 percent of GNP.

Kennedy spent 9.4 percent of the GNP on defense and Reagan, by contrast, spends less than seven percent. In the last 70 years, the communists have succeeded in subjugating 1,727 billion people, or 36.1 percent of the world's population. They have taken over 18.7 million square miles of territory—that is 32.5 percent of the earth's land surface—in the process. Reagan's commitment to defense notwithstanding, seven percent of the GNP seems wholly inadequate.

The Soviets have produced twice as many fighter aircraft as we have together with our NATO allies. They have also manufactured four times as many helicopters, five times as many artillery pieces, 12 times as many ballistic missiles and 50 times as many bombers. In the area of short-range missiles, Soviet forces have a 14.6 to 1 advantage. In intermediate-range missiles, the ratio is 1.2 to 1, and in strategic missiles it is 1.5 to 1. Remember the awful destruction caused by Hitler's 43 submarines in World War II? Well, Russia has 300, 150 of which are nuclear. Eight are circling off the coast of Florida right now.

In short, the threat to our freedom is not diminishing. The real job of government is not to give us 963 social programs but to protect our liberty. We ought to be living up to the principles of our forefathers. We ought to be vocal about waste and fraud in government. We ought to be asking each and every one of our representatives in Congress: "Why are we keeping 4,000 military bases open? How many federal employees work in my state and what are they doing? What are you voting for and voting against?"

OUR FUTURE IS AT STAKE

In 1984, the Commission officially presented its findings to President Reagan during a White House conference. One of the questions addressed to me from the group of nearly 200 reporters on hand was, "Why isn't there anything in your report about taxing the rich?"

I explained that we were not asked to examine the tax structure, that it was not within the parameters of our investigation. I asked my interrogator a question in turn.

"Who's rich?"

"Anybody who makes more than $75,000 a year," she replied.

I said, "You're right; $75,000 is rich."

But at the Democratic Convention that same year, many of the candidates were calling for a 10 percent surcharge on the incomes of those who they claimed were rich—the people earning $60,000 a year. At the time, our Commission figured that this initiative would collect only $1.65 billion a year, or eight-tenths of one percent of the deficit. Why were the Democrats cheering in the aisles at this kind of talk? Because economic illiteracy, jealousy and envy are the fuel that politicians run on.

I told the reporter about what the Democrats had pledged and I said I would go them one better. "Let's put a 100 percent tax on all incomes over $75,000 a year."

She said, "That would be good."

And I replied, "Fine. Now we'll be able to run the government for 7.2 days."

Taxing the rich is not the solution; adopting waste-cutting measures like the ones the Grace Commission proposed is. When New York City went bankrupt, it had no choice but to attempt to put its fiscal house in order. But the trouble with the federal government is that it simply cannot go bankrupt; it will just print more money or borrow more. Now, if I'm having an argument with a congressman and we talk about spending $1.00 and I say, "You can knock it out," and he says, "No, I'm leaving it in, I respond, "Where do you get that buck?"

He says, "Tell Jim Baker to borrow it over at the Treasury."

"Where does he get the interest?"

"Borrows it."

"Where does he get the interest on the interest?"

"Borrows it."

"Next year it's $1.05. Where does he get that?"

"Borrows it."

Well, take a little calculator out and figure out what happens when you borrow something, then you borrow the interest, and then you borrow the interest on the interest. In our report to President Reagan, we warned that one dollar borrowed now will have cost $71.00 by the year 2000. In a little more than 12 years, the debt will be $13 trillion and the interest on that will be $1.5 trillion. By the same token, if the Commission's recommendations were followed, we could save $9.9 trillion.

We need a knowledgeable, informed electorate that doesn't depend on the nightly news for what it knows about what goes on in this country. We need citizens willing to make Congress accountable for the travesty which passes for democratic government today.

Until we have them, we will continue to be bamboozled by Congress which, in its turn, knuckles under to the bureaucratic establishment and the 500 special interest groups entrenched on Capitol Hill. We can start by making the government fiscally responsible, but whether we can muster the political will to do so is up to us alone.

The stakes are high; what kind of future can we build for ourselves unless we mend our ways? What kind of future for our children and their heirs will big government and institutionalized fiscal irresponsibility yield? What we are committing now is child abuse on an unimaginable scale. When our sons and daughters grow up and realize what we've done to them, will they ever forgive us?

ABOUT THE AUTHOR

J Peter Grace is chairman and chief executive officer of W. R. Grace & Co., a New York corporation dealing primarily with chemicals, natural resources and consumer-oriented businesses. Mr. Grace has held his position at W. R. Grace for more than four decades, the longest tenure for a chief executive officer of any major industrial concern. Throughout his career, Mr. Grace has maintained an active role in public affairs. A registered Democrat, he has served as a bipartisan advisor to Presidents Eisenhower, Kennedy and Reagan. His most publicized assignment was as head of the President's Private Sector Survey on Cost Control, popularly known as the Grace Commission.

MR. PRESIDENT,
READ OUR LIPS: NO NEW TAXES

Warren Brookes
August 1990

or years I have thought of George Roche as a kind of modern-day prophet—but today, I am a believer. How else can we explain that over a year ago he predicted that some of America's most fervent anti-taxers would now be hedging on the question of whether new taxes are necessary? It is ironic indeed that halfway through the 8th year of the longest peacetime expansion in U.S. recorded economic history—in the 90th month to be exact, the president who is the direct political beneficiary of that recovery should even be tempted, as he now so obviously is, to answer that question in the affirmative.

There is little doubt that President Bush faces a serious fiscal challenge. The FY1990 budget deficit now appears to be headed toward $190 billion—nearly $40 billion above FY1989. That is because revenues are growing half as fast (four percent) as predicted (eight percent), and spending is growing much faster (seven percent) than forecast (five percent). That implies a budget deficit for FY1991 of $145-195 billion, depending on whose baseline economic and fiscal estimates you accept. Since the Gramm-Rudman-Hollings target is $64 billion, with a $10 billion leeway, those high forecasts could force a "sequester," or automatic cut, of $60-120 billion.

Any president might be tempted to accept a significant tax increase of $30-$50 billion as part of a "solution." Yet such a tax increase is virtually certain to make the deficit worse, not better. Not only will tax increases stimulate more spending growth, they will do far more harm economically than most politicians and even mainstream economists understand.

TAX CAPITALIZATION:
WHY TAXES COST US 10 TIMES OVER

This is because of something called "tax capitalization," an accounting principle used in measuring the influence of tax assessments on the value of assets such as real estate.

Since that value is a function of the income stream the property can earn, any diversion of that stream to higher taxes or increase in that stream from lower taxes will have a *multiplier* effect on the value depending on the current price earnings ratio of real estate. If the current return on property is approximately 10 percent, every dollar of income represents $10 of value. Every dollar of income diverted to taxes reduces that value by $10. Every dollar of income released by tax reduction increases the value by $10. Thus accountants know that an increase in the tax assessment of a property has an automatic 10 to 1 negative impact on value.

Think of the economy as a single business with both fixed and working capital on which an income stream is earned. To the degree that taxes on that business rise and fall, the income stream is lowered or raised. Thus the capital value of that business falls or rises at the nation's effective price earnings ratio, which on corporate bonds is about 10 to 1.

NEW TAXES KILL PROSPERITY

A $30 billion tax increase on the economy may not seem like much in a $5.5 trillion GNP—but its real impact is a $300 billion "tax capitalization" of the asset base of the nation. Since the nation adds less than $300 billion a year in net new investment, such a tax increase effectively destroys an entire year's capital growth.

That is why President Bush and congressional leaders are now playing with economic dynamite. Not only will a $30 billion tax increase generate a likely $40 billion rise in spending, it will kill *all* capital expansion for at least a year and send the stock market down by at least 300-500 points.

This is why Bush was so right when he told a Republican audience in Boston in 1987, "There's no quicker way to kill prosperity than to raise taxes." In Chicago on September 13, 1988, he told a national audience of business leaders and economists, "The surest way to kill the recovery is to raise taxes. That will stifle everything from investment and personal savings to consumer spending. It will clamp down on growth. It will invite a recession." But now Bush is equivocating. The spring 1990 budget summit was clearly intended to explore all options, including raising taxes.

A TALE OF TWO MASSACHUSETTS

No wonder Massachusetts Governor Michael Dukakis, wallowing in the slough of his own 83 percent negative performance despond, with a $2.3 billion 18-month deficit yawning before him, suddenly cheered up and flew to Washington to gloat that Bush's "no-tax" pledge had been "a fraud." The governor is unusually well-equipped to identify such duplicity. In 1974, he ran on a similar promise that it was "a lead pipe cinch" that he would *not* have to raise taxes in 1975. But of course he did, passing the largest tax increase in state history, some $500 million. That broken pledge cost him dearly in the 1978 Democratic primary, when a political neophyte conservative businessman named Ed King threw him out in a shocking landslide upset—running on the explicit promise to roll back the state's highest-in-the-nation property taxes, à la Proposition 13 in

California of which Dukakis had said, "The people of Massachusetts are too smart to fall for a dumb idea like that!"

It seems no accident that in the middle- and working-class communities where property taxes were two and three times the national average, King won pluralities of 15-20 points. In the affluent communities where taxes were at or below the nation, Dukakis scored his only majorities.

Before President Bush makes any deals with the Democrats for higher taxes in return for modest budget reforms or alleged spending cuts, he would do well to study and learn from the Dukakis/Massachusetts experience. It demonstrates the direct connection between taxation and economic growth—between political capital and economic capital. Taxes, he will discover, have not merely a direct but a powerful multiplier effect on both.

During the 1970s when the Massachusetts tax burden as a percent of personal income suddenly soared by 25 percent from about the national average to fifth highest in the nation, its average real personal income growth suddenly plummeted from 91 percent of the U.S. level to 57 percent. By contrast, during the 1980s when the Massachusetts tax burden fell over 17 percent, to five percent *below* the nation, its real personal income grew nearly 45 percent *faster* than the nation's. To put it in another way, from 1970 to 1978, when it became "Taxachusetts," the Bay State fell from 33rd in growth rate among states to 47th, and its per capita personal income fell from 10 percent above the nation to less than two percent above—while its tax burden jumped almost 25 percent.

By contrast from 1978 to 1983, while its tax burden fell 17 percent, it rose from third slowest growing in the nation to third fastest, and its per capita income rose from three percent above the nation to 14 percent above it—the largest and fastest turnaround in U.S. history, from the Taxachusetts Swamp to the Massachusetts Miracle in only five years.

FROM FISCAL RESTRAINT TO SPENDING BOOM ...

Sadly, it is now all too clear that Mike Dukakis had no idea what caused this turnaround or he would not have fought it at every step and then so willingly risked squandering it the way he did. In June 1984, a booming and fiscally flourishing Massachusetts had its bond rating raised to AA. The same month, the state manufacturing base rose to 684,000 jobs, the highest level since the late 1960s in a state whose economy was literally exploding, after surviving the worst U.S. recession in postwar history with surprising ease. State revenues were growing at a 12-14 percent annual rate, 30 percent faster than its spending level, and unemployment was dropping by the month.

Unfortunately, that huge revenue surge merely encouraged a newly re-elected and rejuvenated Dukakis to go on a spending spree, partly to pay off the special interests that had brought him back to office, and partly to build a powerful new campaign army for the 1987-88 national run.

State payrolls which had fallen by 6,000 under King re-exploded by 23,000 under Dukakis. State borrowing for housing development doubled in four years. State executive department spending, which had been going down in real terms under King, took off and rose to triple-inflation rate levels, 30-40 percent faster than the nation's.

The results were neither pretty nor hard to predict. A state that had been running four percent annual surpluses through FY1986 suddenly started running annual deficits of six percent. An FY1986 state surplus of more than $600 million suddenly turned into a $1 billion deficit by FY1989. A state that had been trying to fund its huge pension liability was secretly borrowing from it by the end of 1988, and running $300 million overdrafts at major Boston banks. Revenues that had been rising nearly 13 percent a year from FY1984 through FY1987 fell to a two percent annual rise FY1988 through FY1990, and are down this year one percent from 1989.

... TO TOTAL FISCAL DISASTER

Above all, an economy that had been booming at one of the fastest rates in the nation began to fall apart under the pressure of that government explosion. As we speak, the once proud manufacturing job level is below 560,000 jobs, a 124,000 job plunge in a four-year period when the nation's manufacturing jobs have actually risen by nearly 100,000. The state's total employment in March was 70,000 *lower* than in March of 1989, and its unemployment was 61,000 *higher,* rising from 3.3 percent to 5.4 percent. In spite of more than $400 million in special employment and training programs for welfare mothers, the welfare case load is almost 2,000 higher than it was when that program started in 1984.

In March, the state's bond rating was lowered for the third straight time, this time to BBB by Standard and Poors and Baa by Moody's. Not only is that the *lowest* bond rating of the 50 states, it is only one very small step above junk bonds. Last December, just to meet its current obligations to distribute local aid to the cities and towns, Massachusetts had to obtain a $1.2 billion line of credit from Japanese banks—a line that comes due this September. In fact, the state warned cities and towns it could not make all its June local aid distributions, even though the state Supreme Court has ordered it to reinstate some $200 million it cut last fall.

Despite significant $300 million plus tax increases in 1988 and 1989, the state is now staring at a total fiscal disaster. State spending that was supposed to have been cut in FY1989, instead rose by 11.5 percent. Through April, the current FY1990 budget was in the red by a little under $800 million, headed for a fiscal year gap of over $1 billion. The state legislature is now trying to resolve the differences between a $1.3 billion tax increase passed by the House and $1.6 billion passed by the Senate. Both were rushed through as the Japanese creditors were calling in their notes. The day that latter increase was passed, two of the state's oldest institutions checked out. Boston Gear decided to move to North Carolina taking all of its manufacturing jobs with it and the FDIC took over the venerable Merchant's Bank as insolvent.

Those were merely the latest evidences of the fallout from what one of the bond rating vice presidents called "the worst case of fiscal mismanagement I have ever seen...."

THE DESTRUCTION OF POLITICAL CAPITAL

At the heart of that bond-rating problem was not so much an impoverished economy as the disastrous slide in political capital that made either serious budget-cutting or significant tax increases virtually impossible until immediate bankruptcy was threatened. Over 70 percent of Massachusetts voters now have "no confidence" in state government. The mobs outside the State House recently have had a curiously familiar East European flavor.

This destruction in political capital is now directly causing an equally severe destruction in economic capital. Over the past six months, regulators have forced the four major Boston banks to set aside over $2.2 billion in additional reserves against losses on real estate loans. Those losses, in turn, are the direct result of a sudden collapse of the real estate market. That market's unprecedented boom in values had been built almost entirely on the capitalization of the major property tax-cut and cap called Proposition 2-1/2 passed by the state in 1980, which stimulated a 22 percent annual rise in property values from 1981 to 1988. But that growth rate collapsed in 1989, when it became clear that there was no way the state could continue to fund the Proposition 1-1/2 property tax cap with large local aid distributions.

That signaled the likelihood that the cap would not only begin to be over-ridden by fiscally starved communities (nearly 30 have already done so), but might eventually be amended by a desperate legislature. That in turn meant that taxes on property could once again soar and values could once again have to decline.

The results of anxiety about tax levels were almost immediately devastating to the state's real estate market which went from boom to bust within less than 12 months, forcing scores of Bay State banks onto the FDIC credit watch list because of large real estate loans gone sour.

That precipitate reversal in the state economy's fortunes is as clear proof of the direct role of taxation in economic growth and capital formation as the unexpected and rapid rise in those fortunes had been nearly a decade before.

WHAT CAUSED THE MASSACHUSETTS MIRACLE AND ITS DEMISE?

While much has been written about the reasons for Massachusetts' 1978-1983 turnaround, the high-tech boom, the MIT-Harvard Route 128 complex, state development initiatives, industrial revenue bonds, the defense budget, you name it, none of those reasons hold water when tested by economic analysis. After all, in 1978, Massachusetts had all of those factors going for it in abundance. It has been one of the leading high tech and defense spending states since the 1950s. Harvard and MIT have been around as long as anyone can remember.

But in 1978, what Massachusetts did have that it didn't want or need was not only the fifth highest tax burden in the nation but the highest property taxes, some say, in the world. At the time California passed Proposition 13, its property tax burden was about three percent of market value and over six percent of personal income. At that same time the Massachusetts property tax burden was 4.5 percent of market value, and over nine percent of personal income. The direct effect of such a massive property tax burden was to depress artificially the value of state property assets. During the 1970s total market-based real estate values in Massachusetts actually fell about three percent, while in the nation as a whole they rose by over 35 percent in real terms.

Small wonder that at the same time the state's share of new capital investment fell from an already anemic two percent of the nation in 1970 to less than 1.2 percent in 1978, and its job growth rate dropped to less than half that of the nation's. Little wonder also that the political capital of liberal governors, both Republican and Democrat, fell with it, paving the way both for the 1978 election of Edward King and the 1980 passage of Proposition 2-1/2.

That combination forced state spending growth to fall in real terms to less than one percent a year and the state's tax burden to fall back to 14.6 percent, a massive three-percentage point drop. By 1983 Massachusetts' personal income was back up to 13 percent above the nation and headed to its current 23 percent lead, and the state became number three in growth.

Skeptics say, but how can tax cuts explain *all* or even the major share of such an amazing turnaround? The answer is remarkably simple—and it is summed up in a single phrase that accountants and investors, especially property investors, understand all too well but economists invariably ignore—tax capitalization.

TAX CAPITALIZATION AT WORK IN MASSACHUSETTS

I've already discussed tax capitalization, but it is a lesson worth repeating: When you buy a piece of property, its value is directly the result of the net income you can expect to earn from it either as a business or as a simple home investor. That income in turn is directly affected by the amount of taxes you have to pay on this investment or this income or both. The higher the tax, the lower the income. The lower the income, the lower the value of the base investment.

What this means is that taxes are in fact "capitalized" as losses, at the average rate of return (or about 10 percent), a price earnings ratio of 10 to 1. Every real estate investor knows that when property taxes go up $100, value falls by $1000, and vice versa; when taxes are cut, value rises. This is neither mystic nor theoretical. It operates as accounting *law*. It is really no different from the relationship between interest rates and bond prices. Those rates are a form of tax on borrowing. The higher the rates the lower the bond is worth and vice versa.

In 1980 Massachusetts voters mandated a nominal property tax cut of $1.2 billion in discounted present value. They also set a cap that allowed no more than a 2.5 percent rise in tax assessments per year. Over a period of six years this meant an implicit tax reduction of some $7 billion.

In 1981 the instant effect of the implementation of Proposition 2-1/2 was to convert the Massachusetts real estate market from one of the nation's most depressed to one of its hottest. From 1981 to 1987, property values soared at a 22 percent annual rate, the most in the nation. The state's equalized value base shot up from $89 billion to more than $224 billion—a real increase in real estate wealth of more than $90 billion.

Now you say, what has that boom in paper real estate wealth got to do with the economy? Well, think of what the infusion of $90 billion in new capital value would mean to a state economy whose total gross domestic product was then less than $90 billion and whose net annual business capital investment was then less than $1.5 billion a year and whose total tangible worth was less than $400 billion.

To put it on a national perspective, consider that a Massachusetts-style infusion of wealth would translate into $3.6 trillion in added tangible worth to the nation during the period of 1981-1986 when that total tangible worth grew only $4.4 trillion. Thus the Massachusetts tangible net worth growth from 1981 to 1986 from property values alone was the equivalent of nearly doubling the nation's net worth growth in the same period.

Is it really any wonder that its per capita income jumped from seven percent above the nation in 1981 to 24 percent in 1987, the greatest rise of any state in U.S. history?

Now if you understand this, you will begin to understand why tax capitalization may well explain both the surprisingly positive benefits of national tax reductions, and the equally astonishing negative impacts of national tax increases.

TAX CAPITALIZATION AFFECTS EVERYTHING

Understand that all taxes represent a diversion of income from the nation's basic capital structure, whether that capital is property, or plant and equipment, or merely working capital needed to keep a business going and a payroll met.

When you increase the taxes on anything—sales, property, income, capital, payrolls—you are automatically diverting some of the income stream that goes to support the capital that in turn supports those activities. In the aggregate, you have to be reducing the nation's total capital asset base. And if the price earnings ratio of that base is roughly 10 to 1, every dollar you take away from that income to capital stream means you are reducing the value of that asset base by 10 dollars.

Thus when Congress decides to raise taxes by $30 billion, its real impact is $300 billion *off* the capital asset base of the economy. That may not seem like much to a country whose total capital base is now over $20 trillion—but remember, that base value is not growing all that rapidly. Consider the fact that in 1989, the nation's net rise in private domestic investment was only $225 billion after allowing for depreciation or capital consumption, and less than $110 billion of that net went to non-residential business fixed investment.

A $30 billion tax hike of any kind will cost the U.S. *all* of the net rise in real domestic investment and then some, killing most real economic growth in the process. Conversely, a $30 billion tax cut will have the opposite effect; it will more than double the capital expansion of the nation.

To this day, even conservatives tend to downplay the actual effect of both the Kennedy and Reagan tax cuts. Yet consider that the last time we had nearly nine years of uninterrupted expansion was during the 1960s, which were punctuated by a 29 percent cut in federal income tax rates across the board. In both cases, the immediate effect was to expand the capital asset value of the nation enormously—and the best surrogate for that was and is the stock market. From 1960 to 1968 the S & P 500 rose 44 percent in constant dollars.

But, following massive tax increases on capital and income in 1969, the S & P 500 fell in constant dollars by 30 percent during the 1970s. It is significant that the total movements up and then down in equity values is almost exactly the multiplier of price-earnings ratios—10 or 15 to 1—times the annualized amounts of the tax cuts and subsequent tax increases.

For example, during the 1980s, we have seen the S & P 500 rise in real terms by 84 percent. If that rise had been applied to all of the equities in the market in 1980 (many of which were removed during leveraged buyouts), it would have raised their total value by some $800 billion—or slightly more than 13 times the effective annualized Reagan tax cut of $60 billion a year. In short, the rise and fall of the tax burden has a direct multiplier effect on the nation's equity asset base.

Once you understand this, you will no longer be tempted to think that tax increases are "modest" or "necessary," especially to "reduce the deficit"! As President Bush himself warned in his speech to Pittsburgh steel workers in 1988, "I've been in government a long time and I've seen what happens when government raises a dollar in revenues—Congress spends $1.50." And at the same time that higher tax dollar is killing $10 of capital assets on which employment and growth directly depend.

SOCIAL SECURITY TAXES AND THE WAGE BUST

If you still doubt this relationship, I ask you to consider one more key example. Since 1972, average weekly wages have fallen dramatically in real terms by 16 percent. In the prior 17 years, they *rose* 30 percent.

If you want to know why, consider one thing: Since 1972, the maximum combined employer/employee Social Security tax rose over 675 percent from $936 a year to the current figure of more than $7,200. In that period while total wages and salaries rose by 312 percent, total Social Security contributions rose by 526 percent.

If Social Security tax rates had remained at 1972 levels, workers would now be paying $144 billion less each year than they now do. That means that the working capital that supports those wages and those jobs is $1.44 trillion less than it would be if there had not been that soaring Social Security tax increase. The annual wage effects alone of that higher working capital base easily translate into two percent real annual wage increases instead of the nearly one percent annual wage losses we experienced.

That demonstrates the economic potential of Senator Daniel Patrick Moynihan's proposal to give back the $55 billion higher Social Security payments than are now required to pay current benefits. That reduction would translate into an immediate $550 billion rise in the real working capital of this country—a doubling of the effective capital increase per year. The Democrats were foolish not to grab this idea and run with it. President Bush and Treasury Secretary Nicholas Brady were so transfixed by the deficit they were relieved when the Democrats dropped the ball.

LOW TAXES AND HIGH GROWTH: THE NEW HAMPSHIRE MODEL

By now it should be obvious to you that the so-called Massachusetts Miracle was not a miracle at all, but the simple and direct operation of an economic law that is as fixed as the law of supply and demand. Unfortunately, in the middle of that multiplier effect, the state turned from a strong fiscal policy of tight spending control that made the tax cut real to a very loose policy of spending every nickel of an incredible 12-14 percent a year revenue growth. Instead of using that growth to generate still more political and economic capital, they squandered it on their political machinery.

This was in sharp contrast to Massachusetts' neighbor to the north, New Hampshire, which has used the political capital of its commitment to low taxes to build the best performing economy in the nation over the last two decades. It has also demonstrated the ideal model for fiscal and economic policy for the nation as well. For this I commend a 1989 study by Colin and Rosemary Campbell, economists of Dartmouth College, a follow-up to their 1976-77 study. The Campbells have been keeping a close eye on New Hampshire and Vermont for the last 12 years because they provide a nearly perfect economic laboratory.

New Hampshire, with the lowest overall tax burden of the nation (no state sales or income tax), is the classic "supply-side" limited government economic model, with 53 percent of its revenues collected and administered by local government and the lowest welfare-recipients-to-population ratio in the nation.

Vermont, right next door, is the quintessential liberal welfare state with one of the top 15 tax burdens, 39 percent higher than New Hampshire's and one of the most generous welfare benefit programs in the nation. Its strong centralized state government raises about 60 percent of all revenues collected in the state.

The question is, how have these two models fared in the generally strong New

England high-tech economy? Since 1970, New Hampshire has increased its total personal income in constant dollars by 139 percent, nearly double the nation's growth of 71 percent and New England's growth of 69 percent. Per capita income has soared by 69 percent, compared with 43 percent for the nation, from a level four percent below the nation to 13 percent above it.

By contrast, Vermont's per capita income has risen only 48 percent, some 30 percent slower than New Hampshire's, and 15 percent slower than in the New England region as a whole. Since 1970 Vermont's per capita income has fallen from 93 percent of New Hampshire's to less than 82 percent.

The same contrast holds up in regard to employment. From 1970-1987, New Hampshire's job growth was 98 percent, half again as fast as Vermont's 65 percent and more than double the nation's 44 percent.

Thus, New Hampshire's model outperforms Vermont's on every economic indicator by 40 to 50 percent. One could argue this was because of its proximity to the Boston market. The trouble with that argument is that New Hampshire's job growth has been *triple* that of Massachusetts for two decades, and 66 percent faster than the nation's. Its personal income growth was nearly *double* that of Massachusetts in the 1970s and 70 percent faster than the nation's since 1970.

But what does the New Hampshire low-tax, "laissez-faire" model mean for the poor in limiting government services? The Campbells' answer is: "Most public services in New Hampshire are as good as those in Vermont." There are two reasons for this: First, because New Hampshire's more rapid economic growth has since 1970 generated greater gains in revenue income (585 percent) to all government since than Vermont (397 percent).

Second, because New Hampshire's more locally controlled government administers services in a more cost-effective way than Vermont's more centralized bureaucracy, requiring 11 percent fewer bureaucrats per 10,000 population than Vermont. On education, for example, Vermont spends 39 percent per capita and 14 percent per student more than New Hampshire. But it pays its teachers identical average salaries and has about the same low teacher-to-student ratio. So all of Vermont's extra spending goes into administrative bureaucracy. On education performance, New Hampshire has the highest SAT scores in the nation, 24 points higher than Vermont's and its high school completion rate is three points higher.

On health care, New Hampshire outspends Vermont by 26 percent, and on police and fire protection 42 percent more, reflecting its somewhat more urban environment. But New Hampshire's highways, among the best surfaced and best plowed in the nation, cost taxpayers 23 percent less per capita to maintain than Vermont's.

The one area where Vermont does spend a lot more is welfare. Vermont has some of the most generous welfare benefits in the nation, eight percent above New York and 42 percent above New Hampshire. So it is no surprise that Vermont's total welfare caseload is nearly double that of New Hampshire for a state with half the population, and the share of its population on welfare is 3.3 times that of New Hampshire, with 43 percent more Medicaid recipients.

In spite of this—or perhaps because of it—Vermont's poverty rate has stayed stubbornly high at 12.1 percent for the last two decades. Meanwhile, New Hampshire has cut its welfare caseloads by nearly 60 percent since 1970 and its poverty rate by 43 percent, from 14.9 percent, a level higher than Vermont's, to 8.5 percent, the best performance against poverty of any state in the nation.

Most of all, New Hampshire dispels the notion that strong economic growth and low welfare produce more income inequity. Not only does New Hampshire have the lowest income inequity (or gini coefficient) of any state in the nation, (19 percent lower than the nation) but over the last seven years that index dropped 21 percent, while the national index rose nearly six percent. At the same time, Vermont with its progressive income tax and more generous welfare programs has seen income inequity rise five percent to a level 13 percent higher than New Hampshire's.

In sum, New Hampshire has proved that the low-tax/local-government model not only produces the best economic growth for its citizens and reduces poverty the most, but it provides better, more cost-effective human services for those in need and a more equitable society in which a rising tide is lifting all of the boats as President Kennedy argued it should.

New Hampshire also serves as a clear example that when a political pledge of trust against state-wide taxes is taken, that pledge becomes a veritable political goldmine that goes on year after year yielding a mother lode of economic capital for the citizens and political capital for politicians.

ABOUT THE AUTHOR

Warren Brookes was an award-winning syndicated columnist for the *Detroit News* whose articles appeared regularly in the *Wall Street Journal, Reader's Digest, Policy Review* and approximately 50 daily newspapers nationwide. The author of *The Economy in Mind,* published in 1982, he specialized in looking at the economic side of political and social issues. The well known annual *Media Guide* gave him four stars every year, making him the only journalist to earn that distinction.

A JOURNALIST'S VIEW OF BLACK ECONOMICS

William Raspberry
March 1990

I am intensely interested in the subject of the economics of black America. However, I am neither a businessman, an economist, nor a social scientist. I'm a "newspaper guy." That is not an apology. I like being a newspaper guy, and I like to think I am a pretty good one. I point it out simply to warn you up front that what you will hear from me is neither economic analysis nor nuts-and-bolts business proposals. I like to think about things in general and my proposal is that we ought to approach this subject in that fashion.

MYTHS ABOUT RACE

One of the things I would like us to think about is a myth: a myth that has crippled black America, sent us off on unpromising directions, and left us ill-equipped to deal with either political or economic reality. That myth is that race is of overriding importance, that it is a determinant not just of opportunity but also of potential, a reliable basis for explaining political and economic realities, a reasonable way of talking about geopolitics, and the overwhelming basis on which to deal with the relationships between us.

When I refer to race-based explanations of the plight of black America as myth, I do not mean to suggest that all such explanations are false. My reference is to the definition of myth as a "traditional account of unknown authorship, ostensibly with a historical basis, but serving usually to explain some observed phenomenon."

The historical basis of our preoccupation with race is easy enough to see. America did not invent slavery. Slavery as an institution predates the Bible. But American slavery was peculiarly race-based. Since slavery is the basis for the very presence of black people in America, small wonder that race has assumed such importance in our mythology. But slavery was more than just involuntary, unpaid servitude. Unlike other populations, to whom enslavement seemed a reasonable way of dealing with conquered enemies, America was never happy with the concept of one group of human beings holding another group of human beings in bondage. I suppose it was taken as a sin against God. But rather than forego the economic benefits of slavery, American slaveholders resolved the dilemma by defining blacks not as fellow human beings but more like beasts of burden. There is nothing ungodly about a man requiring unremunerated work of an animal. Didn't God give man dominion over the animals? Now it may have been that Africans were a special kind of animal: capable of thought, and human language, and even worship. But as long as whites could persuade themselves that blacks were not fully human, they could justify slavery.

Thus was born and reinforced the myth of inherent white superiority, which later became the basis for racial separation, for Jim Crow laws, for unequal opportunity and all sorts of evil. Nor is it just among whites that the myth survives. I must say that this fact never really hit home for me until a few years ago when a reader of my column suggested it. Mary Pringle, a Virginia educator, said it occurred to her that Americans generally have lost the myths that give meaning to their lives, and that black Americans in particular suffer from the loss. The predominant surviving myth of black Americans, she said, is that of racism as the dominant influence in their lives.

Myths, she was careful to point out, are not necessarily false. Indeed, whether positive or negative, they are almost always based on actual group experience. But the nature of the operative group myth can make a profound difference in group outcomes. "Racism is a reality, but it has been overcome by many and given way to opportunity and success." Those who have overcome it, she argued, have been moved by different myths: myths that paint them as destined for success rather than doomed to failure, myths that lead them to see themselves as members of a special group capable of overcoming all odds. That is the kind of myth that blacks need to cultivate, she said, and added:

"Racism, though it is a reality, has been a destructive myth, giving greater power to the odds against success than exist in reality making it harder even to *try*. What we need is a stronger, more powerful myth that is constructive and evokes a sense of identity and energy to move ahead."

I think Mary Pringle's insight is profound. As with most keen insights, once it occurs to you, you can see supporting evidence on every hand. Black youngsters in the inner cities are moved by the myth that blacks have special athletic gifts, particularly with regard to basketball. Asian youngsters are influenced by the myth that they have special gifts for math and science. Jewish youngsters accept the myth that their group has a special gift for the power of the written word.

Now all these myths are, by themselves, worthless. But when they evoke a sense of identity and the energy to move ahead something happens. People *work* at the things they believe they are innately capable of achieving. So it is not un-common to see a black kid working up to bedtime, practicing his double-pump scoop, his behind-the-back dribble, his left-handed jump shot. And after a few months of work, if he has any athletic talent at all, he *proves* the myth. Asian-American youngsters, convinced that they may have special aptitude for math or science, reinforce that myth and make it reality—staying up until two in the morning working on their math and science; Jewish youngsters, convinced that they have a special gift for the written word, work at writing.

Those are all positive myths, and they are obviously powerful. But negative myths are powerful, too. The myth that blacks cannot prevail in intellectual competition, that Chinese youngsters cannot play basketball, that Jews are specially vulnerable to guilt trips—these are negative myths whose acceptance has led to failure because they feed the assumption that failure is inevitable. Objective reality is the arena in which we all must perform. But the success or failure of our performance is profoundly influenced by the attitudes—the myths—we bring to that reality. Two things flow from the racism-is-all myth that we have used to account for our difficulties. The first is that it puts the solution to our difficulties outside our control. If our problems are caused by racism, and their solutions dependent on ending racism, our fate is in the hands of people who, by definition, don't love us.

A SKEWED DEFINITION OF CIVIL RIGHTS

The second outcome of the myth is our inclination to think of our problems in terms of a failure of racial justice. "Civil rights," which once referred to those things whose fair distribution was a governmental responsibility, now refers to any discrepancy. Income gaps, education gaps, test score gaps, infant-mortality gaps, life-expectancy gaps, employment gaps, business participation gaps—all now are talked about as "civil rights" issues.

The problems indicated by all these gaps are real. But describing them as "civil rights" problems steers us away from possible solutions. The civil rights designation evokes a sort of central justice bank, managed by the government, whose charge is to ladle out equal portions of everything to everybody. It prompts us to think about our problems in terms of inadequate or unfair distribution. It encourages the fallacy that to attack racism as the source of our problems is the same as attacking our problems. As a result, we expend precious resources—time, energy, imagination, political capital—searching (always successfully) for evidence of racism, while our problems grow worse.

Maybe I can make my point clearer by reference to two other minorities. The first group consists of poor whites. There are in America not just individuals but whole pockets of white people whose situation is hardly worse than our own. And yet these poor whites have their civil rights. They can vote, live where their money permits them to live, eat where their appetites and their pocket-books dictate, work at jobs for which their skills qualify them. But they are in desperate straits. It doesn't seem to occur to us that the full grant and enforcement of our civil rights would leave black Americans in about the same situation that poor white people are now in. That isn't good enough for me.

There is another minority whose situations may be more instructive. I refer to recently arrived Asian-Americans. What is the difference between them and us? Certainly it isn't that they have managed to avoid the effects of racism. Neither the newly arrived Southeast Asians nor the earlier arriving Japanese-Americans, Chinese-Americans, and Korean-Americans are necessarily loved by white people. But these groups have spent little of their time and energy proving that white people don't love them.

OPPORTUNITY KNOCKS: WHO ANSWERS?

The difference between them and us is our operating myths. Our myth is that racism accounts for our shortcomings. Theirs is that their own efforts can make the difference, no matter what white people think. They have looked at America as children with their noses pressed to the window of a candy store: "If only I could get in there, boy, could I have a good time." And when they get in there, they work and study and save and create businesses and job opportunities for their people. But we, born inside the candy store, have adopted a myth that leads us to focus only on the maldistribution of the candy. Our myth leads us into becoming a race of consumers, when victories accrue to the producers.

Interestingly enough, this is a fairly recent phenomenon. There was a time when we, like the more recent arrivals in this country, sought only the opportunity to be productive, and we grasped that opportunity under circumstances far worse— in law, at least—than those that obtain now. Free blacks and former slaves, though denied many of the rights that we take for granted today, were entrepreneurial spirits. They were artisans and inventors, shopkeepers and industrialists, financiers and bankers. The first female millionaire in America was Madame C. J. Walker. At least two companies founded at the turn of the century are now on the *Black Enterprise* list of the 100 top black firms in the country.

Black real estate operatives transformed white Harlem into a haven for blacks. The early 1900s saw the founding of a number of all-black towns: Mound Bayou, Mississippi; Boley, Oklahoma; Nicodemus, Kansas; and others. Boley at one time boasted a bank, twenty-five grocery stores, five hotels, seven restaurants, a water-works, an electricity plant, four cotton gins, three drug stores, a bottling plant, a laundry, two newspapers, two colleges, a high school, a grade school, four department stores, a jewelry store, two hardware stores, two ice cream parlors, a telephone exchange, five churches, two insurance agencies, two livery stables, an undertaker, a lumber yard, two photography studios, and an ice plant [from J. DeSane, *Analogies and Black History: A Programmed Approach*]. Not bad for an all-black town of 4,000.

As Robert L. Woodson observed in his book, *On the Road to Economic Freedom:*

"The Harlem and Boley experiences, which matched aggressive black entrepreneurial activity with the self-assertion drive of the black masses, was multiplied nationwide to the point that, in 1913, fifty years after Emancipation, black America had accumulated a personal wealth of $700 million. As special Emancipation Day festivals and parades were held that year in cities and towns across the country, blacks could take pride in owning 550,000 homes, 40,000 businesses, 40,000 churches, and 937,000 farms. The literacy rate among blacks climbed to a phenomenal 70 percent—up from five percent in 1863."

OVER-LEARNING THE CIVIL RIGHTS LESSON

What has happened since then? A lot of things, including a good deal of success that we don't talk much about. But among the things that have happened are two that have created problems for us. First is the overemphasis on integration, as opposed to desegregation and increased opportunity. Hundreds of thriving restaurants, hotels, service outlets, and entertainment centers have gone out of business because we preferred integration to supporting our own painstakingly established institutions. Indeed, aside from black churches and black colleges, little remains to show for that entrepreneurial spurt of the early decades of this century.

The other thing that has happened is that we over-learned the lessons of the civil rights movement. That movement, brilliantly conceived and courageously executed, marked a proud moment in our history. The upshot was that black Americans, for the first time in our sojourn here, enjoy the full panoply of our civil rights. Unfortunately, that period also taught us to see in civil rights terms things that might more properly be addressed in terms of enterprise and exertion rather that in terms of equitable distribution. Even when we speak of business now, our focus is on distribution; on set-asides and affirmative action.

ENTREPRENEURS AND SELF-HELP

Our 1960s' success in making demands on government has led us to the mistaken assumption that government can give us what we need for the next major push toward equality. It has produced in us what Charles Tate of the Booker T. Washington Foundation recently described as a virtual antipathy toward capitalism. Even middle-class blacks seldom talk to their children about going into business. Instead our emphasis is on a fair distribution of jobs in businesses created and run by others. We ought to have a fair share of those jobs. But the emphasis, I submit, ought to be finding ways to get more of us into business and thereby creating for ourselves the jobs we need. That is especially true with regard to the so-called black underclass who tend to reside in areas abandoned by white businesses.

In addition to figuring out ways of getting our unemployed to jobs that already exist, we need to look for ways to encourage blacks in those abandoned neighborhoods to create enterprises of their own. What I have in mind are not merely the shops and Mom & Pop stores that we still patronize (but whose owners are far likelier to be Vietnamese or Koreans than blacks), but also an entrepreneurial approach to our social problems. I am not suggesting that government has no role in attacking these problems. It has a major role. What I am suggesting is that we need to explore ways of creating government-backed programs that instead of merely making our problems more bearable go in the direction of solving those problems. We are forever talking about the lack of day care as an impediment to work for welfare families. But why aren't we lobbying for legislation that would relax some of the anti-entrepreneurial rules and permit some of the money now spent on public welfare to be used to establish child-care centers run by the neighbors of those who need the care? Why aren't we looking for ways to use the funds that are already being expended to create small jitney services to transport job-seekers to distant jobs?

SUCCESS IS THE GOAL

I said at the beginning that I am not a theoretician, but I do have one little theory that may have some relevance to our subject. It is this: When people believe that their problems can be solved, they tend to get busy solving them—partly because it is the natural thing to do and partly because they would like to have the credit. When people believe that their problems are beyond solution, they tend to position themselves so as to avoid blame for their nonsolution. Now none of the black leadership will tell you that they think the problems we face are beyond solution. To do so would be to forfeit their leadership positions. But their behavior, if my theory is correct, suggests their pessimism.

Let me offer an example of what I am talking about. Take the woeful inadequacy of education in the predominantly black central cities. Does the black leadership see the ascendancy of black teachers and school administrators and the rise of black politicians to positions of local leadership as assets to be used in improving those dreadful schools? Rarely. What you are more likely to hear are charges of white abandonment, white resistance to integration, white conspiracies to isolate black children even when the schools are officially desegregated. In short, white people are responsible for the problem.

But if the youngsters manage to survive those awful school systems and make their way to historically black colleges—that is, if the children begin to show signs that they are going to make it—these same leaders sing a different song. Give our black colleges a fair share of public resources, they say, and we who know and love our children will educate them. The difference, I submit, is that they believe many of our high school students won't succeed, and they conspire to avoid the blame for their failure. But they believe that most of our college youngsters will make it and they want to be in position to claim credit for their success.

I suspect something like that is happening in terms of our economic well-being. Many of us are succeeding, in an astonishing range of fields, and the leadership does not hesitate to point out—with perfect justification—that our success is attributable to the glorious civil rights movement: that black exertion and courage made our success possible. But many of us aren't succeeding. Teenage pregnancy, dope trafficking, lawlessness and lack of ambition make us doubt that they ever will succeed. But do our leaders suggest that the reasons have to do with the inadequacy of the civil rights movement, or with any lack of exertion and courage on the part of the leadership? No. When we see failure among our people, and have reason to believe that the failure is permanent, our recourse is to our mainstay myth: Racism is the culprit. Mistakenly, we credit black pride for our successes and blame prejudice for our shortfalls.

I leave it to others to suggest the specifics by which we will move to increase the economic success of black America. I will tell you only that I believe it can be done—not only because it is being done by an encouraging number of us, but also because it has been done by earlier generations who struggled under circumstances of discrimination, deprivation, and hostility far worse than anything we now face. My simple suggestion is that we stop using the plight of the black underclass as a scourge for beating up on white racists and examine both the black community and the American system for clues to how we can transform ourselves from consumers to producers.

I used to play a little game in which I would concede to members of the black leadership the validity of the racism explanation. "Let us say you're exactly right, that racism is the overriding reason for our situation, and that an all-out attack on racism is our most pressing priority," I would tell them.

"Now let us suppose that we eventually win the fight against racism and put ourselves in the position now occupied by poor whites. What would you urge that we do next?

"Pool our resources? Establish and support black businesses? Insist that our children take advantage of the opportunities that a society free of racism would offer? What should be our next step?

"Well, just for the hell of it, why don't we pretend that the racist dragon has been slain already—and take that next step right now?"

ABOUT THE AUTHOR

William J. Raspberry is a columnist for the *Washington Post*. His twice-weekly column is nationally syndicated by the Washington Post Writers Group. *Time* magazine has written: "Raspberry has emerged as the most respected black voice on any white U. S. newspaper." He joined the *Post* in 1962 and held a variety of positions until he began his urban affairs column. From 1956 to 1960, he was reporter-photographer-editor for the *Indianapolis Recorder*. He then served two years in the U.S. Army. In 1965, Raspberry won the Capital Press Club's "Journalist of the Year" award for his coverage of the Watts riots in Los Angeles.

REAGAN WAS RIGHT:
GOVERNMENT IS THE PROBLEM

Charlton Heston
December 1990

n September 9-10, 1990, Hillsdale College formally launched its FreedomQuest campaign. With a goal of $151 million, it is the largest small college fund-raising effort ever undertaken.

The two-day gala event began with a special "Firing Line" debate, featuring host William F. Buckley, Jr., Rep. Dick Armey, actor, writer and director Charlton Heston, and former U.N. Ambassador Jeane Kirkpatrick for the affirmative side, adopting the resolution: "Government is not the solution, it is the problem." Opposing this team were former senators Gary Hart and George McGovern, Rep. Patricia Schroeder, and actor Dennis Weaver. Moderated by the New Republic *senior editor Michael Kinsley, the debate aired on PBS stations to an estimated audience of over three and a half million viewers.*

The opening arguments of one of the participants, Charlton Heston, are presented here along with additional remarks Mr. Heston delivered on September 10 upon accepting Hillsdale College's Freedom Leadership Award.

Heston: It is seldom that liberty of any kind is lost all at once. David Hume, the great Scottish philosopher, said that. I am a Scot myself. He was bloody right. For more than half a century, the shining Republic created by the blood of the Continental Army and a few great men has been nearly nibbled to death by the Democratic ducks in the Congress and a warmly cooperative Supreme Court.

There is now no aspect of American life, public or private, that the federal government does not invade, instruct and finally coerce to its will. Farm and factory, home and school, university and research center, club and playground— all are overlaid with a spidery network of laws, guidelines, restrictions and Draconian penalties that stifle the spirit, the energy, the creative capacity of what was once the freest nation on earth. In this hemisphere, now that Ortega and Noriega have fallen, the collectivists' sentiments discredited around the world fly best, I fear, in Cuba and Washington, D.C.

Of course, government is the problem. The armies of bureaucrats proliferating like gerbils, scurrying like lemmings in pursuit of the ever-expanding federal agenda, testify to that amply. Tom Jefferson, the only genius we ever had, said that government is best which governs least. I am amazed you Democrats are still comfortable with Mr. Jefferson as your designated logo.

QUESTIONS DIRECTED TO MR. HESTON:

Rep. Pat Schroeder: I certainly hope that you are also going to stand strong with us and keep the federal government out of bedrooms. I know people who are on your side also like to get...into the private lives of folks. And I've always found it really amazing in that your side often trusts corporations and fat cats to do anything and they want them deregulated, but they want to regulate the private lives of people. I hope you clearly are against that also.

Heston: Well, as the fellow that took down the original dictation on the Ten Commandments, I am naturally opposed to adultery.

Schroeder: Would you have federal adultery policed?

Heston: No.

Sen. George McGovern: Mr. Heston, I made reference to the savings and loan crisis. This is probably the most embarrassing and expensive financial scandal in the 200-year history of the country. Some people think that a major contributor to that was the breakdown of government regulation–we actually weakened the regulatory agencies and it was the kind of an atmosphere in the country to let people do what they wanted to in the private sector. What's your assessment of how well that theory has worked in the savings and loan industry where everybody was more or less allowed to run wild without any kind of government supervision?

Heston: I think certainly there was grievous dereliction of duty there on the part of the government, specifically the Congress. We lost the Speaker of the House, Jim Wright; we are about to lose the senior senator from California, Alan Cranston, because of their involvement. There were certainly congressmen and senators in both parties that were involved in this. But I don't think the handling of the program speaks well for the function of government.

McGovern: ...as I understand your view here tonight, you would intend, wherever possible, to eliminate government supervision and government regulation. Obviously, we have a lot of scandalous behavior on the part of both the Congress and the executive branch, but is your argument that things would have been better in the savings and loan industry if we had less government regulation and less government supervision?

Heston: Certainly it would have been better if the little cadre in Congress had not, in kind of a quiet meeting in the [Congressional] cloak room, said, "Well, look, let's guarantee loans up to $100,000." That was a little careless!

Dennis Weaver: Chuck, I just wondered—you don't mind if I call you Chuck, do you? You said government is not the solution; it's the problem. What do you consider to be the solution in situations like we have in our inner cities where our young people there are unemployed at a horrendous rate of [something] like 50 percent? And we have so much crime going on there because there's really no incentive for these young people. I just wonder what your solution would be?

Heston: I think you have to consider very carefully what kind of regulations must be put in place. I think there's an instinct to pass a law, any law, and see if it flies or not. We are both Californians. As you know, we are considering Proposition 128, which is a massive environmental control bill. Now you can't be against controlling the environment—clean air—all that. That's like being against apple pie. But they are just starting to figure out that that bill passed as currently worded in this fall's election is going to cost California taxpayers $4 billion.

Weaver: Do you realize what it would cost them if it isn't passed? They're life supports.

Heston: I think that's an example of excessive government activity without gains.

Sen. Gary Hart: I'd like to provide three or four examples of government services and see which ones you think the government should *not* do: cleaning up toxic waste dumps, protecting worker safety on the job, delivering Social Security checks to elderly people, regulating airline services, or providing poor children the opportunity for advancement through a Head Start program.

Heston: I think a good case is the minority children who are getting insufficient housing, insufficient education. I think government is going at it the wrong way. I think what we have to do is improve the schools, provide employment opportunities—not provide affirmative action programs that amount to mandated quotas in jobs, educational opportunities, things of that kind.

CHARLTON HESTON ACCEPTS THE FREEDOM LEADERSHIP AWARD

I am delighted to be at Hillsdale College and am honored by the award with which I have been presented. I have looked forward to visiting this heartland campus for some time, especially upon the occasion of the "Firing Line" debate that enlivened last evening. It was wonderful to be in such distinguished company as Jeane Kirkpatrick and Bill Buckley and the opposing team of debaters, even if they seemed a little daunted by history.

I first met your president, George Roche, when we served on a presidential task force on the arts and humanities in 1981. We deliberated for some four months before completing our report and submitting it to President Reagan. I am proud to say that once our job was over, we dissolved the task force. It is no more. Anybody who knows much about Washington, D.C. knows just how rare a feat that was.

In wending my way through the imposing corridors and rabbit warrens of our nation's capitol, on a variety of often trivial errands, I sometimes wondered whether behind some walnut door with a brass knob in an obscure corner of a marble corridor I would find an ancient gentleman with a green eye shade and sleeve garters writing with a quill pen. Likely as not, he would be finishing revisions on a report first submitted in 1910.

All the time I have known him, George has politely urged me to visit Hillsdale. And upon each occasion when an invitation was extended, I have said, "Yes, I really want to do that." But various circumstances have prevented it until now. You should have been more eloquent, George; I didn't know what you had here. As another visitor to the Hillsdale campus declared a few years ago, "This isn't a college–this is a 1940 movie set of what a college *ought* to be." I absolutely concur.

I congratulate Hillsdale on its extraordinary success. I wish there were even as few as 10 Hillsdale Colleges around the country–they would be enough to transform American education overnight. I suppose God in His grace will not grant that in my lifetime. I understand, however, why tenured professors from large prestigious universities take salary cuts to come and teach here. I understand why hundreds of thousands of people know about this little rural school and why it has been able to gain national attention for its fight to remain independent.

I suspect that one of the reasons why this has happened and why Hillsdale is thriving (well, you have only been at it since 1844, so I suppose you ought to have gotten somewhere) is the quality of its leadership. I believe that we live in the century of the common man, but I also believe in extraordinary men and women who make a real difference in the world. I think that some of them are leading this college and thus you are to be congratulated.

ABOUT THE AUTHOR

Charlton Heston, recipient of the Academy Award for Best Actor for his performance in *Ben-Hur* in 1959, has also received many international awards. He served six terms as President of the Screen Actors Guild, was chairman of the American Film Institute, and was a member of the National Council on the Arts. In 1978, he received the Jean Hersholt Humanitarian Award from the Academy of Motion Picture Arts and Sciences.

CUTTING GOVERNMENT
DOWN TO SIZE: WILL IT WORK?

Robert Novak and Mark Shields
January 1990

This issue features two of America's most well-known journalists, Robert Novak and Mark Shields. Since their debate took place at Hillsdale's Shavano Institute for National Leadership seminar, "Political Reform in the 1990s," on January 17, the day after war broke out in the Persian Gulf, some of the more serious comments refer to this event. But on the whole, we hope that the reader will enjoy the humorous side of their presentations too. While their deep and wide-ranging differences on the question of big government are obvious and instructive, Novak and Shields roast each other here in an entertaining debate.

ROBERT NOVAK: The moderator for this session gave me some very good news when he indicated he would make sure that the time was even, because Mark always tries to get more time when we have these joint appearances, and I'm glad somebody's going to be fair. Fairness is not just a liberal Democratic issue, you know. I'm glad to be here, but I'm doubly glad that Mark Shields is here. It's good for Mark, who, unlike Jim Wright, is a *real* liberal Democrat who believes that government is wonderful, believes the more you spend the better off you are and who never saw a tax increase that he didn't like. It's also good for Mark to be here in the presence of the patriotic people in this Shavano audience, people who believe in the private sector, the kind of people he never sees, since he is permanently lodged inside the Washington Beltway.

In case you think I'm being over-critical, I think it's also important for Mark to be here because he is an American success story. I don't think it's going to be in his regular introduction, but Mark spent most of his adult life as a professional political consultant. The problem was that nearly all his candidates lost! He took over the Muskie campaign when Muskie had a 77 percent popularity rating and he brought him down in the course of a year to seven percent. When candidates discovered that hiring this little fellow guaranteed they were going to lose, pretty soon they stopped hiring him. So, his family was destitute—he didn't have a dime, and he switched professions. He moved from politics to journalism, and today, ladies and gentlemen, Mark Shields is a millionaire journalist and that's what makes America great!

Unfortunately, Mark and I have been agreeing on something lately, and that is our misgivings about the policy of the United States in the Persian Gulf. I will say this: There are some people, of course, who were out in the street before the war, during the war, after the war demonstrating against the Contras, and against El Salvador. And there are still some Vietnam demonstrators left over. But I believe that once American fighting men and women are committed to action, then all citizens should give the troops 100 percent support. It's been a funny time for me, because I was in the Army in the Korean War, and I supported the Vietnam War to the bitter end. I also supported the Dominican intervention, the Grenadian intervention and the Panamanian intervention. So why, until 7 p.m. EST on January 16 did I have so many public and private misgivings about the Persian Gulf? Well, there are a lot of reasons. If we can intervene here, is there no place we cannot intervene? What other petty dictator shouldn't we intervene against? I am deeply concerned that we are spending too much money for defense, and we are going to have a hell of a time trying to cut the current budget now. I also believe there are a hundred million Arabs, and a lot more Muslims, with whom we have bought some trouble. Those problems are all in the future, and I hope they will be solved.

There has been another development during the months leading up to this war that fits the subject of this debate perfectly, and that is the whole question of President Bush's rhetoric about "a new world order." We're to understand, of course, that this means an order with the United States in the driver's seat. Regardless, that sounds a lot like super-government to me. I don't share the President's confidence in super-government on the international–or national– scale. The Gulf war also recalls some misgivings I have on the domestic scene about the Bush administration. I recently picked up the "Kennedy family news-letter," the *Boston Globe,* and there was a column by a good friend of Mark and mine, Tom Oliphant. He was writing about an interview with Teddy Kennedy, in which Kennedy said that he was glad that at the start of this new Congress he and his Democratic colleagues had helped get an extra $50 billion–for various "worthy purposes"–during budget negotiations with the administration; it wasn't nearly enough, of course, but according to the Senator it was a start.

Hey! Did you know that? Did you know that the President broke his pledge on taxes, that he cut the Republican Party in half to give Ted Kennedy $50 billion more to spend? Did you wonder why it was that Ted Kennedy had been talking about the budget so much, saying we had to have a tax increase? When Ted Kennedy says we have to have a tax increase, that it is the time for Americans to put their hands on their wallet. Let me tell you something about this budget "deal." It calls for $180 billion in *additional* federal spending over the next five years. It has $138 billion in *additional* taxes. The deficit doesn't go down; it goes up. The first estimates said $50 billion or so, but the actual figures will certainly be much higher now. The Bush administration never even went through the motions of trying to cut spending; the only thing it got out of the budget deal was some mechanisms that they said would restrain the Congress from future spending increases, at the cost of these tax increases.

Of course, surprise, surprise, the first thing that Congress did was to renege on these inadequate mechanisms. Men like Ted Kennedy say, "You can't do it, even if it's desirable, there's no way you can cut the budget." In truth, it's just the opposite: it can be done, and it's the people in Washington, D.C. who don't think it's desirable or feasible. The "four percent solution," widely supported by fiscal conservatives, was one plan which should have been seriously considered: It has three elements: (1) no new taxes; (2) a freeze on defense spending; and (3) a four percent increase in domestic spending. This plan allowed for a $450 billion protected deficit reduction instead of $500 billion for the next five years. Why didn't the Bush administration push that? Why didn't the Democratic House leadership even let Republican members put it up for a vote?

It is ironic that sound laissez-faire reforms are rejected at home precisely at a time when the rest of the world is starting to heed the ideas and philosophy of the fellow pictured on my necktie—Adam Smith. (I had breakfast with Mark this morning and he said, "Bob, you wore your Adam Smith tie! If I had known, I'd have worn my Karl Marx.)

Adam Smith's monumental study of the free market, *Wealth of Nations*, published, appropriately enough, in 1776, is said to be the book that is the most quoted and least read of any book with the exception of the Bible. Smith, who was not, thank God, a trained economist, said that the way to get a nation's economy growing is to lower taxes, limit regulation, and to get the cotton-pickin' hands of government off the economy. And the funny thing is, it *always* works. It worked in the 18th, 19th and when it's been tried, it's worked in the 20th century. But the 20th century has been the century of big government.

Ronald Reagan was such a success because he recognized this and attempted to cut government down to size. Reagan, I have to tell you, is my favorite 20th-century American president. My second favorite is Calvin Coolidge. What Reagan and Coolidge had in common was a firm belief that government was the problem, not the solution. They have been pilloried by the press for their shared predilection for getting a little shut-eye during the 24-hour period. But I guarantee that no president of the United States has ever done damage to this country when he was making "Z"s in the White House!

That's why it bothered me so much when George Bush and his administration came into office saying, "We're going to be burning the midnight oil." I have seen a lot of midnight oil-burners: Lyndon Johnson, Richard Nixon, Jimmy Carter, and our old republic has a hard time surviving them. What such ambitious public servants do, with the willing aid of the bureaucracy, is to expand the scope and size of government.

Government is a dingy business. Employees in the federal branch are by their nature dispirited, and the people in the Beltway establishment—the media, the special interests, the bureaucracy and Congress–are completely out of touch with the American public. They have no idea how counter-productive big government is to our economy and our culture.

After centuries of experience, these people still don't know that big government doesn't work. All over Eastern Europe, people are saying, "Get the government off our backs," but in this country, with a Republican president, we're increasing the load. Contrary to Kennedy's comment about the budget, it is more than just a matter of money; it is a mindset that says, "Even if it has never worked, keep doing it, again and again. Even if affirmative action has resulted in racially discriminatory quotas and the worst race relations on the college campus that we've ever had, keep doing it. Even if welfare results, as every sociologist knows, in greater poverty and dislocation in the inner city, keep doing the same thing."

The notion that the American people want all this government, but that they just don't want to pay for it, is the biggest canard foisted on us by today's politicians and media. What the country needs is a leader, and a leader who will make his first priority speaking over the heads of the Beltway types to say, "No more. Let's really cut government down to size."

MARK SHIELDS: I'd like to thank the moderator for that introduction; it was a lot nicer than the one I received recently in Baltimore, where the master of ceremonies simply said, "Now, for the latest dope from Washington, here's Mark Shields." I admit straightforwardly that I stole that line from one of my favorite Republican senators, Alan Simpson of Wyoming, a man of enormous wit. Once, when asked his church preference, Simpson answered, "red brick," which always endeared him to me.

I do appreciate the invitation to be here today; it's an invitation I do not deserve, but I have bursitis and I don't deserve that either (appearing with Bob Novak is the closest thing I can find to bursitis). Actually, Bob and I are friends, in spite of our genuine and serious political differences. There is nothing I wouldn't do for Bob Novak, and there's nothing Bob wouldn't do for me, so we go through life doing nothing for each other.

I was asked on the way in to this Shavano seminar where our "Capital Hill Gang" cohort Pat Buchanan was, and I answered that Pat would have been here today, but he had a conflict in his schedule: He was receiving the Man of the Year award from the Friendly Sons of the Spanish Inquisition.

In spite of Bob's cruel words, I want to be kind to him. He was recently voted one of the best minds in the Washington press corps. (Being voted one of the best minds in the Washington press corps is a little like making the Ten Best Dressed list in Albania.) But Bob is a respected member of the press, and I am happy to be here with him.

I did, in fact, misspend a large part of my youth and early middle age in elective politics. Bob remembered "President Muskie." I worked for a lot of other Democratic candidates, too, and I went to very few inaugural balls, let me tell you. But after the Democrats lost in 1988, for the fifth time in the last six presidential elections, the party leaders gathered at a "secret meeting," which, of course, Evans & Novak reported on. There they agonized in deep soul-searching introspection about what had happened. This lasted about 13 micro-seconds, and what the Democrats concluded they need in 1992 is a Southerner at the top of the ticket. On every Democrat's dance card for 1992 is the name of Chuck Robb, the former governor of Virginia, son-in-law of the late Lyndon Johnson and a Marine Corps combat veteran from Vietnam. He was elected to the Senate from Virginia in 1988, and the Republicans were hard pressed to find anyone to run against him who wasn't under indictment or in detox.

I like Chuck Robb personally, but I do not think the people of the United States are ready for a president from Virginia. If you think about it, Virginia's not a state; it's a museum piece: Williamsburg, Monticello, Mount Vernon; people in Virginia suffer from terminal nostalgia. They talk about General Lee and Mr. Jefferson like they're out on a coffee break and expected back momentarily. Richmond is a sort of hotbed of "social rest." This always reminds me of the old line about how many Virginians does it take to change a light bulb? The answer is three: One to change the light bulb, and two to reminisce about what a great light bulb the old light bulb was.

Bob's mention of Ted Kennedy reminded me of a fundamental political truth, one that is borne out by the time we're going through right now in the Persian Gulf. I obviously share Bob's feelings about Americans who are committed in battle in the Persian Gulf and support them completely. But the war will not always elicit total public support. To illustrate: When Ted Kennedy entered the presidential race in 1980 to oppose Jimmy Carter, it may have been Bob Novak, it may have been Rowland Evans, it may have been *Heloise's Hints,* but somebody who was very smart remarked at the time that Kennedy would never again be as high in the polls as the day he entered.

This prediction proved to be right. There was an idealized reminiscence of his brothers, but as Bob Strauss, the former Democratic Party chairman and former Jimmy Carter campaign manager, quipped, what Ted Kennedy proved in the 1980 campaign was that Rose didn't have triplets. I think the same could be said right now of the war in the Persian Gulf. It will not be as popular a year from now as it is today.

Americans are wonderful people. I say that without any hint of self-congratulation; we truly are. We have rallied to our president in a time of national emergency, and we have obviously rallied to support our brave fighting men and women. But the sobering reality is that the current leadership has not prepared our nation for any sense of sacrifice, and it has not laid out the case as to what constitutes victory. What are our goals, what do they entail and what kind of long-term commitments are we making, not simply in the Persian Gulf, but elsewhere around the world?

We have been told already that this is going to be painless, ouchless and quick. There will be no inconvenience, no sacrifice required of me, or of any of the other 250 million Americans, except our 450,000 soldiers—men and women who are ready to give everything.

I find that really unAmerican, in the true sense of the word. For those of us who lived through World War II—which was a communal experience, when every citizen felt that he or she belonged to the American community and was responsible for its welfare—it is especially disturbing. Any time Americans are at risk, under fire, anywhere in the world, then all of us have a responsibility to share that sacrifice in some way.

Much has been said about the "lessons" of Vietnam that have been supposedly learned over the past twenty years, and the one that seems to be repeated more and more often by our friends on television is, "We learned from Vietnam that there could be no more gradual build-ups, no more gradual escalations. From now on, we are going to mount a quick, complete, muscular response in reaction to military threats." I don't think *that* was the lesson of Vietnam. The lesson of Vietnam was, and remains, that you don't commit Americans to battle until you commit the American people. You don't ask American soldiers to put their lives on the line while we here at home are still undecided and indecisive about what's going on, and what our mission is.

What is going to happen when the Iraqi military machine collapses? Do we put a friendly government in Baghdad? What happens when it loses the first popular election that we've mandated? I don't think we've thought our actions in the Gulf through, and I can tell you that the chairman of the House Intelligence Committee put it very bluntly recently, that no American will be truly safe traveling across the ocean for the next ten years, and that we have unleashed forces of terrorism, the likes of which we in this country have always been blessedly spared and mercifully free.

There is one more thing. Those men and women of my generation learned as schoolchildren the poem that runs, "In Flanders fields the poppies grow...," but there won't be any Flanders fields in Saudi Arabia. Our allies don't allow the Christian cross; they don't allow the Star of David, and they don't allow the American flag. That there will be no tragic Flanders fields in the Middle East may be some sort of consolation, but it is a poor one. Let us pray that the war in the Gulf is short, quick and decisive, but let us not forget this.

I have devoted some time to discussing the Middle East because of the timing of this debate, just hours after American troops were committed to action. But now, we ought to turn our attention to the topic of government. I find myself in agreement with an earlier speaker in this program, former Civil Service director, Don Devine, and in disagreement with Bob Novak, which probably makes Novak comfortable and Devine uncomfortable: the deadlock between the executive and legislative branches in American government can be blamed in large part on Ronald Reagan.

Why? Well, I should state at the outset that I was one of the few political liberals who wrote positive things about Ronald Reagan. His administration proved to Americans, who had grown disenchanted after Vietnam, Watergate, Jimmy Carter and Gerry Ford, that government could work. Optimism and confidence in the federal government went up while Reagan was in office. Ironically, this was a disaster for the conservative, anti-government movement which Reagan publicly supported. He won two landslide elections by asking the question, "Are you better off than you were four years ago?" In 1980, the American people said "No," and Reagan carried 44 states. In 1984, the American people said "Yes," and he carried 49 states. Ronald Reagan actually confirmed the inescapable truth that American politics is not ideological.

We simply are not terribly introspective or philosophical. Americans—and you know them, and live with them, you claim them as relatives and neighbors and friends—are pragmatists. Ideologues believe what is right, works; Americans believe what works is right. Voters, when asked the question, "How about the federal government—is it a pain in the neck?" reply instantly, "You better believe it." When next asked, "Is it too big?" they shout, "Yes! The government is too big. There's too much red tape. Get those government types off my back, out of my hair, I can't stand them!"

You might be inclined to say "Wow, Americans are pretty conservative!" Sure, when people are asked questions in the abstract about how they feel about the federal government, they'll tend to complain. However, when told that just outside of Pocatella, Idaho, a single can of tunafish has been discovered with a trace of botulism, there is a universal American reaction: "Where are our protectors in the federal government? Why aren't they doing their job? I want a report in my office Monday morning."

What we all seem to want is that small, independent, lean, federal government of our dreams working on our side 24 hours a day—on the cheap. In reality, Americans do want government to do all sorts of things.

Ronald Reagan accomplished another feat in American politics: He defined both parties. He gave the Republican Party an identity it had long lacked. There was nobody in a noncomatose state in 1980 (the comatose states were Wisconsin and Connecticut) who could claim that he or she did not know what Ronald Reagan intended to do as president. He laid it out—specific details: cut the size, scope and spending of government, double the defense budget and cut taxes by a third. (I'm sure that was in there somewhere, always noted in the op-cits in Novak's papers.) Reagan gave the Republicans definition because he came to power on this platform, and even Republicans are occasionally pragmatic. He brought into office with him 32 new Republicans to the House, and a Republican majority to the Senate for the first time in 26 years. This too restored Americans' confidence in the federal government.

American voters *have* made a distinction between the two parties. When asked in all the recent surveys which party is better in dealing with the Soviet Union, voters say "Republicans" by a decisive margin, and that's a legacy of the Reagan era. The same holds true for issues like controlling inflation, and maintaining a strong national defense. However, those same voters, when asked in the very same surveys, which party is better at fighting for the interests of the middle class, protecting the environment, protecting the rights of women and minorities, protecting Social Security and Medicare, the Democrats win by a big margin.

Those first tasks I mentioned are basically identified with the President. As far as representing individual citizens' interests—making sure there isn't a toxic waste dump in the next neighborhood, etc.—these are congressional issues. The current deadlock between the executive and legislative branches makes a lot more sense when you take these factors into consideration. Despite that deadlock, does big government work in our country? I think there are some significant successes. For example, in 1972, all fifty states conducted studies that revealed that only 36 percent of the nation's rivers could be considered safe for fishing or swimming. Seventeen years later, by the same states' assessment, the figure had climbed to 70 percent. That's a positive change in American life, and it wasn't achieved by simply lowering the capital gains tax, which is Bob Novak's basic answer for everything from illiteracy to illegitimacy.

ABOUT THE AUTHORS

Robert D. Novak teamed up with Rowland Evans in 1963 to write "Inside Report." Today syndicated by the *Chicago Sun-Times* and appearing four times weekly in over two hundred newspapers, it is a national institution. Formerly a *Wall Street Journal* correspondent, he is the author of *The Agony of the GOP: 1964* (Macmillan, 1965), and co-author of *Lyndon B. Johnson: The Exercise of Power* (New American Library, 1966), *Nixon in the White House* (Random House, 1971), and *The Reagan Revolution* (Dutton, 1981). He collaborates with Evans on two widely read newsletters on politics and taxation, and the "Evans and Novak" program on CNN. Mr. Novak is also a roving editor for *Reader's Digest* and a regular panelist on "Crossfire," "Meet the Press," and "The Capital Gang," of which he is also the executive producer.

Mark Shields, a columnist for the *Washington Post,* is also known to millions of Americans for his regular appearances on television, and has earned a reputation for being one of the wittiest, most insightful political analysts in America. He has worked for CBS and NBC News covering national elections and conventions; he is a frequent guest on programs like "Nightline," the "Phil Donahue Show" and the "Today Show." Since 1987, he has been a regular commentator on the "MacNeil/Lehrer News Hour." And every Saturday, he joins Robert Novak, Pat Buchanan and Al Hunt on CNN's award-winning program, "The Capital Gang." He is also an author and a former Harvard professor.

TECHNOLOGY
AND THE FUTURE

WHO SPEAKS FOR SCIENCE?

Dixy Lee Ray
August 1988

epeatedly, over the past few years, the American public has been subjected to a litany of catastrophe—to predictions of impending disaster that are claimed to be unique to modern civilization. The oceans are dying, the atmosphere is poisoned, the earth itself is losing its capacity to support life. The reported "hole" in the ozone layer is the most recent scare. Cancer, generally blamed on man-made chemicals, is rampant—so the doomsayers say. Warnings that in the past came from the pulpit and called for eternal punishment in the sulfurous fires of hell have been replaced by equally dire predictions that come from alarmist environmentalists who call for spending billions of dollars in order to avoid doom from the sulfurous effluents of industry. The anticipated catastrophes are our own fault, of course, blamed on the greedy and perfidious nature of modern man.

Well, it's all pretty heady stuff, but is it true? As with so many issues that involve technology, the answer is yes—and no—probably rather more "no" than "yes." What are our real environmental concerns? Cancer-causing chemicals? Radiation, including radon? Carbon dioxide, ozone, and the "greenhouse effect"? Let's take a brief but hard look at each of these examples.

CANCER-CAUSING CHEMICALS

Recall that, with the exception of childhood leukemia (always tragic but relatively rare), cancer is a malady that afflicts predominately older adults and the aged. For most cancers—and there are many different kinds—the causes are complex, interactive, and may include genetic factors. If we look at the fatality records, the facts show that the total of carcinogenic substances targeted by the Environmental Protection Agency, including chemicals in the workplace, in the environment, in food additives, and industrial products, cause fewer than eight percent of all cancer deaths in America. The best scientific evidence points to diet, viruses, sexual practices, alcohol, and, above all, tobacco as accounting for nearly all of the remaining 92 percent. Yet the public, by constantly reported innuendo against industrial chemicals and radiation, is encouraged to believe otherwise. Moreover, a proper look at cancer statistics shows that, aside from a sharp increase in lung cancer caused by cigarette smoking, there have been no significant increases in the rate at which people die from any of the common forms of cancer over the past 50 years. In fact, there have been significant decreases in some types of cancer, e.g. stomach cancer, during these decades of rapid industrialization and the introduction of new man-made chemicals.

Most of the public believes that cancer is caused by toxic substances created by industry. Why? Because they listen to the wrong spokesmen. And national television has elevated sob-sister journalism to a new dramatic high, with emotional, heartrending stories about cases of childhood leukemia and other individual or family tragedies as if they were epidemic. These stories capture public attention and play on natural sympathy–these reactions in turn affect the decisions and budgets of government scientific agencies. In an internal memo the EPA admits, with remarkable candor, "Our priorities, [in regulating carcinogens] appear [to be] more closely aligned with public opinion than with our estimated risks"–and with scientific evidence.

RADIATION EXPOSURE

The simple fact is, we live in a radioactive world–always have, always will. Our bodies receive the impact of 15,000 radioactive particles every second; we don't feel them or suffer any ill effect from such bombardment. One of the difficult aspects of radiation phobia is that our ability to measure radiation has become so accurate and precise that it is now possible to detect unbelievably small amounts, e.g., one part per billion. How much or rather how little is that? How can we visualize one part per billion? One way is by analogy–one part per billion is equivalent to one drop of Vermouth in five railroad carloads of gin! (A very dry martini?) Or–look at it another way–there are now about five billion people living on this planet. Therefore, one family of five persons represents one part per billion of the entire human population.

And what about one part per trillion? That would be one thousand times less. When radioactivity from the Chernobyl accident in the USSR reached the West coast of the United States in April 1986, the popular press warned residents about the dangers of possible fallout, speaking of the number of picocuries of radioactivity detected in the high clouds, without ever explaining that one picocurie is one part per trillion and to receive from that "Chernobyl cloud" as much radioactivity as a patient would get in a diagnostic test for thyroid problems, a person would have had to drink 63,000 gallons of the "radioactive" rainwater–a formidable task!

Remember, everything is radioactive–our homes, buildings, everything we use. So is the forest primeval, our lakes, our streams, the ocean, and even our gardens. Because we have no human sense to detect radioactivity (no smell, sound, or sight reveals it), it has been like magnetism, gravity, or molecules; undetectable until instruments were built that can measure it with incredible precision. Now we know that even the ground we walk on is radioactive. In the words of Walter Marshall, Lord Marshall of Goring:

"In my own country, the United Kingdom, I like to point out that the average Englishman's garden occupies 1/10 of an acre. By digging down one metre, we can extract 6 kilograms of thorium, 2 kilograms of uranium, and 7,000 kilograms of potassium—all of them radioactive. In a sense all of that is radioactive waste, not man-made, but the residue left over when God created this planet."

It is radioactive decay that keeps the earth's core molten and provides warmth from inside that makes planet Earth habitable. It is the heat of radioactive decay that provides the driving force for movement of the earth's surface plates, and keeps the continents slowly moving and in turn contributes to both earthquakes and volcanic eruptions. Information about the essential and beneficial aspects of radioactivity, particularly in medical life-saving procedures, never reaches the public. Only the alarmists are heard. The negative effects of their warnings are serious. And, on the other hand, radon has become a national health problem because of our well-meant but stupid insistence on sealing up our homes and buildings to conserve energy without consideration of possible ill effects. Fear of radioactivity rests squarely on ignorance.

CARBON DIOXIDE AND THE GREENHOUSE EFFECT

The current scare is about carbon dioxide buildup, and the "greenhouse effect." It is true that the concentration of carbon dioxide in the atmosphere has been increasing. It is also true that the rate of carbon dioxide increases (and methane, hydrocarbons, sulphur oxides, nitrogen oxides, and few other substances) is now approximately one percent per year. Since increases of carbon dioxide have also occurred in the geological past, without the help of human industry, it is unclear whether the burning of fossil fuel is the cause of the present increase, however much it may be adding to the current totals. Moreover, it is not known what the consequences, if any, of this increase, may be or how long it may last. But this does not stop the doomsayers from hypothesizing about radical climate transformations and other adverse effects in the future.

It is prudent to recall that the climatic history of our planet is one of often quite dramatic change. There have been ice ages and warm periods lasting 800 years. There have even been shifts in the earth's polarity. And we know that drastic changes in climate can affect all living creatures, including humans. What we do not know is what caused severe climatic changes in the geological past, but we can be sure they were not due to human industrial activity. Most likely, the causes were and still are colossal cosmic forces, quite outside human ability to control them. Now that we live in an industrial, technological society, there is no reason to believe that such cosmic forces have ceased to exist. Why must we always blame modern man?

In these three areas of environmental concern (and in many others, including acid rain, the ozone layer, and pesticides), there is clearly a dichotomy between what is known and understood by the predominant body of scientific experts—and what the public believes because of the information it gets. But what the public perceives to be true, even if it is wrong, has enormous consequences since it is public opinion that determines how public funds are spent.

EDUCATE THE PUBLIC

The answer to this vexing problem of what the public believes is always the same: Educate the public. How? It seems so reasonable to conclude that once people understand how good and safe and environmentally benign a technology is, they will accept, if not welcome it. It seems reasonable to expect the public to be grateful for techniques that can mean responsible cures for environmental problems. But clearly it doesn't work that way because calm reason and alarmist environmentalism do not co-exist.

Also, how is the public going to know that the technology under consideration, like nuclear power, for example, is good and safe and environmentally benign? Will the public believe it on your say-so? Or on mine?—assuming, of course, that we have some way to communicate directly with the public. Is the plant manager a credible source of assurance to the public? Or do you think that:

- the generators of electricity are credible?
- the nuclear industry is credible?
- the chemical industry is credible?
- the representatives of government agencies are credible?
- research scientists and engineers are credible?

The course of public events, especially in nuclear science and now increasingly in the chemical industry as well, has, over the past 10-12 years, demonstrated that none of the groups just listed are trusted. The public is far more likely to believe the opponents of science and technology than to believe its supporters. If you are reluctant to accept that proposition, consider for a moment how you would fare on "60 Minutes" or "20/20" or "Crossfire" or on any of the many television and radio programs where controversial issues, even highly complex technical ones, are treated in an adversarial debate-like format as if questions of scientific fact could be settled, not by evidence, but by argument. I have likened this way of informing the public in scientific matters to a hypothetical situation in which a television broadcast program on criminal justice features a "balanced" panel made up of three judges and three criminals. That, of course, is being fair–presenting both sides. At least that is the way it works in science and technology. In such a format, the opposition always "wins" because whoever is against any technology has only to make a charge, however, preposterous; he doesn't have to prove it. The burden falls on the supporter of science to prove that the charge is groundless. It is a difficult situation, and it is one that we tend to handle badly.

There was a time, in my long-ago youth, when experts were believed. It was a time when most people and most institutions were presumed to be well-meaning and honest until and unless proved to be otherwise. It was also a time of unprecedented increase in our knowledge about the world, of belief in ourselves, and in our ability through understanding and logic to provide adequate solutions to technical problems. It was a time of optimism and progress. It was a time of improvement in the conditions of living that made our society and our nation the envy of the world. It was a time when the use of knowledge was expected, when the myriad applications of science through technology made living on this earth easier and better, and gave us more time to enjoy it by increasing our life span beyond three quarters of century. The funny thing is, it's still that kind of time...but it seems that hardly anyone enjoys it anymore. Too many people have exchanged confidence for despair, too many have come to fear technology and to hate and reject anything nuclear or chemical-related. Despite all the evidence of our physical well-being beyond the dreams of all previous generations, we seem to have become a nation of easily frightened people, the healthiest hypochondriacs in the world!

What has brought this condition about? What has made us lament rather than rejoice, so quick to believe the worst about ourselves and so reluctant to recognize the good? Well, among other possible explanations, we have simply done a rotten job of teaching science. Oh, not to those students who will become scientists–we're quite good at that–but at the equally important job of teaching science to all those others, the overwhelming percentage of the student population who will not enter science or engineering as a profession; there we fail miserably.

And so, we must ask further, if not from the schools and colleges, where do most people get their information about science and about important applications of technology in modern society? The answer is easy: mainly from television, and, to a lesser extent, from the print media and radio. Who decides the content of this information? Not scientists, but reporters, news directors, and editors. It is said that Professor John Kemeny, chairman of the President's Enquiry into the accident at Three Mile Island, commented after dealing with the press about his report:

"I left Washington fully expecting to read the following story someday in one of our morning newspapers, 'Three scientists named Galileo, Newton and Einstein have concluded that the earth is round. However, the *New York Times* has learned authoritatively that Professor John Doe of Podunk College has conclusive evidence that the earth is flat.' "

CREDIBILITY

If we want people properly educated in science and therefore more competent to make rational decisions on technical matters that affect them, then we must learn more about the different worlds in which scientists and reporters live and work. We have to recognize that scientists, technologists, and engineers do not and cannot inform the public directly. The media informs the public. And in doing so, the media acts as an information filter. The bottom line is that science and the media must learn to work together for a common purpose, because there is simply no other mechanism that can provide the necessary scientific information to society for social decision-making. So far, unfortunately, this rapport between science and the media shows no signs of developing.

Consider the differences in the ways of working, of motivation, and of rewards for scientists and for reporters. First, the scientists. For them, the volume of work is far less important than its quality. Scientists work at their own pace. There is no intractable daily or weekly deadline. Scientists work within a well-recognized discipline which is only a small part of the scientific whole. A scientist's work is judged by his peers, and unless peer-approved, it won't be published. For a scientist, all funding and professional advancement is based on peer-reviewed work. For all of these reasons, therefore, scientists are very careful about making claims. Those who value their standing in their peer community will be cautious not to overstate, and feel compelled to provide context for what they say. This is often interpreted by the non-scientific community as uncertainty, doubt, hedging, or even as evidence of disagreement among scientists.

In the media, however, a reporter's key to advancement is the volume of his work, maximizing minutes of air time or inches of print. Competition for time and space is fierce. For the reporter, deadlines are externally imposed, are short, and must be met. Narrow disciplines in journalism are non-existent; a reporter must cover them all. A reporter's work is judged not by his peers, but by an editor or news director and what attracts attention is of paramount importance. Good reporting is compact, without space for qualifications and context. On television,

60 seconds is the usual maximum for a story. Under such circumstances, reporters cannot read scientific papers. Most of their work is done on the telephone and they search out "experts" who will give them good one-liners.

Remember that the media are self-appointed defenders of the public faith, and most accept them in this role. Reporters inform the public about peril because this is what the public expects. The fastest way for a reporter to succeed, to become established and recognized, is to raise the specter of imminent peril and then take up the cudgels on behalf of society to deal with it.

There could hardly be two more diverse professions and it is no wonder that misunderstanding and misrepresentation arise. The good scientist strives to be precise by qualifying his statements and staying within the context of a scientific discipline. This is usually done in a deliberate manner. The good reporter strives for a fast response, for a compact statement that is reasonably accurate. Above all, a good reporter makes his statement in a manner designed to make the greatest impact on the audience. Therefore, information flowing from the scientific environment to the media environment inevitably suffers alteration and filtration and this affects public perceptions. In this regard, there appear to be three main problems:

1. An understandable, though unfortunate, emphasis on conflict between technology and social interest makes good press, but often unnecessarily heightens anxiety. The public will accept bad news, but it has been conditioned to reject good news as whitewash.

2. The persistence of false, exaggerated, or misleading information made believable by constant repetition. This leads to dissemination of what we call "factoids."*

Examples of factoids are:
- PCBs cause cancer
- any level of radiation is harmful
- acid rain is caused by sulfur dioxide from burning coal.

There are dozens of such factoids, that is, beliefs that have no evidence to support them. Some come about from the mistaken assumption that if two phenomena occur together or follow one another, they must represent cause-and-effect. Some come from an initial distorted opinion of a scientist desiring publicity for a cause or political position or from a zealous reporter trying to make a name for himself.

*For many of the thoughts presented here, and for the term "factoids," I am indebted to the article, "The Different Worlds of Scientists and Reporters," by G. I. Baskerville and K. L. Brown, published in the University of New Brunswick's "Forestry Focus" and reported in the *Journal of Forestry*.

3. Since good scientists limit their remarks within disciplinary boundaries, and good reporters extrapolate into a broad or common context, the result is often misinterpretation. "I was misquoted," says the scientist—and vows never to talk to a reporter again. Such a reaction is a mistake because it leaves the responsibility of communicating with the media to those scientists who avoid peer review for their work, have a mission or "cause," or are charlatans or quacks. Science has its quota of the latter just as does every profession.

THE SCIENTIFIC COMMUNITY'S RESPONSIBILITY

It is up to good scientists to weed these phonies out, but we don't do it. Rather, we allow, by our silence, such renegade organizations as the Union of Concerned Scientists to present itself as the "voice of the scientific community." They back up the Helen Caldicotts, Barry Commoners, Paul Ehrlichs, Amory Lovinses and other pretenders. While the respected scientific community judges very strictly those at the top of their profession, they simply ignore the incompetents and no-goods at the bottom. It is left to others of courage like the Hon. Patrick F. Kelly, of the U. S. District Court in Kansas, to say in November of 1984 what we should have been saying all along:

> "This Court rejects the opinion testimony of Dr. Karl Morgan and Dr. John Gofman because they both evidence an intellectually dishonest invention of arguments to protect their opinion....This is not a situation where the scientific community is equally divided between two respected schools of thought. It is a case where there is a small but very vocal group of scientists including Dr. Morgan and Dr. Gofman, that holds views not considered credible by experts in the field...."

Dr. Ernest Sternglass, much quoted by the media on radiation matters, has never published his claims about the effect of low-level radiation in a peer-reviewed journal. In an article in *Esquire* published in 1969, Dr. Sternglass predicted that all children in the United States would die as result of fallout from nuclear tests. Twenty years have passed and unfortunately for his credibility but fortunately for children, he was, and is, wrong. But his opinions, long since dismissed by knowledgeable scientists in his field, are still actively sought and quoted by the popular press. Until respected scientists, perhaps through their professional societies or through the National Academy of Science, identify the purveyors of misrepresentation, we have only ourselves to blame for fear, misunderstanding, and the rejection of technology.

We should be very jealous of who speaks for science, particularly in our age of rapidly expanding technology. A misinformed or uninformed public can stop anything even when it is clearly in society's benefit. How can the public be educated? I do not know the specifics, but of this I am certain: The public will remain uninformed and uneducated in science until the media professionals decide otherwise, until they stop quoting charlatans and quacks, and until respected scientists speak up.

ABOUT THE AUTHOR

Governor of Washington from 1977-81, Dixy Lee Ray is the former chairwoman of the Atomic Energy Commission, assistant secretary of state in the U.S. Bureau of Oceans, and director of the Pacific Science Center in Seattle. From 1945-76, she also served on the Zoology faculty of the University of Washington. Recognized by numerous scientific and civic organizations, she was voted Woman of the Year by *Ladies Home Journal* in 1973, the same year she was awarded the United Nations Peace Medal. Four years later, *Harper's* named her among the top ten most influential women in the nation.

FREEDOM AND THE
HIGH TECH REVOLUTION

George Gilder
November 1990

n his stories and essays, Hillsdale College President George Roche celebrates the old frontier of the American West, with its values of freedom, family, faith, and courage. But he also writes of the new frontier in high technology which is leading the worldwide revolt against centralization and tyranny. What is the connection between the old and new frontiers, between a million-fold coming advance in the efficiency of computers and the grinding struggle for food and warmth on the desolate reaches of the Oregon trail?

It is those selfsame values of freedom, family, faith and courage. Today, America is the world leader in technological innovation not because of its government or its Pentagon funding or its accumulated wealth or its natural resources or its continental scope—or any of the blessings to which U.S. success is often ascribed in textbooks—but because of an older ethic of freedom and sacrifice. In short, America's triumphs spring from the very moral codes and disciplines, the religious commitment and faith, which George Roche champions on his own new frontier at Hillsdale College.

WHY SECULARISM IS NOT ENOUGH

Too many people, scientists among them, are prone to believe that technology springs from a culture of secular rationalism in which each generation of children invents anew the codes and disciplines of civilization. But left on their own, children could not even figure out how to tie their shoelaces, let alone temper their appetites or suppress their immediate pleasure in order to fulfill long-term future needs. And we have learned that the more we banish religion and morality from the classroom, the more ill-equipped and credulous our children become. If this century teaches any clear lesson, it is Chesterton's: When people stop believing in God, they do not believe in nothing; they believe in anything. After decades of remorseless secular schooling, recent polls show that 55 percent of all Americans now believe in astrology, up from some 30 percent twenty years ago.

What produces technological progress is certainly not astrology, nor is it "modern values." And as Hillsdale recognizes, progress does not spring from the corrosive creeds of modern materialism: it comes instead from traditional spiritual values, dogged work and discipline, devoted to the fruits of the distant future. There is no doubt that teaching mathematics and science is crucial to technological progress. But teaching these subjects is far from sufficient to evoke technological advances. Outside of costly hothouse projects for the military, the USSR is a technological wasteland, despite the fact that its schools are far better than ours at teaching mathematics and science to a far greater proportion of the population.

Ronald Reagan made the key point in an eloquent speech to the students at Moscow State University: "Even as we explore the most advanced reaches of science, we're returning to the age-old wisdom of our culture. As Genesis affirms, in the beginning was the spirit, and it was from this spirit that the material abundance of creation issued forth." Mikhail Gorbachev recently echoed Reagan: "The Soviet Union is suffering from a spiritual decline. We were among the last to understand that in the age of information technologies the most valuable asset is knowledge, which springs from individual imagination and creativity. We will pay for our mistake for many years to come."

THE MYTH OF AMERICA'S DECLINE

Contrary to the trade statistics and misleading productivity data used by many economists, the U.S. has just undergone a phenomenal upsurge of innovation and growth. Even the economic data show that during the 1980s the U.S. increased its share of global exports, manufacturing output, and GNP. In order to comprehend such success, however, it is necessary to understand the technological and business dynamics of the last two decades. Today, the "experts" in the academy and the media tell a story of decline and decay that makes recent history incomprehensible. Is it really likely that the capitalist triumph of recent years was achieved through a collapse of growth and innovation? Unlike most of these experts, however, Gorbachev got the message.

The chief development was the microchip, the computer etched on a tiny sliver of silicon the size of a fingernail. Beginning with the computer industry, the impact of the chip reverberated across the entire breadth of the U.S. economy and galvanized the electronics industry into a force with revenues today greater than all U.S. automobile, steel, and chemical manufacturers combined. Quite simply, the microchip—and the personal computer industry it inspired—are the central driving force of global economic growth.

In 1980, the U.S. dominated the computer industry, controlling more than 80 percent of the world market. Most of these revenues were produced by less than ten companies, the IBM Corporation plus "the BUNCH" as it was called, including Burroughs, Univac, NCR, Control Data, and Honeywell. However, all of these firms, including IBM, lost ground during the ensuing decade, despite the fact that the computer industry grew five times in size and its cost effectiveness improved some ten thousand-fold. This is an amazing and important story and it bears profound lessons. Imagine for a moment that someone told you back in 1980 that even though the computer industry was about to go though a period of extraordinary growth, all of the U.S. firms then dominant in the industry would suffer drastic losses of market share during the decade and some would virtually leave the business. What would you have predicted for 1990?

Would you imagine that U.S. companies would still command nearly 70 percent of world computer revenue? Despite lavish government programs around the world designed to overtake the U.S. in computing–the major target of every industrial policy–the U.S. held its own in market share and more than tripled its lead in real revenues and profits.

AN ENTREPRENEURIAL EXPLOSION

I t was an industrial miracle. Before we try to copy the strategies of countries that failed, we should try to understand the meaning of America's surprising success. What happened was an entrepreneurial explosion: the completely unexpected emergence of some *fourteen thousand* new software firms. These companies were the catalyst. The U.S. also generated thousands of computer hardware and microchip manufacturers, and they also contributed heavily to the miracle of the 1980s. But the efflorescence of software was decisive. Giving dominance to the U.S. were thousands of young people turning to the personal computer with all the energy and ingenuity that previous generations invested in their Model T automobiles.

A high school hacker and Harvard dropout, Bill Gates of Microsoft, wrote the BASIC language for the PC and emerged ten years later as the richest man in America. Scores of others followed in his wake, with major software packages and substantial fortunes, which–like Gates'–were nearly all reinvested in their businesses.

During the 1980s, the number of software engineers increased about 28 percent a year, year after year. The new software firms converted the computer from the cult tool of a priesthood of data processing professionals–hovering over huge air-conditioned "mainframes"–into a highly portable, relatively inexpensive appliance that anyone could learn to use. This entrepreneurial explosion was a total surprise. It is safe to say that of all the hundreds of reports on technological competitiveness released in the U.S., Europe and Japan during the 1970s not one pointed to software hackers as the critical element–not one suggested that getting Bill Gates to drop out of Harvard would be crucial to the success of American computer technology during the 1980s.

But the transformation of the computer into a commodity appliance was largely achieved in this unexpected and entirely unplanned way. With hardware and software, the transformation was made possible by thousands of new companies that were as flexible and innovative as the new desktop computers and software programs they were producing. Although the "experts" claim that the industry is in a slump, entrepreneurial leaders such as Sun, Compaq and Conner, Microsoft and Intel, remain among the fastest growing firms in the U.S. economy today. The '80s generation of some 120 microchip firms is the fastest growing in history. And the software hackers keep on innovating.

In contrast to the American approach to the computer industry over the last decade, the Europeans have launched a series of unsuccessful national industrial policies, led by national "champion" firms, imitating a spurious vision of IBM. Their only modest successes have come from buying up American firms in trouble. Following similar policies, the Japanese have performed scarcely better. For all their splendid technological achievements, the one field in which Japan did not triumph in the 1980s was computers. Rather than imitate the American model which allows thousands of computer companies to flourish in a competitive environment, the Japanese, like the Europeans, adopted the old centralized IBM model. They gambled that big companies, big capital and big mainframe systems with dumb (i.e., passive) terminals attached would be the wave of the future. They gained virtually no market share until the late 1980s when they began producing laptop computers. By early 1990, they had won only four percent of the American market.

Meanwhile, American entrepreneurs have launched a whole series of new computer industries: supercomputers, graphics computers, supermini computers, minisupercomputers, desktop workstations, multimedia systems, network computers, cellular computers, file server computers, notebook computers, transaction processors, script entry computers–all accompanied by new software. The latest U.S. innovation is an array of special purpose supercomputers. As much as a hundred-fold cheaper than ordinary supercomputers, these new devices handily outperform them for special functions such as reading Pap smear tests, doing three dimensional graphics, executing Navier-Stokes equations (for complex fluid flows), recognizing speech, compressing and rendering video images, and many other uses. Thinking that the "game" was general purpose supercomputers, the Japanese have about caught up in that field, but still find themselves in the wake of American entrepreneurs who constantly change the rules.

Free market enterprise will always beat industrial policy. But today the U.S. government is doggedly trying to kill its entrepreneurial culture with deadly capital gains taxes–retaxing profits already taxed at high rates at the corporate level–and it has launched a national campaign against the so-called "junk bonds" or high-yield securities that over the last four years have financed some

80 percent of computer industry expansion. The result is to constrict capital access and hike the cost of capital for American companies which are forced to compete with foreign firms that face virtually no capital gains taxes. The problem doesn't stop with taxes: American companies also confront a growing body of contradictory and unsound environmental and bureaucratic regulations. And liability laws, which habitually favor plaintiffs and drain billions of dollars from those with "deep pockets," gravely threaten American enterprise. Even though U.S. computer and software industries remain the world leaders, these problems have to be confronted.

AMERICAN COLLEGES AS SEEDBEDS OF INNOVATION

D espite the fact that most of the rationales for over-taxation, regulation and litigation arise on campus, the American system of higher education is an important source of competitiveness. By contrast with U.S. high schools, U.S. colleges are competitive, because they have to face thousands of rivals–unlike most foreign universities which have local monopolies. As a result, our institutions attract would-be entrepreneurs from around the world. The lesson of the American system of higher education is that what breeds competitiveness is competition.

Under the stress of this competition among institutions, U.S. colleges and universities created an entirely new culture of technology within the last ten years. Beyond the 28 percent annual increase in software engineers, the number of trained computer scientists rose 46 percent a year throughout the 1980s–that is, every year, 46 percent more than the year before. In 1980 there were 11,000 computer scientists in the U.S.; in 1986, there were 41,800; and in 1990 the figure exceeded 100,000. Not only did American colleges and universities expand existing computer science programs, but they also launched thousands of new programs. To respond to the radically new technologies and computer languages spawned by earlier graduates, these universities often had to invent entirely new courses. Hundreds of colleges provided adult education in a variety of high technology fields.

Perhaps the key figure in the high technology revolution was a professor at Caltech named Carver Mead. He foresaw as early as the 1960s that he and his students would eventually be able to build computer chips extraordinarily more dense and complex than experts believed was possible or than anyone at the time could design by hand. Therefore he set out to create programs to computerize chip design.

By the end of the 1980s, largely as a result of the work of Mead and his students, any trained person with a workstation computer costing some $20,000 could not only design a major new chip but could also manufacture prototypes on his desktop.

Just as digital desktop publishing programs led to the creation of some ten thousand new publishing companies, so desktop publishing of chip designs and prototypes unleashed tremendous entrepreneurial creativity in the microchip business. During the decade of the 1980s the number of new chip designs produced in the United States rose from just under ten thousand a year to well over one hundred thousand. And it all began with one obscure college professor teaching a few students, year after year, who went on to found scores of small companies and thus share this new microchip breakthrough with the world.

THE 1990s: A NEW HIGH TECH REVOLUTION AHEAD

In the 1990s, we are about to see a dramatic acceleration of the progress first sown in American universities and colleges by the likes of Carver Mead. Right now, it is possible to put twenty million transistors on a single sliver of silicon the size of your thumbnail; by the year 2000, it will be a billion. To understand what a billion transistors means, think of the central processing units of twenty Cray 2 supercomputers, which are the most powerful computers on the market today, each of which costs some $20 million.

Just after the turn of the century, American (and Japanese) computer companies will be able to put the computer power of twenty Cray 2 supercomputers on a *single chip* and manufacture it for under $100. Of course, in an industry of revolutionary surprises the chip won't necessarily take the form of twenty general purpose supercomputers. But the dimensions of progress are summed up by that measure. It signifies that, in the next decade or so, we are going to see about a million-fold rise in the cost effectiveness of computing hardware. This impending advance of a million-fold improvement in computer efficiency is the most important fact in the world economy today. Gorbachev apparently senses it, and so do his generals. But do the "gloom and doom" experts have the slightest conception that this is going on? Do they have any idea of the explosive impact such progress will bring? To get an idea of the likely effect, we should examine the impact of a much smaller but still huge advance achieved earlier.

In 1977, virtually all computer power was commanded by large mainframe computers, mostly from IBM, with dumb terminals attached. Ten years later, by 1987, less than one percent of the world's computer power was commanded by such large computer systems. In 1987, there were some 80 million personal computers in the world. In 1990, it has been estimated there are over fifty million personal computers in the United States alone; by comparison, the U.S. has more than three times as much computer power per capita as Japan.

The 1990s' counterpart of the mainframe computer—similarly vulnerable to the onrush of more powerful tools—is the television industry. Just as there were a few thousand mainframe computers linked to dumb terminals, there are today just over 1,400 television stations and a handful of networks supplying millions of dumb terminals known as television sets, or "idiot boxes." The experts will tell you that the Japanese made the right decision when, ten years ago, they launched a multibillion dollar program to develop "high definition television." In fact, it is widely assumed that HDTV will dominate electronics by the end of the next decade. The advice of the experts, therefore, is "catch-up-and-copy," summoning a massive government effort to create our own high definition television sets.

HDTV does represent a significant advance; the new sets have a resolution five times higher than current models. The television industry may well improve its technology in other respects. But all these gains will be dwarfed by the coming technology of the telecomputer: the personal computer upgraded with supercomputer powers for the processing of full-motion video. As we've seen, the computer industry will improve its cost effectiveness about a million times during the next decade. Unlike HDTV, which is mostly an analog system specialized for the single purpose of TV broadcast and display, the telecomputer is a fully digital technology. It creates, processes, stores and transmits information in the non-degradable form of numbers, expressed in bits and bytes. This means the tele-computer will benefit from the same learning curve of steadily increasing powers as the microchip with its billion transistor potential and the office computer with its ever-proliferating software. With tens of thousands of hardware and software firms in the U.S., the computer industry is an entrepreneurial force vastly more innovative and vigorous than the television broadcast and manufacturing indus-tries. And the television set, even with the benefit of high definition cosmetics, is still just a passive receiver.

The digital computer or telecomputer can receive full motion video just as well as any television set can. Indeed the computer can dispense with most of the complex conversion processes of analog HDTV and accept perfect digital signals from fiber optic telephone lines. The computer, however, is not only a receiver; it is also a processor of video images, capable of windowing, zooming, storing, editing, and replaying. Furthermore, the computer can originate and transmit video images that will be just as high quality and much cheaper than the current television and film industries can provide.

This is a huge difference. It goes beyond the possibility of receiving perhaps a hundred one-way TV channels to having access to as many channels as there are computers attached to the network: millions of potential two-way channels around the world. With every desktop a possible broadcasting station, thousands of U.S. firms are already pursuing the potential market of video systems as universal and simple to use as the telephone is today. Imagine a world in which you can have access to any theater, church, business, college classroom, or library anywhere. The freedom which will be extended to the individual by this technological innovation is beyond compare.

GORBACHEV AND HIS GENERALS GET THE MESSAGE

Most Americans have never heard of Carver Mead, the leading protagonist of the high tech revolution, but once again, Gorbachev got the message. Many people imagine that the breakdown of the Soviet system was the result of a popular uprising, or a demand for consumer goods, or a hunger for democracy. But the views of the people have never mattered under communism. What matters are the views of the generals. Whatever reforms Gorbachev might have wanted to carry forth, he could not have moved forward without the support of the generals. Gorbachev's generals were not moved by any lust for freedom or desire for more McDonald's in downtown Moscow. They were moved by the increasing impact of microchip and other computer technology on the future of warfare and the ability of the state to control the individual.

At a recent Moscow conference, a leading American libertarian declared that he opposed the military industrial complex in the U.S. as much as in the Soviet Union. It is a statement that goes unchallenged in most American centers of learning. But in Moscow, his commentator and other Soviets protested. They declared that without the U.S. military industrial complex, he could not even be celebrating liberty in Moscow and no one would be discussing free markets in the Kremlin.

When President Reagan introduced the Strategic Defense Initiative, it was widely denounced and caricatured as an impossible dream of a perfect shield in the sky. But neither Reagan nor any of his advisors ever imagined that it could be perfect. They did know that it would be good enough to send a message to Gorbachev and his generals. Nonetheless, the experts in the academy, the media, and even in the defense establishment said it was impossible to program the needed equipment. For one thing, they argued, in order to master the command, control and communications of such a system, you would need a supercomputer a hundred times more powerful than the most powerful supercomputers of the day.

Now we know that the experts once again underestimated American ingenuity. The new supercomputers will indeed be a hundred times as powerful as existing computers. But it will be possible to put one of them in each of the many thousands of interceptors in the missile defense array. It will be possible to create a completely decentralized kind of strategic defense in which the previous perplexities of command control and communications can be entirely overcome. Such weapons will be crucial in defense against accidental attacks or Third World madmen like Saddam Hussein. For the first time it will also be possible to create defensive equipment with pattern recognition powers usable against terrorists as well as military aggressors. The message received by Gorbachev and his generals was not merely the potential capability of SDI. It was the recognition that a totalitarian government, no matter how many scientists, engineers, and mathematicians it produces, and no matter how many five-year plans it devises, cannot keep pace with the fruits of freedom in an open society.

AN IMAGE OF SAND AND GLASS

If Gorbachev and his generals could get the message, perhaps we can now dare to pass it on to American college campuses and faculties, which, unlike Moscow, are still benighted by the shades of Karl Marx. Let us send them instead an image of sand and glass. The sand comes in the form of a silicon microchip inscribed with a logical pattern as complex as a street map of the United States, switching its traffic flawlessly in trillionths of seconds. The glass comes in the form of fiber optic threads as thin as human hair and as long as Long Island, fed by laser diodes as small as a grain of salt and brighter than the sun. Each system, in place today for AT&T between Chicago and the East Coast, can send the equivalent of a thousand Bibles a second across the land and indeed could transmit the entire contents of the Library of Congress down one fiber in eight hours. Using copper technology, by contrast, it would take five hundred years.

This image is not some far-off dream. It is here now and will be gathering momentum for the next decade. Together the two technologies made from ordinary sand—fiber optics and silicon chips—will form a global network of computers and cables, a worldwide web of glass and light that leaves all previous history in its wake. Consisting of technologies that defy the normal constraints of time and space, this vision also transcends the materialist superstitions that have governed most of human history. For thousands of years, the route to power was the control of land and armies. Today when you can put "worlds on a grain of sand," control of specific territories declines in importance. What matters is not the control of lands but the liberation of minds.

The American frontier, celebrated by George Roche and Hillsdale College, is a frontier of mind and spirit, and it epitomizes the disciplines and values that have brought about the technological revolution, which itself opens new frontiers of mind and spirit. But it is not any peculiarly American character trait that has made our nation the world leader on this technological frontier. It is American freedom beckoning to the world with a vision, not of service to the state, but of service to others—it is the values of freedom, family, faith and courage defended by schools like Hillsdale College, and which are embodied in our Constitution and our Judeo-Christian heritage. As we move through the 1990s, with its promise of million-fold gains in computing, it is crucial that our schools transmit the values of American freedom and faith to future generations. As President Reagan told the Moscow students: "In the beginning was the spirit and it was from this spirit that the material abundance of creation issued forth."

ABOUT THE AUTHOR

George Gilder, senior fellow of the Hudson Institute and author of the best-selling *Wealth and Poverty* (Basic Books, 1981), writes regularly for *Forbes, the Wall Street Journal,* and *National Review.* His other books include *Sexual Suicide* (Quadrangle, 1973), reissued as *Men and Marriage* (Pelican, 1986), *Visible Man* (Basic Books, 1978), *The Spirit of Enterprise* (Touchstone, 1984), *Microcosm: The Quantum Revolution in Economics and Technology* (Simon & Schuster, 1989), and *Life After Television: The Coming Transformation of Media and American Life* (Whittle Communications, 1990). Mr. Gilder has also served as a fellow of the Kennedy School of Government at Harvard University.

FAITH, FREEDOM AND CULTURE

WE CANNOT SEPARATE
CHRISTIAN MORALS AND THE
RULE OF LAW

Russell Kirk
April 1983

wo there are by whom this world is ruled," said Pope Gelasius I, near the end of the fifth century. In that phrase may be found the beginning of the doctrine of the "two swords"—of the separation of church and state. In every century, after one fashion or another, church and state have had occasion to fall out—even in this American Republic.

Recently the Supreme Court of the United States found unconstitutional a Kentucky statute requiring that the Ten Commandments be posted in public schools. The placards in question bore a notice stating that "the secular application of the Ten Commandments is clearly seen in its adoption as the fundamental legal code of Western Civilization and the common law of the United States." But the Supreme Court ruled, five justices against four, that this educational employment of the Decalogue breached the famous wall of separation (*Stone* v. *Graham,* decided November 17, 1980). This decision carried to an extreme the doctrine of the two swords: the concept that although the spiritual authority and the temporal authority exist in symbiosis, still a gulf must be fixed between the two.

Presumably the majority of the justices who handed down this decision were not expressing hostility toward Judaism or Christianity; but certainly they did not acknowledge any religious consecration of the American Republic. Beyond this present "neutrality" in the courts may lurk the prospect of hostility between church and state, even here in America. And so one thinks of the words of T. S. Eliot: "If you will not have God—and he is a jealous God—you should pay your respects to Hitler or Stalin."

The vast quantity of litigation in federal and state courts concerning church schools, employees of churches, church tax exemptions, and related questions, suggests that the old established relationships between church and state in America have become strained. Litigation may, and does often, become effectual harassment. It is possible, for instance, for American Civil Liberties Union types to harass out of existence public displays of the Nativity at Christmas time. Also it is possible, or may become possible, for the state to harass the church into compliance with political passions of the moment. It is quite conceivable that there is developing among us, even now, a humanitarian "civil religion," an American Erastianism, which might supplant Christian teaching as the basis of public order.

GRIM DESCENT

Now the purpose of law is to keep the peace. When this end is half forgotten, and instead the law is used by some as a means of extortion from others, or as an instrument for class advantage, or as a tool for social direction, or merely for the gratifying of malice—why, the law itself tumbles into injustice. Toward that we have been sliding in this Republic; and most of the world has stumbled the whole way down that grim descent.

True law necessarily is rooted in ethical assumptions or norms; and those moral principles are derived, in the beginning at least, from religious convictions. When the religious understanding, from which a concept of law arose in a culture, has been discarded or denied—well, the laws may endure for some decades, through what sociologists call "cultural lag"; but in the long run, the laws also will be discarded or denied, after having been severed from their ethical and religious sources.

With this hard truth in mind, I venture to suggest that the corpus of English and American laws—for the two arise for the most part from a common root of belief and experience—cannot endure forever unless it is animated by the spirit that moved it in the beginning: that is, by religion, and specifically by the Christian religion. Certain moral postulates of Christian teaching have been taken for granted, in the past, as the ground of justice. When courts of law ignore those postulates, we grope in judicial darkness.

Nowadays those postulates are being ignored; nay, we suffer already from a strong movement to exclude from courts of law such religious beliefs, and to discriminate against those unenlightened who fondly cling to the superstitions of the childhood of the race. Permit me to offer two recent examples of this anti-religious tendency in judicial concerns.

Consider the attempt made not long ago to disqualify a federal judge who was about to hand down—and subsequently did hand down—a decision in a case concerned with an extension of time for ratifying the proposed Equal Rights Amendment. Judge Marion Callister is an active communicant of the Church of Jesus Christ of the Latter-Day Saints, and formerly was a bishop in that church. The Mormon Church has declared its opposition to the Equal Rights proposal. Therefore the U.S. Department of Justice sought to have Judge Callister disqualified from hearing the case, on the ground that his religious views would prejudice him. Presumably, if we are to grant this premise, a Catholic jurist, or a Missouri Synod Lutheran, or a member of any other denomination that has declined to embrace the enthusiasts of ERA, also would be found disqualified. On the other hand, a judge who could demonstrate that his conscience lay untroubled by any religious scruples would be found qualified by our Department of Justice.

RELIGION DIVISIVE?

My second instance is certain litigation about an ordinance regulating abortion in the city of Akron, Ohio. The American Civil Liberties Union, representing two abortion clinics and an abortionist-physician, challenged in a federal district court various provisions of the Akron ordinance. The most curious aspect of the case was the ACLU's argument about "divisiveness": put succinctly, the ACLU contended that any restraint upon abortion must be unconstitutional, because such statutes or ordinances are founded upon a religious belief to the effect that human life commences at the conception of the fetus. In short, any law rooted in religious dogmas is no law at all—or so the zealots of the ACLU contend.

The Supreme Court has yet to instruct us that Christian and Hebraic beliefs are inadmissible in a court of law, and that a new civil religion of "scientism" has supplanted them. The two cases I mentioned a moment ago are not yet the law of the land; they suggest, nevertheless, the direction in which our juridical assumptions have been drifting.

This retreat from the Christian postulates of American law (for there are such Christian postulates, just as there are Muslim postulates of Arab law) soon may encounter unhappy difficulties. Many moral beliefs, although sustained by religious convictions, may not be readily susceptible of "scientific demonstration." Our abhorrence of murder and rape may be traced back to the Decalogue and other religious injunctions. If it can be shown that our opposition to such offenses is rooted in religious belief, then are restraints upon murder and rape unconstitutional?

At such absurdities we arrive if we attempt to erect a real wall of separation between the operation of the laws and those Christian moral convictions that move most Americans. Theater of the absurd can become nasty reality: "See my pageant passing," says the playwright, looking out of his window upon the revolutionary mob pouring through the street. The doctrinaires of the American Civil Liberties Union would not be spared, were the religious postulates underlying law to be swept away; for that matter, our very civil liberties themselves are held up by theological pillars. Yet not all is lost; and if we are to try to sustain some connection between Christian moral teaching and the laws of this land, we must understand the character of that link. We must claim neither too much nor too little for the influence of Christian belief upon our structure of law.

CHRISTIAN FOUNDATIONS MINIMIZED

For the past two centuries, the tendency of writers upon the law has been to claim too little for Christian influence upon the foundations of law.

If we turn to that high juridical authority Sir Henry Maine, who was no Christian enthusiast, we find that in his *Early History of Institutions* (published in 1875) he remarks many Christian influences upon law: how Christianity restrained the liberty of divorce; how it affected the Brehon laws; how it altered the character of contracts; how it worked in favor of women with respect to the laws; how it promoted donation; how "the Will, the Contract, and the Separate Ownership were in fact indispensable to the Church as the donee of pious gifts; and they were also essential and characteristic elements in the civilization amid which the Church had been reared to maturity." Parallel treatment of Christian influence could be cited in various other important nineteenth-century writers on legal institutions and jurisprudence—although still more about Christian teaching will be found in the works of seventeenth- and eighteenth-century legal writers.

Twentieth-century commentators, nevertheless, have been somewhat timid about referring to religious sources for law. Take Roscoe Pound, in his *Interpretations of Legal History,* written in 1922. Pound is by no means unfriendly to Christian concepts; he thinks Christian influence has been held in too low esteem; for all that, he grants such concepts no broad sway.

"The prevailing view has been that, after the stage of primitive law is passed, religion has played relatively a small part in legal history," Pound writes.

> "Yet I venture to think that the influence of religious ideas in the formative period of American law was often decisive and that without taking account of Puritanism we shall fail to get an adequate picture of American legal history as it was in the last century. I suspect that some day we shall count religious ideas as no mean factor in the making of what are now the doctrines of English equity. Undoubtedly such ideas played a substantial part in the history of the modern Continental law of obligations. So far as it directs attention to a factor which often may be of the first moment in shaping legal rules and doctrines and institutions, the religious interpretation is by no means to be neglected."

Let it be noted that here Pound is writing of the law—both statutory law and common law—rather than of the sources of the law. "One of the main difficulties and causes of confusion in Jurisprudence," J. C. Gray writes in his *Nature and Sources of the Law* (second edition, 1927), "has been the failure to distinguish between Law and the sources of Law." A country's law is "composed of the rules for conduct that its courts follow and that it holds itself out as ready to enforce." But these rules, Gray continues, though enforced regardless of abstract theories of justice, in part arise from ethical principles. Permit me to add to Gray's observation that ethical principles ordinarily arise from religious perceptions.

RATIONALISTS, DARWINIANS, FREUDIANS

I am suggesting that Pound and Gray, though conceding something to Christian ethics as a source of law, still conceded too little; they wrote in a climate of opinion not cordial toward religious concepts, a climate in which flourished the *dicta* and *obiter dicta* of Justice Oliver Wendell Holmes. I am suggesting that Christian faith and reason have been underestimated in an age bestridden, successively, by the vulgarized notions of the Rationalists, the Darwinians, and the Freudians. Yet I am not contending that the laws ever have been the Christian word made flesh; nor that they can ever be.

My Puritan ancestors of Massachusetts Bay, like their fathers, the "Geneva Men" of Elizabethan England, hoped to make the laws of the ancient Jews into a code for their own time—a foolish notion. My Scottish Covenanting ancestors, too, aspired nearly to that. Upon such misconceptions, my great-great-great-great-great-great-great-great-grandfather on the distaff side, Abraham Pierce, was tried at Plymouth, Massachusetts, in 1625, for indolence on the Sabbath; by a miscarriage of justice, doubtless, he was acquitted.

Such attempts at legal archaism, being absurd, failed before they properly began; for the particular laws of a people ineluctably mirror the circumstances of an age. Hebraic legal institutions would no more suit seventeenth-century England, say, than the English common law of the seventeenth century would have been possible for Jerusalem in the sixth century before Christ. No, what Christianity (or any other religion) confers is not a code of positive laws, but instead some general understanding of justice.

Judges cannot well be metaphysicians—not in the execution of their duties upon the bench, at any rate, even though the majority upon the Supreme Court of this land, and judges in inferior courts, seem often during the past three decades to have mistaken themselves for original moral philosophers. The law that judges mete out is the product of statute, custom, convention, precedent. Yet back of statute, custom, convention, and precedent may be discerned, if mistily, the forms of Christian doctrines, by which statute and custom and convention and precedent have been much influenced in the past. And the more that judges ignore Christian assumptions about human nature and justice, the more are they thrown back upon their private resources as abstract metaphysicians–and the more the laws of the land fall into confusion and inconsistency.

PERIL OF JUDICIAL METAPHYSICS

Prophets and theologians and priests and pastors are not legislators, ordinarily; yet their pronouncements may be incorporated, if sometimes almost unrecognizably, in statute and custom and convention and precedent. The Christian doctrine of natural law cannot be made to do duty for the law of the land, were this tried, positive justice would be delayed to the end of time. Nevertheless, if the Christian understanding of natural law is cast aside utterly by magistrates, mocked and flouted, then positive law becomes patternless and arbitrary.

Would it be preferable to have the law arise from the narrow, fanatic speculations of some ideologue? Just that disaster has befallen the law in Russia, China, and other lands, a matter with which the gentlemen and ladies of the American Civil Liberties Union do not much concern themselves.

I am saying that Christian doctrine, in the United States as in Britain, is not the law; yet it is a major source of the law, and in particular a major foundation of jurisprudence, that science so neglected in nearly all American law schools. This reality was understood by the two principal legal scholars of the formative era of American law, Joseph Story and James Kent; and to them I turn now.

Story and Kent sustained the long-established understanding of the relationship between Christian morals and the law of the land. Sir Matthew Hale, Justice of the King's Bench, ruled in Taylor's Case (1676) that "the Christian religion is part of the law itself." In Woolston's Case (1729), King's Bench found that "Christianity in general is parcel of the common law of England and therefore to be protected by it." (Both were cases concerned with blasphemy.) These precedents, cited by Sir William Blackstone in his *Commentaries,* were accepted by those American champions of common law Justice Story and Chancellor Kent. There runs through Story's *Commentaries* and Kent's *Commentaries* the assumption that in America also the common law is bound up with Christian doctrine.

In important decisions in their courtrooms, Story and Kent sustained the especial standing of the Christian religion in common law. In *Terret* v. *Taylor* (1815), Story recognized that the Episcopal Church in Virginia derived its rights from the common law; in *Vidal* v. *Girard's Executors* (1844), he accepted Daniel Webster's argument that the Christian religion was part of the common law of Pennsylvania. Kent, when Chief Justice of New York, found in *People* v. *Ruggles,* that the defaming of Christianity might be punished under common law. He wrote in his decision (1811): "The people of this state, in common with the people of this country, profess the general doctrines of Christianity, as the rule of their faith and practice."

Story's and Kent's decisions, and their arguments in their respective *Commentaries,* remained powerful influences upon later important federal and state decisions that touched upon questions of morals—for instance, the United States Supreme Court's stern warning against bigamy and polygamy, written by Chief Justice Waite and Justice Field (in 1879), who called these customs crimes against "the laws of all civilized and Christian countries." Even though weakened by the ambiguity of a series of Supreme Court decisions during the past three decades, the opinions of Story and Kent continue in some degree to affect court rulings on public morality.

NOT AN ESTABLISHMENT OF RELIGION

Did Story and Kent imply that an establishment of religion existed in the United States? Not so: both jurists strongly expressed their approval of the separation of church and state. In 1813, touching upon the practice of the New England Puritans, Story denounced (and somewhat misrepresented) the Puritan error of "the necessity of a union between church and state." In his *Commentaries,* he remarked that "Half the calamities with which the human race have been scourged have arisen from the union of Church and State." And in *Vidal* v. *Girard's Executors,* Story noted in his decision that "although Christianity may be a part of the common law of the State, yet it is so in this qualified sense, that its divine origin and truth are admitted, therefore it is not to be maliciously and openly reviled and blasphemed against, to the annoyance of believers or the injury of the public." In a letter to Story, Kent expressed his full concurrence in the Vidal decision.

In effect, Story and Kent tell us that Christianity is not the law of the land in the sense that Christian teachings might be enforced upon the general public as if they were articles in a code; Story and Kent had no intention of emulating in the nineteenth century the Geneva Men's ambition to resurrect the laws of the Jews. Rather, the two great American commentators point out that Christian moral postulates are intricately woven into the fabric of the common law, and cannot be dispensed with, there being no substitute for them in ethical concerns; and that the Christian religion, as the generally recognized faith (in one profession or another) of the American people, is protected against abuse by defamers, that the peace may be kept and the common good advanced.

It is not Christianity as an exclusive creed, but rather Christianity as the Western, or English, or American form of what C. S. Lewis calls the "Tao," or the underlying morality of natural law, that is a source of common law and of jurisprudence. Story and Kent affirmed their belief in the Christian connection with common law, and their belief in the need for separation of church and state—without lack of consistency.

The relationship of federal and state governments to Christian belief, as implied in the first clause of the First Amendment, was taken up by Story in his *Commentaries:*

"It was impossible that there should not arise perpetual strife and perpetual jealousy on the subject of ecclesiastical ascendency, if the national government were left free to create a religious establishment. The only security was in extirpating the power....

"Probably at the time of the adoption of the Constitution, and of the amendment to it now under consideration, the general if not the universal sentiment in America was that Christianity ought to receive encouragement from the state so far as was not incompatible with the private rights of conscience and the freedom of religious worship. An attempt to level all religions, and to make it a matter of state policy to hold all in utter indifference, would have created universal disapprobation, if not universal indignation."

EVEN DOUGLAS BOWED

There is no national establishment of religion, but American governments acknowledge the benefits of religion and desire to encourage religious faith—this, Joseph Story's view, remained the general consensus of the Supreme Court of the United States, with few and partial exceptions, until very recent years. Justice William O. Douglas wrote in the Zorach case (1952):

"We are a religious people whose institutions presuppose a Supreme Being. We guarantee the freedom to worship as one chooses. We make room for as wide a variety of beliefs and creeds as the spiritual needs of man deem necessary. We sponsor an attitude on the part of government that shows no partiality to any one group and that lets each flourish according to the zeal of its adherents and the appeal of its dogma....To hold [that government may not encourage religious instruction] would be to find in the Constitution a requirement that the government show a callous indifference to religious groups. That would be preferring those who believe in no religion over those who do believe....But we find no constitutional requirement which makes it necessary for government to be hostile to religion and to throw its weight against efforts to widen the effective scope of religious influence."

It will be noted that Justice Douglas referred to religion in general, rather than to the Christian religion in particular; American pluralism had grown more diverse with the passage of more than a century. But also it should be noted that so late as the Zorach case even the more liberal justices of the Supreme Court did not interpret the "wall of separation" doctrine (a phrase that originated in a letter written by Thomas Jefferson, not in any public document) as a declaration of hostility against Christian churches. Story and Kent were heard, at least through echoes, as late as a quarter of a century ago.

A less amicable relationship between state and church has been developing since 1952—although it is true that a series of recent decisions by the United States Supreme Court, somewhat dogmatically reaffirming the separation of church and state, have the beneficial effect of securing church schools and churches themselves against various attempts at direction by the agencies of the federal government or of the several states.

What we call "law" does not exist in an intellectual and moral vacuum. To cut off law from its ethical sources is to strike a baleful blow at the rule of law. Yet such blows are inflicted upon the law today—ordinarily in the names of liberation and modernity.

APOLLO VS. DIONYSIUS

The wisest brief treatise on the present plight of the law with which I am acquainted is the Cardozo Lecture delivered in 1962 by Huntington Cairns, entitled, "Law and Its Premises." Dr. Cairns emphasizes that the forces of order, symbolized in ancient times by the god Apollo, are attacked in every age by the forces of license, symbolized by the god Dionysius. In our time, that struggle affects the whole of the law. Cairns writes:

"From the beginnings of Western thought, law has been a field of knowledge derived from a larger whole, the understanding of which has been held to be indispensable to any effort to reach the standards applicable to human affairs. At the same time, there has been a volitional element in the legal process stemming from the contrary view that law is not derived from a larger whole; man devises his own standards and law need not be understood in terms of any ultimate order. These two ways of seeing law are in conflict today, and the consequences of this conflict in the long run could be fatal."

In this contest during the present century, the Dionysian powers are those influences that would sweep away altogether any influence of Christian postulates—along with classical wisdom—upon modern law; and the Apollonian powers set their faces against this emasculation of the law. Christian belief is not the only source of ethical principle behind our laws; but it is the most powerful and popular source. If all connection between the Christian religion and the verdicts of courts of law is severed in this country, the law must become erratic and unpredictable at best (when it is supposed to be regular in its operation), and tyrannical rather than protective.

Some moral convictions must be the foundation of any system of law. In this country, were the Christian postulates swept away, by what moral principles might they be supplanted? Not by the amorphous notions labelled "liberalism," now thoroughly unpopular, called by Santayana "a mere adventitious phase." No, the Christian moral understanding presumably could yield, in the long run, only to the commandments of the Savage God—enforced by some Rough Beast, his hour come round at last.

WHAT IS MAN?

How will this struggle over the nature of law, with the followers of Apollo on one side and the votaries of Dionysius on the other, be terminated? Will the Christian sources of the law be effaced quite speedily—as already they have been in Eastern Europe—or will the Christian moral imagination and right reason rise up again in strength, even in our courts of law? No man can say. It would be easy to accept, with the Eastern sages in Chesterton's poem, "The Ballad of the White Horse," "the inevitability of gradualism"—that is, the steady diminishing of religious remnants and the steady advance of the Dionysians. Yet that cannot be the way of the Cross.

> "The men of the East may spell the stars,
> And times and triumphs mark,
> But men signed of the cross of Christ
> Go gaily in the dark.
> * * * *
> "Night shall be thrice night over you,
> And heaven an iron cope.
> Do you have joy without a cause,
> Yea, faith without a hope?"

In the domain of the law today, as in all other realms of human endeavor, there is waged a battle between those who believe that we human creatures are made in the image of a Creator, and those who believe that you and I are not much more than fleshly computers. Even within the courts of law, created to help keep the peace, this war is fought to the knife.

Witness to the truth, my friends, and go gaily in the dark wood of our twentieth century.

ABOUT THE AUTHOR

President of two educational foundations, editor of the quarterly *University Bookman,* and founder of *Modern Age,* Russell Kirk is the author of more than thirty books, which collectively have sold over a million copies, most notably: *The Conservative Mind* (Regnery, 1953, now in its 7th printing), *Enemies of the Permanent Things: Observations of Abnormity in Literature and Politics* (3rd edition, Open Court, 1988), *The Wise Men Know What Wicked Things Are Written on the Sky* (Regnery Gateway, 1987), *The Roots of American Order* (Intercollegiate Studies Institute, 3rd edition, 1990), and *Eliot and His Age: T.S. Eliot's Moral Imagination in the Twentieth Century* (3rd edition, Open Court, 1988). His award-winning gothic fiction includes *Watchers at the Gate* (Arkham House, 1984) and *Lord of the Hollow Dark* (Christendom Press, 2nd edition, 1989). The only American to hold an earned doctor of letters from St. Andrews University, he lectures widely on politics, history, literature, religion and contemporary issues. In one of his final acts before leaving office, President Ronald Reagan publicly presented Dr. Kirk with the Presidential Citizen's Medal.

THE GREAT LIBERAL
DEATH WISH

Malcolm Muggeridge
May 1979

he great liberal death wish" is a subject that I have given a lot of thought to and have written about, and it would be easy for me to present to you a long piece that I have written on the subject. But somehow in the atmosphere of this delightful college, I want to have a shot at just discussing this notion of the great liberal death wish as it has arisen in my life, as I have seen it, and the deductions I have made from it. I should also plead guilty to being responsible for the general heading of these lectures at Hillsdale, namely, "The Humane Holocaust: The Auschwitz Formula."

Later on I want to say something about all this, showing how this humane holocaust, this dreadful slaughter that began with 50 million babies last year, will undoubtedly be extended to the senile old and the mentally afflicted and mongoloid children, and so on, because of the large amount of money that maintaining them costs. It is all the more ironical when one thinks about the Jewish holocaust that Western audiences, and the German population in particular, have been shuddering over, as it has been presented on their TV and cinema screens. Note: this new compassionate or humane holocaust, if, as I fear, it gains momentum, will quite put that other in the shade. And as I shall try to explain, what is even more ironical, the actual considerations that led to the Jewish holocaust were not, as is commonly suggested, due to Nazi terrorism, but were based upon the sort of legislation that advocates of euthanasia, or "mercy killing," in this country and in Western Europe, are trying to get enacted. It is not true that the Jewish holocaust was simply a war crime, as it was judged to be at Nuremberg. In point of fact, it was based upon a perfectly coherent, legally enacted decree approved and operated by the German medical profession before the Nazis took over power. In other words, from the point of view of the *Guinness Book of Records* you can say that in our mad world it takes about thirty years to transform a war crime into a compassionate act.

But I am going to deal with that later. I want first of all to look at this question of the great liberal death wish. And I was very delighted that you should have gotten here for this CCA program the film on Dostoevsky for which I did the commentary, because his novel, *The Devils,** is the most extraordinary piece of prophecy about this great liberal death wish. All the characters in it, the circumstances of it, irresistibly recall what we mean by the great liberal death wish. You cannot imagine what a strange experience it was doing that filming in the USSR. I quoted extensively from the speech that Dostoevsky delivered when the Pushkin Memorial was unveiled in Moscow, and his words were

* Sometimes translated as *The Possessed.*

considered to be, in terms of then current ideologies, about the most reactionary words ever spoken. They amounted to a tremendous onslaught on this very thing that we are talking about, this great liberal death wish, as it existed in Russia in the latter part of the last century. The characters in the book match very well the cast of the liberal death wish in our society and in our time. You even have the interesting fact that the old liberal, Stephan Trofimovich Verkovensky, who is a sort of male impersonator of Mrs. Eleanor Roosevelt, with all the sentimental notions that go therewith, is the father of Peter Verkovensky, a Baader Meinhof character, based on a Russian nihilist of Dostoevsky's time, Sergey Nechayef. To me, it is one of the most extraordinary pieces of modern prophecy that has ever been. Especially when Peter Verkovensky says, as he does, that what we need are "a few generations of debauchery—debauchery at its most vicious and most horrible—followed by a little sweet bloodletting, and then the turmoil will begin." I put it to you that this bears a rather uneasy resemblance to the sort of thing that is happening at this moment in the Western World.

Now I want to throw my mind back to my childhood, to the sitting room in the little suburban house in south London where I grew up. On Saturday evenings my father and his cronies would assemble there, and they would plan together the downfall of the capitalist system and the replacement of it by one which was just and humane and egalitarian and peaceable, etc. These were my first memories of a serious conversation about our circumstances in the world. I used to hide in a big chair and hope not to be noticed, because I was so interested. And I accepted completely the views of these good men, that once they were able to shape the world as they wanted it to be, they would create a perfect state of affairs in which peace would reign, prosperity would expand, men would be brotherly, and considerate, and there would be no exploitation of man by man, nor any ruthless oppression of individuals. And I firmly believed that, once their plans were fulfilled, we would realize an idyllic state of affairs of such a nature. They were good men, they were honest men, they were sincere men. Unlike their prototypes on the continent of Europe, they were men from the chapels. It was a sort of spillover from the practice of nonconformist Christianity, not a brutal ideology, and I was entirely convinced that such a brotherly, contented, loving society would come to pass once they were able to establish themselves in power.

My father used to speak a lot at open air meetings, and when I was very small I used to follow him around because I adored him, as I still do. He was a very wonderful and good man. He had had a very harsh upbringing himself, and this was his dream of how you could transform human society so that human beings, instead of maltreating one another and exploiting one another, would be like brothers. I remember he used to make quite good jokes at these outdoor meetings when we had set up our little platform, and a few small children and one or two passers-by had gathered briefly to listen. One joke I particularly appreciated and used to wait for even though I had heard it a hundred times ran like this: "Well ladies and gentlemen," my father would begin, "you tell me one thing. Why is it that it is His Majesty's Navy and His Majesty's Stationery Office and His Majesty's Customs but it's the *national* debt? Why isn't the debt His Majesty's?" It always brought the house down.

Such was my baptism into the notion of a kingdom of Heaven on earth, into what I was going to understand ultimately to be the great liberal death wish. Inevitably, my father's heroes were the great intellectuals of the time, who banded themselves together in what was called the Fabian Society, of which he was a member—a very active member. For instance, Bernard Shaw, H. G. Wells, Harold Laski, people of that sort—all the leftist elite—like Sydney and Beatrice Webb, belonged to this Fabian Society, and in my father's eyes they were princes among men. I accepted his judgment.

Once I had a slight shock when he took me to a meeting of the Fabian Society where H. G. Wells was speaking, and I can remember vividly his high squeaky voice as he said—and it stuck in my mind long afterward—"We haven't got time to read the Bible. We haven't got time to read the history of this obscure nomadic tribe in the Middle East." Subsequently, when I learned of the things that Wells *had* got time for, the observation broke upon me in all its richness.

Anyway, that for me was how my impressions of life began. I was sent to Cambridge University, which of course in those days consisted very largely of boys from what we call public schools, and you call private schools. Altogether, it was for me a quite different sort of milieu, where the word "socialist" in those days—this was in 1920 when I went to Cambridge at 17—was almost unknown. We who had been to a government secondary school and then to Cambridge were regarded as an extraordinary and rather distasteful phenomenon. But my views about how the world was going to be made better remained firmly entrenched in the talk of my father and his cronies.

In the meantime had come the First World War, to be followed by an almost insane outburst of expectations that henceforth peace would prevail in the world, that we would have a League of Nations to ensure that there would be no more wars, and gradually everybody would get more prosperous and everything would be better and better. That rather lugubrious figure, Woodrow Wilson, arrived on the scene, to be treated with the utmost veneration. I can see him now, lantern-jawed, wearing his tall hat–somehow for me he didn't fill the bill of a knight in shining armor who was going to lead us to everlasting peace. Somehow the flavor of Princeton about him detracted from that picture, but still I accepted him as an awesome figure.

My stay at Cambridge was a rather desolate time. I never much enjoyed being educated, and have continued to believe that education is a rather over-rated experience. Perhaps this isn't the most suitable place in the world to say that, but such is my opinion. I think that it is part of the liberal dream that somehow or other–and it was certainly my father's view–people, in becoming educated, instead of on Sundays racing their dogs or studying racing forms, or anything like that, would take to singing madrigals or reading *Paradise Lost* aloud. This is another dream that didn't quite come true.

Anyway, from Cambridge I went off to India, to teach at a Christian college there, and I must say it was an extremely agreeable experience. The college was in a remote part of what was then Travancore, but is now Kerala. It was not one of the missionary colleges, but associated with the indigenous Syrian Church, which is a very ancient church, dating back to the fourth century, and now there are a million or more Syrian Christians. In its way it was quite an idyllic existence, but of course one came up against naked power for the first time. I had never thought of power before as something separate from the rest of life. But in India, under the British raj, with a relatively few white men ruling over three or four hundred million Indians, I came face to face with power unrelated to elections or any other representative device in the great liberal dream that became the great liberal death wish.

However, it was a pleasant time, and the Indian nationalist movement was beginning, and Gandhi came to the college where I was teaching. This extraor-dinary little gargoyle of a man appeared, and held forth, and everybody got tremendously excited, and shouted against imperialism, and the Empire in which at that time the great majority of the British people firmly believed, and which they thought would continue forever. If you ventured to say, as I did on the boat going to India, that it might come to an end before long, they laughed you to scorn, being firmly convinced that God had decided that the British should rule over a quarter of the world, and that nothing could ever change this state of affairs. Which again opened up a new vista about what this business of power signified, and how it worked, not as a theory, but in practice. We used to boast in those days that we had an Empire on which the sun never set, and now we have a commonwealth on which it never rises, and I can't quite say which concept strikes me as being the more derisory.

That was India, and then I came back to England and for a time taught in an elementary school in Birmingham, and married my wife Kitty. (I wish she were here today because she's very nice. We've been married now for 51 years, so I am entitled to speak well of her.) She was the niece of Beatrice and Sydney Webb, so it was like marrying into a sort of aristocracy of the Left. After our wedding, we went off to Egypt, where I taught at the University of Cairo, and it was there that the dreadful infection of journalism got into my system. Turning aside from the honorable occupation of teaching, I started writing articles about the wrongs of the Egyptian people, how they were clamoring, and rightly so, for a democratic setup, and how they would never be satisfied with less than one man/one vote and all that went therewith. I never heard any Egyptian say that this was his position, but I used to watch those old pashas in Groppi's cafe smoking their hubble-bubble pipes, and imagined that under their tabooshes was a strong feeling that they would never for an instant countenance anything less than full representative government. That at least was what I wrote in my articles, and they went flying over to England, and, like homing pigeons, in through the windows of the *Guardian* office in Manchester, at that time a high citadel of liberalism. That was where the "truth" was being expounded, that was where enlightenment reigned. In due course, I was asked to join the editorial staff of the *Guardian,* which to me was a most marvelous thing.

I may say that the work of teaching at Cairo University was not an arduous job, essentially for three reasons. One was that the students didn't understand English; the second that they were nearly always on strike or otherwise engaged in political demonstrations, and thirdly they were often stupified with hashish. So I had a lot of leisure on my hands. (Incidentally, to be serious for a moment, it seems to me a most extraordinary thing that at that time you wouldn't have found anybody, Egyptian or English or anybody else, who wasn't absolutely clear in his mind that hashish was a most appalling and disastrous addiction. So you can imagine how strange it was forty years later for me to hear life peeresses and people like that insisting that hashish didn't do any harm to anybody, and was even beneficial.)

Anyway, these were the golden days of liberalism when the *Manchester Guardian* was widely read, and even believed. Despite all its misprints, you could make out roughly speaking what it was saying, and what we typed out was quite likely, to our great satisfaction, to be quoted in some paper in Baghdad or Smyrna as being the opinion of our very influential organ of enlightened liberalism. I remember my first day I was there, and somehow it symbolizes the whole experience. I was asked to write a leader–a short leader of about 120 words–on corporal punishment. At some headmasters' conference, it seemed, words had been spoken about corporal punishment and I was to produce appropriate comment. So I put my head into the room next to mine, and asked the man who was working there: "What's our line on corporal punishment?" Without looking up from his typewriter, he replied: "The same as capital, only more so." So I knew exactly what to tap out, you see. That was how I got into the shocking habit of pontificating about what was going on in the world; observing that the Greeks did not seem to want an orderly government, or that one despaired sometimes of the Irish having any concern for law and order; weighty pronouncement tapped out on a typewriter, deriving from nowhere, and for all one knew, concerning no one.

We were required to end anything we wrote on a hopeful note, because liberalism is a hopeful creed. And so, however appalling and black the situation that we described, we would always conclude with some sentence like: "It is greatly to be hoped that moderate men of all shades of opinion will draw together, and that wiser councils may yet prevail." How many times I gave expression to such jejeune hopes! Well, I soon grew weary of this, because it seemed to me that immoderate men were rather strongly in evidence, and I couldn't see that wiser councils were prevailing anywhere. The Depression was on by that time, I am talking now of 1932-33. It was on especially in Lancashire, and it seemed as though our whole way of life was cracking up, and, of course, I looked across at the USSR with a sort of longing, thinking that there was an alternative, some other way in which people could live, and I managed to maneuver matters so that I was sent to Moscow as the *Guardian* correspondent, arriving there fully prepared to see in the Soviet regime the answer to all our troubles, only to discover in a very short time that though it might be an answer, it was a very unattractive one.

It is difficult to convey to you what a shock this was, realizing that what I had supposed to be the new brotherly way of life my father and his cronies had imagined long before, was simply on examination an appalling tyranny, in which the only thing that mattered, the only reality, was power. So again, like the British raj, in the USSR I was confronted with power as the absolute and ultimate arbiter. However, that was a thing that one could take in one's stride. How I first came to conceive of the notion of the great liberal death wish was not at all in consequence of what was happening in the USSR, which, as I came to reflect afterward, was simply the famous lines in the "Magnificat" working out, "He hath put down the mighty from their seat and hath exalted the humble and meek," whereupon, of course, the humble and meek become mighty in their turn and have to be put down. That was just history, something that happens in the world; people achieve power, exercise power, abuse power, are booted out of power, and then it all begins again.

The thing that impressed me, and the thing that touched off my awareness of the great liberal death wish, i.e., my sense that Western man was, as it were, sleep-walking into his own ruin, was the extraordinary performance of the liberal intelligentsia, who, in those days, flocked to Moscow like pilgrims to Mecca. And they were one and all utterly delighted and excited by what they saw there. Clergymen walked serenely and happily through the anti-god museums, politicians claimed that no system of society could possibly be more equitable and just, lawyers admired Soviet justice, and economists praised the Soviet economy. They all wrote articles in this vein that we resident journalists knew were completely nonsensical. It is impossible to exaggerate to you the impression that this made on me. Mrs. Webb had said to Kitty and me: "You'll find that in the USSR Sydney and I are icons." As a matter of fact they were Marxist icons.

How could this be? How could this extraordinary credulity exist in the minds of people who were adulated by one and all as maestros of discernment and judgment? It was from that moment that I began to get the feeling that a liberal view of life was not what I'd supposed it to be—a creative movement that would shape the future—but rather a sort of death wish. How otherwise could you explain how people, in their own country ardent for equality, bitter opponents of capital punishment and all for more humane treatment of people in prison, supporters, in fact, of every good cause, should in the USSR prostrate themselves before a regime ruled over brutally and oppressively and arbitrarily by a privileged party oligarchy? I still ponder over the mystery of how men displaying critical intelligence in other fields could be so astonishingly deluded. I tell you, if ever you are looking for a good subject for a thesis, you could get a very fine one out of a study of the books that were written by people like the Dean of Canterbury, Julian Huxley, Harold Laski, Bernard Shaw, or the Webbs about the Soviet regime. In the process you would come upon a compendium of fatuity such as has seldom, if ever, existed on earth. And I would really recommend it; after all, the people who wrote these books were, and continue to be regarded as, pundits, whose words must be very, very seriously heeded and considered.

I recall in their yellow jackets a famous collection in England called the Left Book Club. You would be amazed at the gullibility that is expressed. We foreign journalists in Moscow used to amuse ourselves, as a matter of fact, by competing with one another as to who could wish upon one of these intelligentsia visitors to the USSR the most outrageous fantasy. We would tell them, for instance, that the shortage of milk in Moscow was entirely due to the fact that all milk was given nursing mothers—things like that. If they put it in the articles they subsequently wrote, then you would score a point. One story I floated myself, for which I received considerable acclaim, was that the huge queues outside food shops came about because the Soviet workers were so ardent in building socialism that they just wouldn't rest, and the only way the government could get them to rest for even two or three hours was organizing a queue for them to stand in. I laugh at it all now, but at the time you can imagine what a shock it was to someone like myself, who had been brought up to regard liberal intellectuals as the samurai, the absolute elite, of the human race, to find that they could be taken in by deceptions that a half-witted boy would see through in an instant. I never got over that; it always remained in my mind as something that could never be erased. I could never henceforth regard the intelligentsia as other than credulous fools who nonetheless became the media's prophetic voices, their heirs and successors remaining so still. That is when I began to think seriously about the great liberal death wish.

In due course, I came back to England to await the Second World War, in the course of which I found myself engaged in Intelligence duties. And let me tell you that if there is one thing more fantastical than news, it is Intelligence. News itself is a sort of fantasy; and when you actually go collecting news, you realize that this is so. In a certain sense, you create news; you dream news up yourself and then spread it. But that is nothing to the fantasy of Intelligence. Of the two, I would say that news seems really quite a sober and considered commodity compared with your offerings when you are an Intelligence agent.

Anyway, when in 1945 I found myself a civilian again, I tried to sort out my thoughts about the great wave of optimism that followed the Second World War—for me, a repeat performance. It was then that I came to realize how, in the name of progress and compassion, the most terrible things were going to be done, preparing the way for the great humane holocaust, about which I have spoken. There was, it seemed to me, a built-in propensity in this liberal world view whereby the opposite of what was intended came to pass. Take the case of education. Education was the great mumbo-jumbo of progress, the assumption being that educating people would make them grow better and better, more and more objective and intelligent. Actually, as more and more money is spent on education, illiteracy is increasing. And I wouldn't be at all surprised if it didn't end up with virtually the whole revenue of the Western countries being spent on education, and a condition of almost total illiteracy resulting therefrom. It is quite in the cards.

Now I want to try to get to grips with this strange state of affairs. Let us look again at the humane holocaust. What happened in Germany was that long before the Nazis got into power, a great propaganda was undertaken to sterilize people who were considered to be useless or a liability to society, and after that to introduce what they called "mercy killing." This happened long before the Nazis set up their extermination camps at Auschwitz and elsewhere, and was based upon the highest humanitarian considerations. You see what I am getting at? On the basis of liberal humanism, there is no creature in the universe greater than man, and the future of the human race rests only with human beings themselves, which leads infallibly to some sort of suicidal situation. It is to me quite clear that that is so; the evidence is on every hand. The efforts that men make to bring about their own happiness, their own ease of life, their own self-indulgence, will in due course produce the opposite, leading me to the absolutely inescapable conclusion that human beings cannot live and operate in this world without some concept of a being greater than themselves, and of a purpose which transcends their own egotistic or greedy desires.

Once you eliminate the notion of a God, a creator, once you eliminate the notion that the creator has a purpose for us, and that life consists essentially in fulfilling that purpose, then you are bound, as Pascal points out, to induce the megalomania of which we have seen so many manifestations in our time—in the crazy dictators, as in the lunacies of people who are rich, or who consider themselves to be important or celebrated in the Western world. Alternatively, human beings relapse into mere carnality, into being animals. I see this process going on irresistibly, of which the holocaust is only just one example. If you envisage men as being only men, you are bound to see human society, not in Christian terms as a family, but as a factory-farm in which the only consideration that matters is the well-being of the livestock and the prosperity or productivity of the enterprise. That is where you land yourself. And it is in that situation that Western man is increasingly finding himself.

This might seem to be a despairing conclusion, but it isn't, you know. First of all, the fact that we cannot work out the liberal dream in practical terms is not bad news, but good news. Because if you could work it out, life would be too banal, too tenth-rate to be worth bothering about. Apart from that, we have been given the most extraordinary sign of the truth of things, which I continually find myself thinking about. This is that the most perfect and beautiful expressions of man's spiritual aspirations come, not from the liberal dream in any of its manifestations, but from people in the forced labor camps of the USSR. And this is the most extraordinary phenomenon, and one that of course receives absolutely no

* "Mystical Experience of the Labor Camps," included in his excellent book, *Underground Notes*.

attention in the media. From the media point of view it is not news, and in any case the media do not want to know about it. But this is the fact for which there is a growing amount of evidence. I was reading about it in a long essay by a Yugoslav writer Mihajlo Mihajlov,* who spent some years in a prison in Yugoslavia. He cites case after case of people who, like Solzhenitsyn, say that enlightenment came to them in the forced labor camps. They understood what freedom was when they had lost their freedom, they understood what the purpose of life was when they seemed to have no future. They say, moreover, that when it is a question of choosing whether to save your soul or your body, the man who chooses to save his soul gathers strength thereby to go on living, whereas the man who chooses to save his body at the expense of his soul loses both body and soul. In other words, fulfilling exactly what our Lord said, that he who hates his life in this world shall keep his life for all eternity, as those who love their lives in this world will assuredly lose them.

Now, that is where I see the light in our darkness. There's an image I love—if the whole world were to be covered with concrete, there still would be some cracks in it, and through these cracks green shoots would come. The testimonies from the labor camps are the green shoots we can see in the world, breaking out from the monolithic power now dominating ever greater areas of it. In contradistinction, this is the liberal death wish, holding out the fallacious and ultimately destructive hope that we can construct a happy, fulfilled life in terms of our physical and material needs, and in the moral and intellectual dimensions of our mortality.

I feel so strongly at the end of my life that nothing can happen to us in any circumstances that is not part of God's purpose for us. Therefore, we have nothing to fear, nothing to worry about, except that we should rebel against His purpose, that we should fail to detect it and fail to establish some sort of relationship with Him and His divine will. On that basis, there can be no black despair, no throwing in of our hand. We can watch the institutions and social structures of our time collapse—and I think you who are young are fated to watch them collapse—and we can reckon with what seems like an irresistibly growing power of materialism and materialist societies. But, it will not happen that that is the end of the story. As St. Augustine said, in effect, and I love to think of it when he received the news in Carthage that Rome had been sacked: "Well, if that's happened, it's a great catastrophe, but we must never forget that the earthly cities that men build they destroy, but there is also the City of God which men didn't build and can't destroy." And he devoted the next seventeen years of his life to working out the relationship between the earthly city and the City of God—the earthly city where we live for a short time, and the City of God whose citizens we are for all eternity.

You know, it is a funny thing, but when you are old, as I am, there are all sorts of extremely pleasant things that happen to you. One of them is, you realize that history is nonsense, but I won't go into that now. The pleasantest thing of all is that you wake up in the night at about, say, three a.m., and you find that you are half in and half out of your battered old carcass. And it seems quite a toss-up whether you go back and resume full occupancy of your mortal body, or make off toward the bright glow you see in the sky, the lights of the City of God. In this limbo between life and death, you know beyond any shadow of doubt that as an infinitesimal particle of God's creation, you are a participant in God's purpose for His creation, and that that purpose is loving and not hating, is creative and not destructive, is everlasting and not temporal, is universal and not particular. With this certainty comes an extraordinary sense of comfort and joy.

Nothing that happens in this world need shake that feeling; all the happenings in this world, including the most terrible disasters and suffering, will be seen in eternity as in some mysterious way a blessing, as a part of God's love. We ourselves are part of that love, we belong to that scene, and only in so far as we belong to that scene does our existence here have any reality or any worth. All the rest is fantasy—whether the fantasy of power which we see in the authoritarian states around us, or the fantasy of the great liberal death wish in terms of affluence and self-indulgence. The essential feature, and necessity of life is to know reality, which means knowing God. Otherwise our mortal existence is, as Saint Teresa of Avila said, no more than a night in a second-class hotel.

ABOUT THE AUTHOR

Malcolm Muggeridge (1903-1990) was the author of such books as *Jesus Rediscovered* (Doubleday, 1979), *Something Beautiful for God* (Harper & Row, 1979) (also a television documentary), *Winter in Moscow* (Little, Brown, 1934), and his autobiography, *Chronicles of Wasted Time* (Regnery Gateway, 1989). His career as a journalist included Moscow correspondent for the *Manchester Guardian;* editor of *Punch;* book reviewer for *Esquire;* and deputy editor of the *London Daily Telegraph*. He was known to millions around the world for his popular documentaries, series and commentaries on the BBC.

HOLLYWOOD VS. RELIGION

Michael Medved
December 1989

y job involves watching as many as six movies every week. This may strike strangers as an all but ideal occupation, but that is only because they forget that I have little choice as to which films I am required to review. As a critic, I am compelled to sample almost every new product which Hollywood offers up to the waiting world. At times, I feel that I deserve hazardous duty pay.

Just recently, I had to endure an extraordinarily offensive film called *Parents*. It has been promoted as a light-hearted comedy about a typical middle-class family in the 1950s, but it is actually a graphic, horrifyingly detailed, and very stylish film about suburban cannibalism. Mary Beth Hurt and Randy Quaid play a friendly neighborhood couple who steal bodies from a local morgue, grind them into meat loaf, and then force-feed this hamburger surprise to their terrified little boy. The meat grinder sequences alone would be enough to give nightmares to any sane viewer.

I have also recently suffered through Blake Edwards' latest offering, *Skin Deep*. This has become a controversial picture even before its release, and the producers have actually encouraged that controversy by promising potential moviegoers "The Most Outrageous Scene of the Decade." Now, just what is this scene? It is a ten-minute sequence about two men fighting in a hotel room while wearing colorful, phosphorescent, glow-in-the-dark condoms. I am not kidding–this was the artistic highlight of a multimillion-dollar major studio project. It is no wonder that my job sometimes gives rise to the feeling that I am actually working as a glorified sewer inspector.

There are rare occasions, however, when a new movie comes along and, against all odds, offers a chance to address some serious issues. Like all other critics, I am eternally grateful for these fleeting moments–even if the film that inspires them happens to be a pretentious and sadly muddled mess.

THE LAST TEMPTATION OF THE CRITICS

This was the case with Martin Scorsese's overwrought epic, *The Last Temptation of Christ*–an unbearably boring two-hour-and-forty-minute extravaganza that proved considerably less interesting than the controversy surrounding it. From Hollywood, most of the noise in that debate involved smug and solemn pronouncements in defense of Mr. Scorsese's First Amendment rights–inconsistently coupled with condemnation of those who chose to exercise *their* First Amendment rights by protesting the film. For several weeks, on the airwaves and in private conversations, you couldn't escape the defenses and denunciations of this particular picture–provided, in most cases, by people who had never seen the movie. Unfortunately, I *did* see the movie in its nearly insufferable entirety—at an early, pre-release screening, and I can assure you that the experience is about as satisfying and uplifting as two hours and forty minutes in the dentist's chair. The prevailing tedium is relieved only by great bouts of gore that seem to splatter the screen at irregular intervals. The film opens with a sequence that shows Jesus himself engaged in crucifying someone else. As the victim's feet are nailed to the cross, blood spurts out and covers Jesus' face.

The members of what you would have to call "the supporting cast" fare no better. In this picture, Mary Magdelene was covered from head to toe with tattoos—resembling no one so much as that character Groucho Marx used to sing about, "Lydia the Tattooed Lady." And she wasn't the only one—you'd think that director Scorsese had discovered in his research about ancient Judea that there were tattoo parlors on every corner catering exclusively to females. In reality, however, it was against Jewish and Biblical law to decorate yourself with even a single, small tattoo. Meanwhile, the actor who played Judas Iscariot, Harvey Keitel, provided us with what must rank as one of the most outrageously miscalculated performances of recent years—delivering all his lines with his Bronx accent firmly intact, and wearing an orange fright wig which made him look like a Biblical Bozo.

The Last Temptation of Christ was, by any honest and objective standards, an artistic disaster—a bitter embarrassment for a genuinely gifted director. Yet many of my colleagues in what passes for "the critical community" hailed it as a masterpiece. One of America's best known movie reviewers even annointed it "The Greatest Film of 1988." The Academy of Motion Picture Arts and Sciences went so far as to nominate Mr. Scorsese for an Academy Award as best director of the year. To me, nothing so forcefully reveals the clouded lens through which Hollywood views the world as the utterly undeserved praise which this film received.

I would argue that the response to *The Last Temptation* represents the film industry's "Circle the Wagons" mentality at its most hysterical and paranoid. Since religious figures across the country were attacking the picture, the members of the Hollywood community felt called upon to defend it. I remember a conversation with one of my colleagues who had prepared what I considered an unaccountably generous review. He explained himself with surprising candor. "If I was too rough on the film," he said, "then people would associate me with Jerry Falwell"—and that was an association he could not accept.

THE GOSPEL ACCORDING TO HOLLYWOOD

The movie industry's resounding endorsement of *The Last Temptation of Christ* is only the latest and perhaps the most grotesque illustration of the overt and pervasive hostility to religion and religious values that has taken root in Hollywood. To maintain a sense of perspective, it is important to remember that this is a relatively recent development in movie history. In the past, the major studios churned out biblical blockbusters like *The Ten Commandments, Samson and Delilah, The Robe* and *Ben Hur,* specifically designed to appeal to religious sensibilities. These sandstorm-and-sandals epics may not stand today as examples of deathless works of art, but they did earn millions at the box office and even won a measure of critical acclaim.

In years past, Hollywood also turned out popular and sympathetic portrayals of contemporary clergymen. Bing Crosby, Pat O'Brien and Spencer Tracy played earthy, compassionate priests who gave hope to underprivileged kids or comforted GI's on the battlefield. Nearly all men of the cloth who appeared on screen would be kindly and concerned, if not downright heroic. In the last ten to fifteen years mainstream moviemakers have swung to the other extreme. If someone turns up in a film today wearing a Roman collar or bearing the title "Reverend," you can be fairly sure that he will be either crazy or corrupt—or probably both.

The 1982 film *Monsignor* offers an especially obnoxious case in point. That distinguished thespian, Christopher Reeve, plays a cardinal—after his success with *Superman* he apparently craved another role where he could wear a cape. This particular prince of the Church not only seduces an idealistic nun, but also invests Vatican money in a series of hideously corrupt business deals involving the mafia and the CIA.

As the world's most visible religious institution, the Roman Catholic Church has become a particularly popular target for contemporary filmmakers. *Agnes of God* offers us the elevating image of young nun Meg Tilly murdering her own baby and attempting to flush the tiny body down the toilet of her convent room. *The Runner Stumbles* presents Dick Van Dyke as yet another priest involved in an affair with a nun, while many more films, including *True Confessions, Mass Appeal* and *The Mission,* use some of the best actors in the business to play well-intentioned idealists who are overwhelmed by the pervasive cynicism and hypocrisy of the church hierarchy. Protestant pastors suffer the same rough treatment at the hands of Hollywood as their Catholic brothers and sisters. In the last two years alone, independent feature films like *Pass the Ammo, Salvation* and *Riders of the Storm* have savagely satirized greedy and greasy evangelists lusting after sex and money.

Even when religion isn't the primary focus of a film, religious figures frequently turn up as convenient heavies. In *Light of Day,* a 1987 stinker written and directed by *Last Temptation* screenwriter Paul Schrader, the family minister is a pious, pompous fraud who impregnates the hero's teenaged sister and then takes no responsibility for the child. *Malone* gives us a chance to watch Burt Reynolds battling a Christian para-military cult in the Pacific Northwest. In *Crimes of Passion,* Tony Perkins is a crazed, sweating skid row preacher attempting to murder prostitute Kathleen Turner in the most sickening and sadistic manner imaginable. Even last summer's horror remake, *The Blob,* offers some oblique commentary on organized religion, when the bespectacled small-town pastor (Del Close) turns out to be a secret drunk. The last scene in the movie shows his crazed sermon threatening the end of the world as he fiendishly contrives to bring the title monster back to earth.

Poltergeist II is an extreme example of the way that mainstream moviemakers have turned traditional thinking on its head. The villain of the piece is a hymn-singing preacher from beyond the grave who leads a band of demonic Bible-belters in attempting to drag a hip suburban family down to hell. The only force that can stop these crazed Christians is a heroic American Indian medicine man—who mobilizes the positive power of an ancient pagan religion.

In explaining the hostility to our Judeo-Christian heritage that characterizes so many of these films, industry insiders firmly deny any deep-seated anti-religious bias. They insist that moviemakers are merely responding to the beliefs and prejudices of the film-going public. According to this argument, they are merely following the honorable capitalist practice of giving the customers what they want.

There is, however, one gigantic flaw in that line of reasoning: all of the movies I've mentioned above—*every single one of them*—flopped resoundingly at the box office. Taken together, these pictures lost hundreds of millions for the people who made them. Hunger for money can explain *almost* everything in Hollywood, but it can't explain why ambitious producers keep launching expensive projects that slam religion. Their mysterious behavior becomes even more difficult to understand when one takes a brief look at the public reception for those exceedingly rare films of recent years that have taken a more sympathetic view of organized faith.

Consider, for example, *Chariots of Fire,* the 1981 Academy Award winner and worldwide box office smash. Its title is taken from a line in the beloved hymn "Jerusalem," and one of the film's two heroes is a Scottish missionary so devout that he refuses to run in the Olympics if it would force him to violate the sabbath. Like *Chariots of Fire, Tender Mercies* confounded the experts with its strong audience appeal. Robert Duvall won an Oscar as a washed-up alcoholic country-

and-western singer whose life is transformed by religious faith. In one of the most artfully underplayed scenes in recent films, he is baptized on screen and most convincingly born again.

Horton Foote, the same great screenwriter who created *Tender Mercies,* also wrote *The Trip to Bountiful,* about a sweet and profoundly religious elderly lady who wants to revisit her tiny home town in Texas once more before she dies. *Places in the Heart* is also set in Texas–with an astonishing concluding scene that shows all the characters in the film, including several who died earlier in the story, taking communion together in a dusty country church.

Witness became one of the top grossing movies of 1985, with Harrison Ford as a fugitive Philadelphia cop who is sheltered in a secluded Amish community in rural Pennsylvania. The portrayal of the Amish and their stubbornly traditional faith is not merely sympathetic–it is idealized. Most recently, *A Cry in the Dark* won yet another Oscar nomination for Meryl Streep with its dramatization of a famous murder case in Australia. Streep plays the wife of a Seventh Day Adventist minister who is falsely accused of murdering her own baby. The unshakable faith of husband and wife, and warm support from their close-knit church community, enables them to survive this nightmare ordeal, which, the film makes clear, was caused at least in part by the anti-religious bigotry of many of their accusers.

These six distinguished films stand apart as proud exceptions to the movie industry's pervasive hostility to religious values and practices. Yet even these sympathetic portrayals fail to show organized faith as relevant in any way to the lives of ordinary urban Americans. Each of the films places religion in an exotic context far removed from the daily lives of most moviegoers. *Chariots of Fire* presents England of the 1920s. *Tender Mercies, The Trip to Bountiful* and *Places in the Heart* all focus on tiny, old-fashioned Texas towns. *Witness* portrays a quaint sect in a pastoral and isolated enclave, while *A Cry in the Dark* concerns itself with another small, misunderstood sect in a lonely corner of Australia. In addition to their remote settings, these films share another important point in common: they all won surprisingly large audiences, especially when compared with the disastrous commercial performance of so many of the most tendentious anti-religious films.

HOLLYWOOD'S MOTIVES

Why hasn't Hollywood gotten the message? The one thing this industry is supposed to be able to do is to read the bottom line. Why, then, do savvy producers continue to authorize scores of projects that portray religious leaders as crazed, conspiratorial charlatans, when similar films have failed so conspicuously and consistently in the past?

It is hard to escape the conclusion that there is a perverse sort of idealism at work here. For many of the most powerful people in the entertainment business, hostility to traditional religion goes so deep and burns so intensely that they insist on expressing that hostility, even at the risk of commercial disaster.

Despite an unprecedented firestorm of free publicity, *The Last Temptation of Christ* performed dismally at the box office. Nevertheless, one of the most prestigious production companies in Hollywood has already announced plans for a new project entitled *Christ the Man*—to be directed by Paul Verhoeven of *Robocop* fame—that is rumored to be even more offensive to traditional believers.

Moviemakers can't stay away from religious themes because of their deep-seated desire to be taken seriously; religion offers one subject which everyone acknowledges as fundamentally serious. If writers and directors take a swipe at religion in one of their films, no matter how clumsy or contrived that attack may be, they can feel as if they've made some sort of important and courageous statement. Hence the makers of *The Blob* can insist that they've created something more than a slick monster movie about a huge strawberry jello that devours a town. By portraying a demented and hypocritical minister as a key character in that town, they've also delivered a "significant" message against religious fanaticism. Such messages win applause in Hollywood, even when they're hopelessly simplistic and one-sided. By sneering at zealots and deriding conventional religious beliefs, a filmmaker can win the respect of his peers, even if his work is rejected by the larger public.

In this context, I will never forget an astonishing private conversation concerning the motivations behind the notorious 1985 fiasco, *King David*. This Godzilla-sized turkey cost $28,000,000 and attracted less than $3,000,000 in ticket sales. It featured Richard Gere in the title role—a bizarre casting choice that led industry wags to refer to it as *An Israelite and A Gentleman*. Most peculiar of all, the film advanced the radical—and totally unsupported—notion that the Biblical king freed himself from his religious "delusions" at the end of his life. The concluding sequence shows a suddenly enlightened David violently rejecting God as he smashes the scale model of the temple he had previously intended to build. A few weeks before the film's release, one of the people who created it spoke to me proudly of its fearless integrity. "We could have gone the easy way and played to the Bible belt," he said, "but we wanted to make a tough, honest film. We don't see David as a gung-ho, Praise-the-Lord kind of guy. We wanted to make him a richer, deeper character."

In his mind, in other words, secure religious faith is incompatible with depth of character.

AN INDUSTRY OUT OF TOUCH WITH AMERICA

It is easy for most moviemakers to assume a patronizing attitude toward religiously committed people because they know so few of them personally. If most big screen images of religious leaders tend to resemble Swaggart or Bakker it's because evangelists on television are the only believers who are readily visible to the members of the film colony. In 1982, a fascinating survey by researchers from the University of Maryland analyzed the attitudes and practices of key decision makers and creative personnel in the movie business. Only three percent responded that they regularly attended church or synagogue. In the country at large, by contrast, the same study indicated that just under fifty percent flock to services on a regular basis.

America is, by every measure, the most openly and actively religious society in the West. But those who function within the smug, self-enclosed hothouse atmosphere of Hollywood seem genuinely unaware of that fact. To them, the national religious revival observed by so many social commentators is a distant phenomenon—a malign and threatening form of mass delusion. Our mighty engines of popular culture are hopelessly out of touch with America. This means, of course, that the movie business is also out of touch with a huge portion of its potential audience. Statistics prove the point. In the 1940s, over 90 million Americans—close to two-thirds of the country—went to the movies every week. Today, the number of filmgoers is less than 20 million per week and, more importantly, surveys show that close to 40 percent of the American people don't even go out to a single movie in the course of a *year*. There is surely a significant overlap between that half of our population that attends church or synagogue every weekend, and that substantial portion of potential filmgoers who avoid all current films.

Make no mistake: it is not just the high ticket prices or the gum on the seats or the easy availability of television that keeps patrons away from the theatres. Tens of millions of Americans have given up on contemporary movies because they see their own deepest values so rarely reflected—or even respected—on screen. Attempts are now in the works to change all that, though the initiative, not surprisingly, is coming from outside the Hollywood community. A number of Christian organizations across the country are preparing to enter the business of feature film production. They have raised millions of dollars and secured the services of experienced filmmakers in order to create an alternative source of movie entertainment—providing motion pictures that reenforce family and spiritual values.

It surely is a welcome development that instead of merely condemning the level of Hollywood's current offerings, some religious leaders are now determined to create better movies of their own. In the process, they may win back part of the mass audience for films that the movie industry has recently lost. If they do, and their projects succeed at the box office, then they have a chance of shaking up the entire movie business and undermining its most cynical assumptions. I wish these people well, and hope that others—both inside and outside the current Hollywood establishment—will come forward to offer new directions in feature films, particularly in the way that today's movies present religious and spiritual issues. My interest in this struggle is, I will confess, at least partially selfish. If current efforts succeed, then in years to come I may be spared the experience of more feature films about suburban cannibalism and condoms that glow in the dark.

ABOUT THE AUTHOR

M ichael Medved is well known to millions of Americans as the co-host of the weekly PBS television program, "Sneak Previews." An honors graduate of Yale, he is the author of seven non-fiction books, including the best-sellers: *What Really Happened to the Class of '65?*, which became the basis for a weekly series on NBC, *Hospital: The Hidden Lives of a Medical Center Staff*, and with his brother, Harry Medved, *The Golden Turkey Awards*. Mr. Medved has been a frequent guest on "The Tonight Show," "Oprah Winfrey," "David Letterman," "ABC Nightline," "Today," "Good Morning America," and other programs. He is active in a wide variety of Jewish causes and is president of the Pacific Jewish Center in Venice, California. He is also a Hillsdale College Life Associate.

POPULAR CULTURE AND
THE WAR AGAINST STANDARDS

Michael Medved
February 1991

hen people meet me and they find out that I make my living as a film critic, they often exhibit two spontaneous but absolutely contradictory reactions. The first comment is, "Boy, you have a great job!" and, usually in the very next breath, they add, "Aren't movies terrible these days?"

The fact is that both statements are accurate. I do have a great job in many ways, and yes, movies are absolutely terrible today. Ironically, it is sometimes those films that are the most profoundly, irredeemably awful that make my job most stimulating. That was certainly the case with one of the most critically praised movies of 1990, *The Cook, the Thief, His Wife and Her Lover*. This is not a film for the faint-of-heart—or the delicate of stomach. It begins with a scene showing the brutal beating of a naked man while the main character gleefully urinates all over him. It ends with that same character slicing off a piece of a carefully cooked and elegantly prepared human corpse in the most vivid and horrifying scene of cannibalism ever portrayed in motion pictures. In between, we see necrophilia, sex in a toilet, the unspeakably bloody and sadistic mutilation of a nine-year-old boy, another victim smeared with feces, a woman whose cheek is pierced with a fork, and an edifying scene with two naked bodies writhing together ecstatically in the back of a truck filled with rotting, maggot-infested garbage. There is, in short, unrelieved ugliness, horror and depravity at every turn.

Naturally, the critics loved it.

Caryn James of the *New York Times* hailed *The Cook, the Thief, His Wife and Her Lover* as "brilliant." Two leading film critics, whose approach to film reviewing I have often considered all thumbs, called the picture "provocative" and awarded their coveted "Two thumbs up" endorsement. Richard Corliss of *Time* magazine went even further and described the film as "excellent, exciting and extraordinary."

For me, this sort of critical praise proved even more disturbing than the film itself. The movie just made me sick, but the positive reviews made me angry. My partner and I had initially decided not to cover the film on "Sneak Previews," the weekly show we host on PBS, because we felt that by discussing it on the air we'd only be granting it additional publicity. Jeffrey Lyons and I don't always agree by any means, but we certainly saw eye to eye on *The Cook, the Thief, His Wife and Her Lover*. And when some of our esteemed colleagues began using words like "brilliant" and "excellent" to describe this putrid, pointless and pretentious piece of filth, we decided that we had to respond. So we did a special segment on our show in the course of which I transgressed one of the great unwritten rules of the so-called critical community: I not only attacked the film itself, but I also attacked my fellow critics who had praised it so lavishly. I objected in particular to the tendency to describe the picture as "a raunchy black comedy" without giving prospective moviegoers any honest indication of the vivid brutality and horrors it contained. I also cited the laudatory response to this hateful film as an indication that Americans are absolutely justified in their deep distrust of film critics.

After I made such statements on nationwide TV, there was a minor—and entirely predictable—firestorm concerning my comments and protesting my alleged "arrogance" and "irresponsibility." One letter from a viewer in Oregon eloquently summarized these protests: "I was angered and disgusted by your unfair and savage attack on *The Cook, the Thief, His Wife and Her Lover*," she wrote, and then went on revealingly,

> "Though I have not seen the film, I certainly plan to do so and your review was way out of line. The one thing we don't need is a Jesse Helms clone on PBS....If you are so full of old-fashioned, judgmental, right-winged bigotry, then that is your problem, but you have no right to pollute the airwaves with your narrow-minded stupidity....Your job is to tell us if a movie is skillful or not, but please stay off your moralistic high horse and keep to the business of reviewing movies."

IGNORING SOUL AND SUBSTANCE

This letter represents just one very small skirmish in what I would describe as the "culture wars" currently raging in our society, but it reveals very forcefully what those wars are all about. My correspondent is saying that it's fine for me to talk about a film being in or out of focus, about sloppy or competent editing, about a convincing or unconvincing performance, but Heaven forfend that I should address its moral content! Heaven forfend that I should discuss in any way the message that a particular film is sending to the movie-going public! This is the very nature of the cultural battle before us. It is, at its very core, a war against standards. It is a war against judgment. Its proponents insist that the worst insult you can offer someone today is to suggest that he or she is judgmental.

One of the symptoms of the corruption and collapse of our national culture is the insistence that we examine only the surface of any work of art. The politically correct, properly liberal notion is that we should never dig deeper—to consider whether a given work is true, or good, or spiritually nourishing—or to evaluate its impact on society at large. Contemporary culture is obsessed with superficial skill and slick salesmanship while ignoring the more important issues of soul and substance. This is one of the consequences of the war on standards—a war that is currently being waged on three fronts: the glorification of ugliness, the assault on the family, and the attempt to undermine organized religion. Each of these fronts is serious enough to merit separate consideration.

THE GLORIFICATION OF UGLINESS

Everywhere around us, in every realm of artistic endeavor, we see evidence of the rejection of traditional standards of beauty and worth. In the visual arts, in literature, in film, in music of both popular and classical variety, ugliness has been enshrined as a new standard, as we accept the ability to shock as a replacement for the old ability to inspire.

This tendency has reached absurd extremes with the recent efforts to elevate the banging and shouting of rap music into some sort of noble art form. Consider, for a moment, the recent obscenity trial of 2 Live Crew. One of the expert witnesses who helped secure the group's acquittal was a professor of literature and Afro-American studies at Duke University, Henry Louis "Skip" Gates. Under oath, mind you, he testified that these poetic souls, whose lyrics exalt anal rape and the mutilation of female genitalia, had created a "refreshing and astonishing" body of work. Professor Gates went on to compare their achievements to those of Shakespeare, Chaucer, and James Joyce. (As the late George Orwell once commented, "There are some ideas so preposterous that only an intellectual could believe them.")

In film, the art form which I most regularly consider, the process of degradation has already reached levels that should lead all thoughtful critics to despair for the future of the medium. Indescribable gore drenches the modern screen, even in movies allegedly made for families. And the most perverted forms of sexuality—loveless, decadent, brutal and sometimes incestuous—are showing regularly at a theater near you. Perhaps you haven't seen *The Grifters,* another critical favorite of the last few months. Oscar winner Anjelica Houston co-stars with John Cusak in a story about the sexual tension between a mother-and-son team of con artists. In the climactic sequence, Houston attempts to seduce her boy in order to steal his money, but this heart-warming family reunion ends with blood spurting endlessly from his severed jugular vein.

This kind of work is regularly described as high art, along with another sort of ugliness that is even more commonly celebrated on movie screens today. Film after film centers on characters who are, fundamentally, despicable—amoral losers who give us nothing to admire, nor even to care about. *Goodfellas,* the winner of nearly all the most prestigious critics' awards for 1990, is a case in point. This gritty tale of small-time Mafia hoods is Martin Scorsese's follow-up to

The Last Temptation of Christ. Technically, it is indeed a brilliant achievement, and it features superb performances by a number of talented actors. Why, then, do most people who see the film leave the theater feeling cold and empty? Because *Goodfellas,* with its fascination for its own collection of lavishly loathsome characters, never engages our sympathy or our concern. This has been a problem with scores upon scores of recent American films. From *Miller's Crossing* to Dennis Hopper's *The Hot Spot,* from *After Dark, My Sweet* to *State of Grace,* to David Lynch's *Wild at Heart* to Robert Redford's *Havana* to Jack Nicholson's *Two Jakes,* Hollywood has been creating central characters with all the warmth and charm of poisonous lizards.

This trend reached its logical conclusion, I suppose, in an absolutely unbearable film called *Homer and Eddie,* in which the heroine, played by Whoopi Goldberg, is a murderer, a thief, and an escaped mental patient who also happens to be dying of a brain tumor. What an inspiring role model for today's youth! You may never have heard of *Homer and Eddie,* or many of the other films I've just mentioned, because they all proved to be pathetic flops at the box office. Despite the presence of major stars, obscenely inflated production budgets, and enthusiastic endorsements from some of my fellow critics, these motion pictures failed to connect with ordinary moviegoers. Hollywood nevertheless persists in shelling out untold millions on projects that emphasize the darkest, most repulsive aspects of American life. To vary the lyrics of the old song, these cinematic artists insist on walking exclusively on "The Slimey Side of the Street."

In years past, in the heyday of Gary Cooper, Jimmy Stewart and Katharine Hepburn, Hollywood was accused of creating characters who were larger than life, more deeply lovable and admirable than people in the real world. Today, the movie business regularly offers us characters who are smaller than life, who are less decent, less intelligent, less noble than our own friends and neighbors. Four years ago, George Roche wrote an eloquent and important book that highlighted the threat within our culture to those values of civility and faith that many of us hold most dear. The name of that book was *A World Without Heroes.* And that is precisely the sort of world that Hollywood portrays again and again on screen. It is a world in which ugliness—and emptiness—emerge as the new standard for our society.

THE ASSAULT ON THE FAMILY

The second front on the war against standards involves an attack on the family that seems to gather new force with every passing year. For thousands of years, society has acknowledged the fact that a permanent partnership between a man and woman, for the purpose of nurturing children, offers the best chance of human happiness and fulfillment. This fundamental notion has not only been challenged in recent years, it has been assaulted with unparalleled ferocity by some of the most powerful forces in our culture.

The popular music business, for instance, has become a global enterprise of staggering proportions that generates billions of dollars every year through the simple-minded glorification of animal lust. Nothing could stand at a further remove from the selflessness and discipline that are essential to successful family life than the masturbatory fantasies that saturate MTV 24 hours a day.

Once upon a time, parents worried about the impact of idolized crooners like Frank Sinatra, Elvis Presley, or the Beatles, but these performers were tender, wholesome romantics when compared to Guns and Roses, Madonna and other paragons who dominate today's music scene. The singers of yesteryear certainly exploited sexuality as part of their appeal, but the fantasies they purveyed in their songs still centered on long-term emotional relationships between men and women. What is most striking about the popular music of the moment is the cold, bitter and sadistic edge to the vision of fleeting sex it promotes.

Another message of the music that is ceaselessly reinforced by television and movies is the perverse but pervasive idea that "kids know best." Teenagers are regularly portrayed as the source of all wisdom, sanity and sensitivity, while their parents are shown as hopeless, benighted clowns. With Bart Simpson regularly turning up on lists of the most admired Americans, we've certainly come a long way from the Andy Hardy model, with young Mickey Rooney learning life lessons from his father, the stern but kindly judge. This new idea that children have all the answers, and have to show the older generation how to live and how to adjust to the brave new world around them, is a holdover from the destructive obsessions of the '60s youth culture, and it poisons the climate for family life.

Even the smash hit motion picture *Home Alone,* which cunningly caters to America's desperate hunger for family entertainment, advances the notion that today's hip kids don't really need their bumbling parents. The seven-year-old hero not only survives in fine style when his parents fly away to Europe and accidentally leave him behind, but the boy also displays remarkable courage and skill in foiling the designs of two adult burglars. Nevertheless, *Home Alone* deserves some credit for showing a more-or-less normal middle class family, since this sort of unit has become an increasingly endangered species in American feature films. According to the Census Bureau, two-thirds of all American adults are currently married, but movies today focus overwhelmingly on single people. If you want to test this premise, all you have to do is pick up a copy of any metropolitan newspaper and read the entertainment section to see what's currently playing at your local theatres. The number of films about single people will outnumber the films about married people by a ratio of five or six to one. And even those relatively rare films that do make an attempt to show life within a family will most often depict a marriage that is radically dysfunctional—with a husband accused of attempting to murder his wife (as in *Reversal of Fortune*), or a wife sleeping with her husband's male (or female) friends, as in *Henry and June,* or *The Sheltering Sky,* or *Alice,* or so many others.

Apparently, some stern decree has gone out from the upper reaches of the Hollywood establishment that love between married people must never be portrayed on screen. If a wedding occurs in the course of a film, it invariably marks the conclusion of a romance, never the beginning or the middle of the love relationship. The top grossing film of 1990 was *Ghost,* one of a series of sex-after-death fantasies that the movie industry has churned out in recent years. In this crafty tear-jerker, the filmmakers seemed to make a point of the fact that the central couple, connected by a love so deep that it survives into the afterlife, have never taken the trouble to get married.

Even those films that seem to celebrate the joys of child-rearing display a contemptuous attitude toward marriage. A few years ago, Hollywood discovered that babies could serve as a major draw at the box office, and attempted to lure moviegoers with a series of diapers-and-formula fantasies. The three most successful of these films—*Three Men and a Baby, Look Who's Talking,* and *Baby Boom*—all featured single people in the parental roles. The underlying message could hardly be more clear: infants may be cute and cuddly and desirable, but they are best enjoyed without the inconvenient entanglements of marriage. This is precisely the sort of irresponsible message that encourages the tragic epidemic of out-of-wedlock births that is sweeping the country.

With its single-minded focus on unmarried characters, the movie industry conveys the idea that it's exciting to live on your own, but boring and stifling to live within a marriage. The unspoken assumption is that married people never experience anything that's interesting enough to be dramatized in a feature film. My favorite contemporary psychologist—who also happens to be my wife, Dr. Diane Medved—recently wrote a book called *The Case Against Divorce.* In the course of that book, she shows how the media's titillating portrayal of the sexy thrills of singlehood has helped to foster the sense that people are missing something if they remain married, and has thereby promoted the rising divorce rate. Of course, there are many other sociological and psychological reasons that couples break up, but can anyone doubt that the popular culture's determined assault on the traditional family has contributed to the problem?

HOSTILITY TO ORGANIZED RELIGION

his brings us to the third front in the current culture wars, and perhaps the most crucial battlefield of all, and that is the attempt to undermine organized religion. A war against standards leads logically and inevitably to hostility to religion, because it is religious faith that provides the ultimate basis for all standards. The God of the Bible is not a moral relativist, and He *is* definitely judgmental. The very nature of the Judeo-Christian God is a Lord who makes distinctions. In the Book of Genesis, God creates the world by dividing the light from the darkness, dividing the waters above from the waters beneath, and so forth. In traditional Jewish homes, when we say farewell to the Sabbath every Saturday night and prepare to move into the secular week, we recite a blessing that praises God for separating aspects of reality, one from the others–for making distinctions. To the extent that we as human beings feel that we are created in God's image, we make distinctions too–and we have standards.

That is a position that is honored by millions upon millions of our fellow citizens, but it is regularly ridiculed in the mass media. One of the national television networks has chosen to promote its most popular show with a scene that mocks a family saying grace. With the Simpsons solemnly gathered around their cartoon dinner table, Bart intones: "Dear God, we pay for all this stuff ourselves, so thanks for nothing." Meanwhile, the federal government pays to display a crucifix immersed in a jar of the artist's own urine, and the nation's most prominent vocalist, Madonna, abuses Christian symbols and sacraments in sexually explicit music videos commonly viewed by children.

In 1989, I spoke at Hillsdale College on the topic, "Hollywood Versus Religion," and I focused on the film industry's self-destructive tendency to portray all religious characters as corrupt, or crazy, or both. I found this pattern particularly perplexing since the major movie projects that attacked traditional faith all turned out to be commercial flops, while the very few films that took a more sympathetic attitude toward religion performed surprisingly well at the box office. I wish that I could report that Hollywood has gotten the message in recent months, but if anything the situation has deteriorated. Since I last spoke on this subject, major studios have given us films such as *Nuns on the Run,* which savagely lampoons every aspect of Catholic practice and belief; *Star Trek V,* in which the villains are a band of crazed believers who follow a mysterious, demonic force that they, and the film's credits, identify as "God"; *Mermaids,* which features Cher as a nymphomaniac single mother and manages the considerable feat of trashing both Judaism and Catholicism in the same film; and *Godfather III,* which focuses on corruption and murder within the Vatican and displays far more sympathy for the mafia than for the Church.

POPULAR CULTURE:
WHY IT'S IMPOSSIBLE TO TUNE OUT

When I try to discuss some of these issues with working professionals in the entertainment industry, they usually offer the same response: "Nobody's forcing people to see these movies," they'll say. "If you object to the messages that you're getting from a piece of creative work, then you can exercise your right to avoid that film, or to switch that channel on your TV set, or to turn your radio off. If something offends you, then it's easy to tune it out." Unfortunately, they're wrong. Popular culture is an overwhelming and omnipresent force in this society; not even the most determined and conscientious efforts can effectively insulate you—or your children—from its powerful reach.

Allow me to illustrate the point with a personal recollection. Last spring, my family and I went with a large group on a Passover retreat to the mountains near Santa Barbara. It was a wonderful experience, and in the middle of the week we took a private side trip to a nearby lake. The weather couldn't have been more perfect—with puffy April clouds in a pure blue sky—and as we got out of the car our daughters, aged one and three, went toddling off toward the ducks at the edge of the water. All of a sudden, the one-year-old was saying one of her first words, "Duckie! Duckie!" and reaching out to the birds with her chubby little arms, while my wife and I looked on with satisfaction.

But within minutes, a group of teenagers, mostly 13- to 15-year-olds, arrived at the lakeshore. They were carrying a "boom box," and coming out of that shiny chrome machine was a rap song with the foulest, ugliest language I have ever heard. It produced a series of angry shouts of four-letter words describing rape and feces and oral sex—all blasting out at a deafening volume. Our little girls had never heard those words before. They were startled. I don't know if it was the words themselves, the violent explosions of that so-called music, or whether it was merely the painful level of that throbbing bass. Whatever it was, my one-year-old started to cry. Naturally, the three-year-old soon joined her, and we had our hands full trying to comfort two frightened little girls. I suppose we could have stayed and made a scene, but the fact is that I don't carry assault weapons in my trunk. Instead, we did the only sensible thing, which was to get into the car and to drive away. We gave up the shores of the lake, the waterfowl, and the beautiful day. We abandoned the scene to these brutish kids, and to the degradation of that hideous noise.

The point is that you can say to yourself, "I'll just tune out the messages of the media," but it's not possible today. In the past, if you talked about popular culture, you meant going to a movie theatre perhaps once a week and paying your money to see a single show. But modern technological advances have brought us boom boxes, and Walkmans, and VCRs, television and MTV. The messages, the images, are everywhere around us, and seep into every corner of our lives.

Is it a coincidence that the war on standards in art, music, television and film corresponds with increasingly destructive behavior on the part of the young people who are the most devoted consumers of these media? In one of his most important columns, George Will asks if it was merely an accident that the horrifying "wilding" attack in Central Park so precisely mirrored the images in popular rap songs celebrating sexual violence and the degradation of women. The members of a new generation of American children will have watched an average of 15,000 murders on television by the time they've reached the age of eighteen. Is it illogical to suspect that some of them might be intrigued enough by all this vicarious violence that they might want to explore similar experiences firsthand?

Is there no connection between the media's obsession with crime and violence and the fact that the number of 14- to 17-year-olds who were arrested in 1990 was thirty times what it was in 1950?

The rate of out-of-wedlock births in this country has increased by 500 percent since 1960, and one out of ten of all teenaged girls will be pregnant in 1991. The Center for Disease Control recently reported that more than a quarter of American females have engaged in sexual intercourse by age fifteen—five times the rate that prevailed as recently as 1970. How can media moguls plausibly maintain that these behavioral trends have nothing to do with the sex-drenched popular culture that plays such a central, all-consuming role in the lives of so many young Americans?

Ironically, the leaders of the entertainment industry regularly downplay the significance of their own work, insisting that the fantasies they have created have no influence on anyone. The networks and the studios have commissioned expensive studies from various experts to support their appallingly illogical contention that violence on screen has no connection to violence in real life, and that intensely sexual material does nothing to encourage promiscuity. This same industry then turns around and asks advertisers to pay hundreds of thousands of dollars for thirty seconds of air time in the hope that this fleeting exposure will directly alter the public's buying behavior! Don't they grasp the internal contradiction here? On the one hand, we're told that an hour of television programming has no real world consequences whatsoever, and on the other we're led to believe that 60-second spots that occasionally interrupt this program are powerful enough to change public perceptions of everything from canned goods to candidates. I happen to believe that the industry is right when it touts the impact of media images, but I can't accept the contention that motion pictures, and song lyrics, and music videos and TV shows are somehow less influential than commercials.

GETTING GOVERNMENT OUT OF THE CULTURE BUSINESS

That is why the current war on standards in the popular culture is such an important struggle for America's future. I believe that this will be *the* issue of the 1990s–the issue of values, of trying to maintain standards against those who are seeking to erase them altogether. Unfortunately, there's a tendency at both ends of the political spectrum to confuse this question with absolutist claims about the need for censorship versus the protections of the First Amendment.

For conservatives, there's the special danger of surrendering to the fundamental liberal temptation, which is to attempt to solve every problem with a new government program. When it comes to the current crisis in values in the popular culture, the governmental initiative that is sometimes recommended is a vastly expanded role for official censorship. I am always surprised at thoughtful conservatives who argue passionately that bureaucratic solutions will never eliminate poverty, or improve medical care, or end racism overnight, but who nonetheless believe that a government program can somehow succeed in the delicate task of raising the moral tone in this country.

Expanded censorship is not the answer, and attempts to move in that direction will invariably prove counter-productive. Take the example of 2 Live Crew, our country's most celebrated poets of the perverse. When we tried to censor them and had them arrested on obscenity charges, we made these thugs into instant folk heroes. They were performing in front of an adults-only crowd of masochists who had been stupid enough to pay money to listen to their feeble-minded filth, when the police appeared to apprehend the stars of the evening and to cart them away in handcuffs. Of course, they became the objects of sympathy, while receiving generous coverage on the evening news.

Largely thanks to the free publicity resulting from governmental attempts to silence them, 2 Live Crew has now sold more than two million copies of their disgusting album, "As Nasty as They Wanna Be." This is a group that had been wallowing in well-deserved obscurity before it became the target of would-be censors. As Talleyrand once commented about a particularly ill-considered policy of Napoleon: "It is worse than a crime; it is a blunder." People on our side of the current culture wars should be calling consistently for less governmental involvement, not more. The fact is that it is the other side that has relied upon federal power to advance its own purposes in the campaign against standards.

The most obvious example is the outrageous abuse of the National Endowment for the Arts, which has played a major role in helping to underwrite and sanction the glorification of ugliness that we previously discussed. When someone like NEA grant recipient Karen Finley feels a deep compulsion to express her spiritual yearnings by taking off her clothes and smearing her genitalia with chocolate, then more power to her. If responsible adults choose to invest their money in paying for the opportunity to witness such enlightening displays, who are we to object? Nor should we attempt to interfere with the paying fans of another federally supported artist, Miss Annie Sprinkle, who delights members of her audience by urinating on them in the course of her act. But it is hardly reasonable to expect the taxpayers of America to subsidize the cost of those experiences for those who feel the need to share them. Whenever specific NEA grants are questioned, the media and the liberal mandarins invariably holler, "Censorship!" But the issue isn't censorship at all, it is *sponsorship*.

On another front in the war against standards, the assault on the family, governmental power is similarly deployed. For many years, perceptive critics have pointed out the way that federal welfare policy promotes and subsidizes promiscuity and illegitimacy. In recent years, the genuine need for AIDS education has provided a new excuse for massive governmental support for radical sexual indoctrination. I am personally acquainted with one mother in the Chicago suburbs who felt compelled to withdraw her sixth grader from the public schools because the required "AIDS Awareness Unit" featured approving and graphic descriptions of anal intercourse, oral sex, and male and female homosexuality—all presented to 11-year-olds! This particular mother could turn to private education as a refuge, but what about the millions who can't afford that alternative, or aren't even aware of what their children are being taught?

We have the right, we have the obligation, to protest such abuses of bureaucratic authority. While it is unreasonable to expect that government provide a solution to the crisis in fundamental values, we certainly should demand that it cease contributing to the problem. Strict governmental neutrality in the ongoing culture wars is not only a legitimate goal, but an attainable one if we fight for it intelligently.

FREE MARKET SOLUTIONS AND A GRASSROOTS REVOLUTION

In the final analysis, the key issues in the current conflict won't be decided in the halls of Congress or the offices of the federal bureaucracy. They will be settled, as fundamental questions are always settled most effectively in America, through the application of free market principles and displays of private-sector determination and resourcefulness. Part of this process will no doubt involve sponsor boycotts, direct protests, letter-writing campaigns, and other forms of organized pressure. These tools are far more appropriate than new governmental regulation, which is, at best, a blunt, sloppy and ineffective instrument. A group called CLEAR TV—Christian Leaders for Responsible Television—has already enjoyed some notable success in this area. They recently pushed Burger King, one of the largest advertisers on network TV, to take out a series of newspaper ads in which the company pledged its support for family values, and promised to apply those values in judging any future television shows it will sponsor.

While environmentalists are employing all means available to persuade major corporations to stop polluting our air and water, we should use similar persuasion to prevent the further pollution of our culture. It's high time to broaden our sense of corporate responsibility to include a serious consideration of the long-term impact of the entertainment that a company may produce or sponsor. As part of the continuing struggle we must do more than protest the bad; we should also begin promoting the good, and providing uplifting alternatives to the trash that currently dominates the scene. It's a sad fact that talented individuals with traditional convictions or religious scruples have too often shunned active involvement in show business because of that arena's long-standing reputation for sleaziness. Unfortunately, this means abandoning the field to the sickos and sybarites, and you see the results on your television and movie screens. Let the call go out immediately: the outnumbered good guys in Hollywood desperately need reenforcements!

Keep in mind that the entertainment industry is one area of endeavor in which a few gifted individuals can still make an enormous difference. The American people have shown that they are ready to respond when given the opportunity, as witness the utterly unexpected $100 million success of a wholesome, life-affirming project like *Driving Miss Daisy*. Even more recently, an unheralded, low-budget picture called *China Cry* demonstrated once again that good values can mean good box office. This off-beat production, funded by a determined group of evangelical Christians, may not be the greatest film ever made, but it's a heart-felt, passionate piece of movie-making about a young mother who undergoes a religious conversion while suffering persecution at the hands of the Chinese Communists. Without well-known stars or any promotion budget to speak of, this audacious little picture has drawn an amazing response from the public—averaging more than $6,000 per screening in its first three weeks of release. This means that in multiplex theatres where it has played alongside big budget major studio productions, it has easily clobbered films such as *Rocky V* or *Goodfellas* or *Predator II*. We need more films like *China Cry,* but we'll only get them if concerned individuals are willing to roll up their sleeves, to dirty their hands, and to get to work—outside the mainstream, if necessary—to change the direction of the popular culture.

The change, when it comes, will amount to nothing less than a grassroots revolution. It won't flow from the top down, but from the bottom up. If we place all our faith in a few bigwigs in Los Angeles, or New York, or Washington, nothing will happen. We must rely instead on a thousand different centers of energy and dedication, in every corner of these United States, to make sure that popular culture will once again reflect–and encourage–the fundamental goodness of our people.

As a film critic, it is sometimes difficult for me to acknowledge that movies aren't the measure of all things. I keep my own sense of perspective through my involvement with Pacific Jewish Center–an educational and religious institution in California I helped to found some thirteen years ago. People constantly ask me, "Why do you spend so much time on that place? You have access to television, to the world stage, and yet you devote every spare moment to your neighborhood, your synagogue, and your personal friends." I know that supporters of Hillsdale College get the same sort of questions: "Why lavish all this attention on this one tiny school? It's in the middle of Michigan, for Heaven's sake, with only a thousand or so students! Wouldn't it be better to forget about this backwater institution and concentrate on the big picture?"

There's a ready answer to that challenge in George Roche's homely recollections of his own education in a one-room schoolhouse high in the Colorado Rockies where they were short on money, books and facilities, but long on grit, determination and individual responsibility. What matters ultimately in the culture wars is what we do in our daily lives–not the big statements that we broadcast to the world at large, but the small messages we send through our families and our neighbors and our communities. And those small messages, reinforcing each other from every direction across this country, can become a force powerful enough to change the world. The future of America will depend not so much on the movers and shakers in the centers of power, but on the hopes that we generate in our own communities, our schools, our churches, synagogues, and families. What we do there will count for even more, in the long run, than what celluloid shadows do on screen.

ABOUT THE AUTHOR

Michael Medved is well known to millions of Americans as the co-host of the weekly PBS television program, "Sneak Previews." An honors graduate of Yale, he is the author of seven non-fiction books, including the best-sellers: *What Really Happened to the Class of '65?,* which became the basis for a weekly series on NBC, *Hospital: The Hidden Lives of a Medical Center Staff,* and with his brother, Harry Medved, *The Golden Turkey Awards.* Mr. Medved has been a frequent guest on "The Tonight Show," "Oprah Winfrey," "David Letterman," "ABC Nightline," "Today," "Good Morning America," and other programs. He is active in a wide variety of Jewish causes and is president of the Pacific Jewish Center in Venice, California. He is also a Hillsdale College Life Associate.

COMMUNISM:
"THE GOD THAT FAILED"

WORDS OF WARNING
TO AMERICA

Aleksandr Solzhenitsyn
September 1975

et me remind you of a recent incident which some of you may have seen in the newspapers, although others might have missed it: Certain of your businessmen, on their own initiative, established an exhibition of criminological technology in Moscow. This was the most recent and elaborate technology, which here, in your country, is used to catch criminals, to bug them, to spy on them, to photograph them, to tail them, to identify criminals. This was taken to Moscow to an exhibition in order that the Soviet KGB agents could study it, as if not understanding what sort of criminals would be hunted by the KGB.

The Soviet government was extremely interested in this technology, and decided to purchase it. And your businessmen were quite willing to sell it. Only when a few sober voices here raised an uproar against it was this deal blocked. Only for this reason it didn't take place. But you have to realize how clever the KGB is. This technology didn't have to stay two or three weeks in a Soviet building under Soviet guard. Two or three nights were enough for the KGB there to look through it and copy it. And if today, persons are being hunted down by the best and most advanced technology, for this, we can also thank your Western capitalists. This is something which is almost incomprehensible to the human mind: that burning greed for profit which goes beyond all reason, all self-control, all conscience, only to get money.

I must say that Lenin foretold this whole process. Lenin, who spent most of his life in the West and not in Russia, who knew the West much better than Russia, always wrote and said that the Western capitalists would do anything to strengthen the economy of the USSR. They will compete with each other to sell us goods cheaper and sell them quicker, so that the Soviets will buy from one rather than the other. He said: They will bring it themselves without thinking about their future. And, in a difficult moment, at a party meeting in Moscow, he said: "Comrades, don't panic, when things go very hard for us, we will give a rope to the bourgeoisie, and the bourgeoisie will hang itself."

Then, Karl Radek, whom you may have heard of, who was a very resourceful wit, said: "Vladimir Ilyich, but where are we going to get enough rope to hang the whole bourgeoisie?"

Lenin effortlessly replied, "They'll supply us with it."

Through the decades of the 1920s, the 1930s, the 1940s, the 1950s, the whole Soviet press wrote: Western capitalism, your end is near. But it was as if the capitalists had not heard, could not understand, could not believe this. Nikita Khrushchev came here and said, "We will bury you!" They didn't believe that, either. They took it as a joke.

Now, of course, they have become more clever in our country. Now they don't say "we are going to bury you."

Nothing has changed in communist ideology. The goals are the same as they were, but instead of the artless Khrushchev, who couldn't hold his tongue, now they say "détente."

In order to understand this, I will take the liberty of making a short historic survey—the history of such relations, which in different periods have been called "trade," "stabilization of the situation," "recognition of realities," and now "détente." These relations now are at least 40 years old.

Let me remind you with what sort of system they started. The system was installed by armed uprising:

- It dispersed the Constituent Assembly.
- It capitulated to Germany—the common enemy.
- It introduced execution without trial.
- It crushed workers' strikes.
- It plundered the villagers to such an unbelievable extent that the peasants revolted, and when this happened it crushed the peasants in the bloodiest possible way.
- It shattered the Church.
- It reduced 20 provinces of our country to a condition of famine.

This was in 1921, the famous Volga famine. A very typical Communist technique: to seize power without thinking of the fact that the productive forces will collapse, that the fields will not be sown, that factories will stop, that the country will decline into poverty and famine—but when poverty and hunger come, then they request the humanitarian world to help them. We see this in North Vietnam today, perhaps Portugal is approaching this also. And the same thing happened in Russia in 1921. When the three-year civil war, started by the communists—and "civil war" was a slogan of the communists, civil war was Lenin's purpose; read Lenin, this was his aim and his slogan—when they had ruined Russia by this civil war, then they asked America, "America, feed our hungry." And indeed, generous and magnanimous America did feed our hungry.

The so-called American Relief Administration was set up, headed by your future President Hoover, and indeed many millions of Russian lives were saved by this organization of yours. But what sort of gratitude did you receive for this? In the USSR not only did they try to erase this whole event from the popular memory—it's almost impossible today in the Soviet press to find any reference to the American Relief Administration—but they even denounce it as a clever spy organization, a clever scheme of American imperialism to set up a spy network in Russia. I repeat, it was a system that introduced concentration camps for the first time in the history of the world—a system that, in the 20th century, was the first to introduce the use of hostages, that is to say, not to seize the person whom they were seeking, but rather a member of his family or someone at random, and shoot that person. This system of hostages and persecution of the family exists to this day. It is still the most powerful weapon of persecution, because the bravest person, who is not afraid for himself, still shivers at the threat to his family.

It is a system which was the first—long before Hitler—to employ false registration, that is, to say: "Such and such people have to come in to register." People would comply and then they were taken away to be annihilated. We didn't have gas chambers in those days. We used barges. A hundred or a thousand persons were put into a barge and then it was sunk. It was a system which deceived the workers in all of its decrees—the decree on land, the decree on peace, the decree on factories, the decree on freedom of the press. It was a system which exterminated all additional parties, and let me make it clear to you that it not only disbanded the parties themselves, but destroyed their members. All members of every other party were exterminated. It was a system which carried out genocide of the peasantry; 15 million peasants were sent off to extermination. It was a system which introduced serfdom, the so-called "passport system." It was a system which, in time of peace, artificially created a famine, causing six million persons to die in the Ukraine in 1932 and 1933. They died on the very edge of Europe. And Europe didn't even notice it. The world didn't even notice it—six million persons!

I could keep on enumerating these endlessly, but I have to stop because I have come to the year 1933 when, with all I have enumerated behind us, your President Roosevelt and your Congress recognized this system as one worthy of diplomatic recognition, of friendship and of assistance. Let me remind you that the great Washington did not agree to recognize the French Convention because of its savagery. Let me remind you that in 1933, voices were raised in your country objecting to recognition of the Soviet Union. However, the recognition took place and this was the beginning of friendship and ultimately of a military alliance.

Let us remember that in 1904, the American press was delighted at the Japanese victories and everyone wanted Russia's defeat because it was a conservative country. I want to remind you that in 1914 reproaches were directed at France and England for having entered into an alliance with such a conservative country as Russia.

The scope and the direction of my remarks here do not permit me to say more about pre-revolutionary Russia. I will just say that information about pre-revolutionary Russia was obtained by the West from persons who were either not sufficiently competent or not sufficiently conscientious. I will just cite for the sake of comparison a number of figures which you can read for yourself in *The Gulag Archipelago,* Volume 1, which has been published in the United States, and perhaps many of you may have read it. These are the figures: According to calculations by specialists, based on the most precise objective statistics, in pre-revolutionary Russia, during the 80 years before the revolution—years of the revolutionary movement when there were attempts on the tsar's life, assassination of a tsar, revolution—during these years about 17 persons a year were executed. The famous Spanish Inquisition, during the decades when it was at the height of its persecution, destroyed perhaps 10 persons a month. In the *Archipelago,* I cite a book which was published by the Cheka in 1920, proudly reporting on its revolutionary work in 1918 and 1919 and apologizing that its data were not quite complete—in 1918 and 1919 the Cheka executed, without trial, more than a thousand persons a month! This was written by the Cheka itself, before it understood how this would look to history.

At the height of Stalin's terror in 1937-38, if we divide the number of persons executed by the number of months, we get more than 40,000 persons shot per month! Here are the figures: 17 a year, 10 a month, more than 1,000 a month, more than 40,000 a month! Thus, that which had made it difficult for the democratic West to form an alliance with pre-revolutionary Russia had, by 1941, grown to such an extent and still did not prevent the entire united democracy of the world—England, France, the United States, Canada, Australia and smaller countries—from entering into a military alliance with the Soviet Union. How is this to be explained? How can we understand it? Here we can offer a few explanations. The first, I think, is that the entire democracy of the world was too weak to fight against Hitler's Germany alone. If this is the case, then it is a terrible sign. It is a terrible portent for the present day. If all these countries together could not defeat Hitler's little Germany, what are they going to do today, when more than half the globe is flooded with totalitarianism? I don't want to accept this explanation.

The second explanation is perhaps that there was simply an attack of panic—of fear—among the statesmen of the day. They simply didn't have sufficient confidence in themselves, they simply had no strength of spirit, and in this confused state decided to enter into an alliance with Soviet totalitarianism. This is also not flattering to the West.

Finally, the third explanation is that it was a deliberate device. Democracy did not want to defend itself. For defense it wanted to use another totalitarian system, the Soviet totalitarian system. I'm not talking now about the moral evaluation of this, I'm going to talk about that later. But in terms of simple calculation, how shortsighted, what profound self-deception! We have a Russian proverb: "Do not call a wolf to help you against the dogs." If dogs are attacking and tearing at you, fight against the dogs, but do not call a wolf for help. Because when the wolves come, they will destroy the dogs, but they will also tear you apart.

World democracy could have defeated one totalitarian regime after another, the German, then the Soviet. Instead, it strengthened Soviet totalitarianism, helped bring into existence a third totalitarianism, that of China, and all this finally precipitated the present world situation. Roosevelt, in Teheran, during one of his last toasts, said the following: "I do not doubt that the three of us"—meaning Roosevelt, Churchill and Stalin—"lead our peoples in accordance with their desires, in accordance with their aims." How are we to explain this? Let the historians worry about that. At the time, we listened and were astonished. We thought, "when we reach Europe, we will meet the Americans, and we will tell them." I was among the troops that were marching towards the Elbe. A little bit more and I would have reached the Elbe and would have shaken the hands of your American soldiers. But just before that happened, I was taken off to prison and my meeting did not take place.

But now, after all this great delay, the same hand has thrown me out of the country and here I am, instead of the meeting at the Elbe. After a delay of 30 years, my Elbe is here today. I am here to tell you, as a friend of the United States, what, as friends, we wanted to tell you then, but which our soldiers were prevented from telling you on the Elbe.

There is another Russian proverb: "The yes-man is your enemy, but your friend will argue with you." It is precisely because I am the friend of the United States, precisely because my speech is prompted by friendship, that I have come to tell you: "My friends, I'm not going to tell you sweet words. The situation in the world is not just dangerous, it isn't just threatening, it is catastrophic."

Something that is incomprehensible to the ordinary human mind has taken place. We over there, the powerless, average Soviet people, couldn't understand, year after year and decade after decade, what was happening. How were we to explain this? England, France, the United States, were victorious in World War II. Victorious states always dictate peace; they receive firm conditions; they create the sort of situation which accords with their philosophy, their concept of liberty, their concept of national interest.

Instead of this, beginning in Yalta, your statesmen of the West, for some inexplicable reason, have signed one capitulation after another. Never did the West or your President Roosevelt impose any conditions on the Soviet Union for obtaining aid. He gave unlimited aid, and then unlimited concessions. Already in Yalta, without any necessity, the occupation of Mongolia, Moldavia, Estonia,

Latvia, and Lithuania was silently recognized. Immediately after that, almost nothing was done to protect Eastern Europe, and seven or eight more countries were surrendered.

Stalin demanded that the Soviet citizens who did not want to return home be handed over to him, and the Western countries handed over 1.5 million human beings. How was this done? They took them by force. English soldiers killed Russians who did not want to become prisoners of Stalin, and drove them by force to Stalin to be exterminated. This has recently come to light—just a few years ago—a million and a half human beings. How could the Western democracies have done this?

And after that, for another 30 years, the constant retreat, the surrender of one country after another, to such a point that there are Soviet satellites even in Africa; almost all of Asia is taken over by them; Portugal is rolling down the precipice.

During those 30 years, more was surrendered to totalitarianism that any defeated country has ever surrendered after any war in history. There was no war, but there might as well have been. For a long time we in the East couldn't understand this. We couldn't understand the flabbiness of the truce concluded in Vietnam. Any average Soviet citizen understood that this was a sly device which made it possible for North Vietnam to take over South Vietnam when it so chose. And suddenly, this was rewarded by the Nobel Prize for Peace—a tragic and ironic prize.

A very dangerous state of mind can arise as a result of this 30 years of retreat: give in as quickly as possible, give up as quickly as possible, peace and quiet at any cost. This is what many Western papers wrote: "Let's hurry up and end the bloodshed in Vietnam and have national unity there." But at the Berlin Wall no one talked of national unity. One of your leading newspapers, after the end of Vietnam, had a full headline: "The Blessed Silence." I would not wish that kind of "blessed silence" on my worst enemy. I would not wish that kind of national unity on my worst enemy.

I spent 11 years in the Archipelago, and for half of my lifetime I have studied this question. Looking at this terrible tragedy in Vietnam from a distance, I can tell you, a million persons will be simply exterminated, while four to five million (in accordance with the scale of Vietnam) will find themselves in concentration camps and will be rebuilding Vietnam. And what is happening in Cambodia you already know. It is genocide. It is full and complete destruction but in a new form. Once again their technology is not up to building gas chambers. So, in a few hours, the entire capital city—the guilty capital city—is emptied out: old people, women, children are driven out without belongings, without food. "Go and die!"

This is very dangerous for one's view of the world when this feeling comes on: "Go ahead, give it up." We already hear voices in your country and in the West— "Give up Korea and we will live quietly. Give up Portugal, of course; give up Japan, give up Israel, give up Taiwan, the Philippines, Malaysia, Thailand, give up 10 more African countries. Just let us live in peace and quiet. Just let us drive our big cars on our splendid highways; just let us play tennis and golf, in peace and quiet; just let us mix our cocktails in peace and quiet as we are accustomed to doing; just let us see the beautiful toothy smile with a glass in hand on every advertisement page of our magazines."

But look how things have turned out: Now in the West this has all turned into an accusation against the United States. We hear many voices saying, "It's your fault, America." And, here, I must decisively defend the United States against these accusations. The United States, of all the countries of the West, is the least guilty in all this and has done the most in order to prevent it. The United States has helped Europe to win the First and the Second World Wars. It twice raised Europe from post-war destruction—twice—for 10, 20, 30 years it has stood as a shield protecting Europe while European countries were counting their nickels, to avoid paying for their armies (better yet to have none at all) to avoid paying for armaments, thinking about how to leave NATO, knowing that in any case America will protect them anyway. These countries started it all, despite their thousands of years of civilization and culture, even though they are closer and should have known better.

I came to your continent—for two months I have been travelling in its wide open spaces and I agree: here you do not feel the nearness of it all, the immediacy of it all. And here it is possible to miscalculate. Here you must make a spiritual effort to understand the acuteness of the world situation. The United States of America has long shown itself to be the most magnanimous, the most generous country in the world. Wherever there is a flood, an earthquake, a fire, a natural disaster, disease, who is the first to help? The United States. Who helps the most and unselfishly? The United States. And what do we hear in reply? Reproaches, curses, "Yankee Go Home." American cultural centers are burned, and the U.N. representatives of the Third World jump on tables to vote against the United States.

But this does not take the load off America's shoulders. The course of history—whether you like it or not—has made you the leaders of the world. Your country can no longer think provincially. Your political leaders can no longer think only of their own states, of their parties, of petty arrangements which may or may not lead to promotion. You must think about the whole world, and when the new political crisis in the world will arise (I think we have just come to the end of a very acute crisis and the next one will come any moment) the main decisions will fall anyway on the shoulders of the United States of America.

And while already here, I have heard some explanations of the situation. Let me quote some of them: "It is impossible to protect those who do not have the will to defend themselves." I agree with that, but this was said about South Vietnam. In one-half of today's Europe and in three-quarters of today's world the will to defend oneself is even less than it was in South Vietnam.

We are told, "We should not protect those who do not have full democracy." This is the most remarkable argument of the lot. This is the leitmotif I hear in your newspapers and in the speeches of some of your political leaders. Who in the world ever, on the front line of defense against totalitarianism, has been able to sustain full democracy? You, the united democracies of the world, were not able to sustain it. America, England, France, Canada, Australia together did not sustain it. At the first threat of Hitlerism, you stretched out your hands to Stalin. You call that sustaining democracy?

And there is more of the same (there were many of these speeches in a row): "If the Soviet Union is going to use détente for its own ends, then we...." But what will happen then? The Soviet Union has used détente in its own interests, is using it now and will continue to use it in its own interests! For example, China and the Soviet Union, both actively participating in détente, have quietly grabbed three countries of Indochina. True, perhaps as a consolation, China will send you a ping-pong team. And the Soviet Union has sent you the pilots who once crossed the North Pole. In a few days you're flying into space together.

A typical diversion. I remember very well the year, this was June of 1937, when Chkalov, Baidukov and Beliakov heroically flew over the North Pole and landed in the state of Washington. This was the very year when Stalin was executing more than 40,000 persons a month. And Stalin knew what he was doing. He sent those pilots and aroused in you a naive delight—the friendship of two countries across the North Pole. The pilots were heroic; nobody will say anything against them. But this was a show—a show to divert you from the real events of 1937. And what is the occasion now? It is an anniversary—38 years? Is 38 years some kind of an anniversary? No, it is simply necessary to cover up Vietnam. And, once again, those pilots were sent here. The Chkalov Memorial was unveiled in the state of Washington. Chkalov was a hero and is worthy of a memorial. But, to present the true picture, behind the memorial there should have been a wall and on it there should have been a bas relief showing the executions, showing the skulls and bones.

We are also told (I apologize for so many quotes, but there are many more in your press and radio): "We cannot ignore the fact that North Vietnam and the

Khmer Rouge have violated the agreement, but we're ready to look into the future." What does that mean? It means: let them exterminate people. But if these murderers, who live by violence, these executioners, offer us détente we will be happy to go along with them. As Willy Brandt once said: "I would even be willing to have détente with Stalin." At a time when Stalin was executing 40,000 a month he would have been willing to have détente with Stalin?

Look into the future. This is how they looked into the future in 1933 and 1941, but it was a short-sighted look into the future. This is how they looked into the future two years ago when a senseless, incomprehensible, non-guaranteed truce in Vietnam was arranged, and it was a short-sighted view. There was such a hurry to make this truce that they forgot to liberate your own Americans from captivity. They were in such a hurry to sign this document that some 1,300 Americans, "Well, they have vanished; we can get by without them." How is that done? How can this be? Part of them, indeed, can be missing in action, but the leaders of North Vietnam themselves have admitted that some of them are still being kept in prison. And do they give you back your countrymen? No, they are not giving them back, and they are always raising new conditions. At first they said, "Remove Thieu from power." Now, they say, "Have the United States restore Vietnam, otherwise it's very difficult for us to find these people."

If the government of North Vietnam has difficulty explaining to you what happened to your brothers, to your American POWs who have not yet returned, I, on the basis of my experience in the Gulag Archipelago, can explain this quite clearly. There is a law in the Archipelago that those who have been treated the most harshly and who have withstood the most bravely, the most honest, the most courageous, the most unbending, never again come out into the world. They are never again shown to the world because they will tell such tales as the human mind cannot accept. Returned POWs told you that they were tortured. This means that those who have remained were tortured even more, but did not yield an inch. These are your best people. These are your first heroes, who, in a solitary combat, have stood the test. And today, unfortunately, they cannot take courage from our applause. They can't hear it from their solitary cells where they may either die or sit 30 years, like Raoul Wallenberg, the Swedish diplomat who was seized in 1945 in the Soviet Union. He has been imprisoned for 30 years and they will not yield him up. And you have some hysterical public figure who said: "I will go to North Vietnam. I will stand on my knees and beg them to release our prisoners of war." This isn't a political act—this is masochism.

To understand properly what détente has meant all these 40 years—friendships, stabilization of the situation, trade, etc. I would have to tell you something, which you have never seen or heard, of how it looked from the other side. Let me tell you how it looked. Mere acquaintance with an American, and God forbid that you should sit with him in a cafe or restaurant, meant a 10-year term for suspicion of espionage.

In the first volume of *Archipelago,* I tell of an event which was not told me by some arrested person, but by all of the members of the Supreme Court of the USSR during those short days when I was in the limelight under Khrushchev. One Soviet citizen was in the United States and on his return said that in the United States they have wonderful automobile roads. The KGB arrested him and demanded a term of 10 years. But the judge said: " I don't object, but there is not enough evidence. Couldn't you find something else against him?" So the judge was exiled to Sakhalin because he dared to argue and they gave the other man 10 years. Can you imagine what a lie he told? And what sort of praise this was of American imperialism—in America there are good roads? Ten years.

In 1945-46 through our prison cells passed a lot of persons—and these were not ones who were cooperating with Hitler, although there were some of those, too. They were not guilty of anything, but rather were persons who had just been in the West and had been liberated from German prison camps by the Americans. This was considered a criminal act: liberated by the Americans. That means he has seen the good life. If he comes back, he will talk about it. The most terrible thing is not what he did but what he would talk about. And all such persons got 10-year terms.

During Nixon's last visit to Moscow, your American correspondents were reporting in Western fashion from the streets of Moscow, going down a Russian street with a microphone and asking the ordinary Soviet citizen: "Tell me please, what do you think about the meeting between Nixon and Brezhnev?" And, amazingly, every last person answered: "Wonderful. I'm delighted. I'm absolutely overjoyed!"

What does this mean? If I'm going down a street in Moscow and some American comes up to me with a microphone and asks me something, then I know that on the other side of him is a member of the state security, also with a microphone who is recording everything I say. You think that I'm going to say something that is going to put me in prison immediately? Of course, I say: "It's wonderful! I'm overjoyed!" What is the value of such correspondents if they simply transfer Western techniques over there without thinking things through?

You helped us for many years with Lend-Lease, but we've now done everything to forget this, to erase it from our minds, not to remember it if at all possible. And now, before I came into this hall, I delayed my visit to Washington a little in order to first take a look at some ordinary parts of America, going to various states and simply talking with people. I was told, and I learned this for the first time, that in every state during the war years there were Soviet-American friendship societies which collected assistance for Soviet people–warm clothes, canned food, gifts and sent them to the Soviet Union. But we not only never saw these; we never received them (they were distributed somewhere among the privileged circles) and no one ever even told us that this was being done. I only learned about it for the first time here, this month, in the United States.

Everything poisonous which could be said about the United States was said in Stalin's days. And all of this is a heavy sediment which can be stirred up anytime. Any day the newspapers can come out with the headlines: "Bloodthirsty American imperialism wants to seize control of the world," and this poison will rise up from the sediment and many people in our country will believe this, and will be infected by it, and will consider you as aggressors. This is how détente has been managed on our side.

The Soviet system is so closed that it is almost impossible for you to understand from here. Your theoreticians and scholars write works trying to understand and explain how things occur there. Here are some naive explanations which are simply funny to some Soviet citizens. Some say that the Soviet leaders have now given up their inhumane ideology. Not at all. They haven't given it up one bit. Some say that in the Kremlin there are some on the Left, some on the Right. And they are fighting with each other, and we've got to behave in such a way as not to interfere with those on the Left. This is all fantasy: Left....Right. There is some sort of a struggle for power, but they all agree on the essentials.

There also exists the following theory, that now, thanks to the growth of technology, there is a technocracy in the Soviet Union, a growing number of engineers and the engineers are now running the economy and will soon determine the fate of the country, rather than the Party. I will tell you, though, that the engineers determine the fate of the economy just as much as our generals determine the fate of the Army. That means zero. Everything is done the way the Party demands. That's our system. Judge it for yourself. It's a system where for 40 years there haven't been genuine elections but simply a comedy, a farce. Thus a system which has no legislative organs. It's a system without an independent press; a system without an independent judiciary; where the people have no influence either on external or internal policy; where any thought which is different from what the state thinks is crushed.

And let me tell you that electronic bugging in our country is such a simple thing that it's a matter of everyday life. You had an instance in the United States where a bugging caused an uproar which lasted for a year and a half. For us it's an everyday matter. Almost every apartment, every institution has got its bug and it doesn't surprise us in the least–we are used to it. It's a system where unmasked butchers of millions like Molotov and others smaller than him have never been tried in the courts but retire on tremendous pensions in the greatest comfort. It's a system where the show still goes on today and to which every foreigner is introduced surrounded by a couple of planted agents working according to a set scenario. It's a system where the very constitution has never been carried out for a single day; where all the decisions mature in secrecy, high up in a small irresponsible group and then are released on us and on you like a bolt of lightning.

And what are the signatures of such persons worth? How could one rely on their signatures to documents of détente? You yourselves might ask your specialists now and they'll tell you that precisely in recent years the Soviet Union has succeeded in creating wonderful chemical weapons and missiles, which are even better than those used by the United States. So what are we to conclude from that? Is détente needed or not? Not only is it needed, it's as necessary as air. It's the only way of saving the earth—instead of a world war to have détente, but a true détente, and if it has already been ruined by the bad word which we use for it—"détente"—then we should find another word for it.

I would say that there are very few, only three, main characteristics of such a true détente. In the first place, there would be disarmament—not only disarmament from the use of war but also from the use of violence. We must stop using not only the sort of arms which are used to destroy one's neighbors, but the sort of arms which are used to oppress one's fellow countrymen. It is not détente if we here with you today can spend our time agreeably while over there people are groaning and dying and in psychiatric hospitals. Doctors are making their evening rounds, for the third time injecting people with drugs which destroy their brain cells.

The second sign of détente, I would say, is the following: that it be not one based on smiles, not on verbal concessions, but it has to be based on a firm foundation. You know the words from the Bible: "Build not on sand, but on rock." There has to be a guarantee that this will not be broken overnight and for this the other side—the other party to the agreement—must have its acts subject to public opinion, to the press, and to a freely elected parliament. And until such control exists there is absolutely no guarantee.

The third simple condition—what sort of détente is it when they employ the sort of inhumane propaganda which is proudly called, in the Soviet Union, "ideological warfare." Let us not have that. If we're going to be friends, let's be friends, if we're going to have détente, then let's have détente, and an end to ideological warfare.

The Soviet Union and the communist countries can conduct negotiations.

They know how to do this. For a long time they don't make any concessions and then they give in a little bit. Then everyone says triumphantly, "Look, they've made a concession; it's time to sign." The European negotiators of 35 countries for two years now have painfully been negotiating and their nerves were stretched to the breaking point and they finally gave in. A few women from the communist countries can now marry foreigners. And a few newspapermen are now going to be permitted to travel a little more than before. They give 1/1,000th of what natural law should provide. Matters which people should be able to do even before such negotiations are undertaken. And already there is joy. And here in the West we hear many voices saying: "Look, they're making concessions; it's time to sign." During these two years of negotiations, in all the countries of Eastern Europe, the pressure has increased, the oppression intensified, even in Yugoslavia and Romania, leaving aside the other countries. And it is precisely now that the Austrian chancellor says, "We've got to sign this agreement as rapidly as possible."

What sort of an agreement would this be? The proposed agreement is the funeral of Eastern Europe. It means that Western Europe would finally, once and for all, sign away Eastern Europe, stating that it is perfectly willing to see Eastern Europe be crushed and overwhelmed once and for all, but please don't bother us. And the Austrian chancellor thinks that if all these countries are pushed into a mass grave, Austria, at the very edge of this grave, will survive and not fall into it also. And we, from our lives there, have concluded that violence can only be withstood by firmness.

You have to understand the nature of communism. The very ideology of communism, all of Lenin's teachings, are that anyone is considered to be a fool who doesn't take what's lying in front of him. If you can take it, take it. If you can attack, attack. But if there's a wall, then go back, and the communist leaders respect only firmness and have contempt and laugh at persons who continually give in to them. Your people are now saying—and this is the last quotation I am going to give you from the statements of your leaders—"Power, without any attempt at conciliation, will lead to a world conflict." But I would say that power with continual subservience is no power at all.

But, from our experience, I can tell you that only firmness will make it possible to withstand the assaults of communist totalitarianism. We see many historic examples, and let me give you some of them. Look at little Finland in 1939, which by its own forces withstood the Nazi attack. You, in 1948, defended Berlin only by your firmness of spirit, and there was no world conflict. In Korea, in 1950, you stood up against the communists, only by your firmness, and there was no world conflict. In 1962, you compelled the rockets to be removed from Cuba. Again, it was only firmness and there was no world conflict. And the late

Konrad Adenauer conducted firm negotiations with Khrushchev and thus started a genuine détente with Khrushchev. Khrushchev started to make concessions and if he hadn't been removed, that winter he was planning to go to Germany and to continue genuine détente.

Let me remind you of the weakness of a man whose name is rarely associated with weakness—the weakness of Lenin. Lenin, when he came to power, in panic gave up to Germany everything Germany wanted. Germany took as much as it wanted and said, "Give Armenia to Turkey." And Lenin said, "Fine." It's almost an unknown fact but Lenin petitioned the Kaiser to act as intermediary to persuade the Ukraine and, thus, to make possible a boundary between the communist part of Russia and the Ukraine. It wasn't a question of seizing the Ukraine but rather of making a boundary with the Ukraine.

We—the dissidents of the USSR—don't have any tanks. We don't have any weapons. We have no organization. We don't have anything. Our hands are empty. We have only heart and what we have lived through in the half century of this system. And when we have found the firmness within ourselves to stand up for our rights, we have done so. It's only by firmness of spirit that we have withstood. And if I am standing here before you, it's not because of the kindness or the good will of communism, not thanks to détente, but thanks to my own firmness and your firm support. They knew that I would not yield one inch, not one hair. And when they couldn't do more they themselves fell back.

This is not easy. In our conditions this was taught to me by the difficulties of my own life. And if you yourselves—any one of you—were in the same difficult situation, you would have learned the same thing. Take Vladimir Bukovsky, whose name is now almost forgotten. Now, I don't want to mention a lot of names because however many I might mention there are more still. And when we resolve the question with two or three names it is as if we forget and betray the others. We should rather remember figures. There are tens of thousands of political prisoners in our country and—by calculation of English specialists—7,000 persons are now under compulsory psychiatric treatment. Let's take Vladimir Bukovsky as an example. It was proposed to him, "All right, we'll free you. Go to the West and shut up." And this young man, a youth today on the verge of death said: "No, I won't go this way. I have written about the persons whom you have put in insane asylums. You release them and then I'll go West." This is what I mean by that firmness of spirit to stand up against granite and tanks.

Finally, to evaluate everything that I have said to you, I would say we need not have had our conversation on the level of business calculations. Why did such and such a country act in such and such a way? What were they counting on? We should rather rise above this to the moral level and, say: "In 1933 and in

1941 your leaders and the whole western world, in an unprincipled way, made a deal with totalitarianism." We will have to pay for this, some day this deal will come back to haunt us. For 30 years we have been paying for it and we're still paying for it. And we're going to pay for it in a worse way.

One cannot think only on the low level of political calculations. It's necessary to think also of what is noble, and what is honorable—not only what is profitable. Resourceful Western legal scholars have now introduced the term "legal realism." By legal realism, they want to push aside any moral evaluation of affairs. They say, "Recognize realities; if such and such laws have been established in such and such countries by violence, these laws still must be recognized and respected." At the present time it is widely accepted among lawyers that law is higher than morality—law is something which is worked out and developed, whereas morality is something inchoate and amorphous. That isn't the case. The opposite is rather true! Morality is higher than law! While law is our human attempt to embody in rules a part of that moral sphere which is above us. We try to understand this morality, bring it down to earth and present it in a form of laws. Sometimes we are more successful, sometimes less. Sometimes you actually have a caricature of morality, but morality is always higher than law. This view must never be abandoned. We must accept it with heart and soul.

It is almost a joke now in the Western world, in the 20th century, to use words like "good" and "evil." They have become almost old-fashioned concepts, but they are very real and genuine concepts. These are concepts from a sphere that is higher than us. And instead of getting involved in base, petty, short-sighted political calculations and games, we have to recognize that the concentration of evil and the tremendous force of hatred is flowing throughout the world. And we have to stand up against it and not hasten to give to it, give to it, give to it, everything that it wants to swallow.

Today there are two major processes occurring in the world. One is the one which I have just described to you, a process of giving up, and giving up and giving up and hoping that perhaps at some point the wolf will have eaten enough. The second process is one that I consider the key to everything and that, I will say now, will bring all of us our future; under the cast-iron shell of communism—for 20 years in the Soviet Union and a shorter time in other communist countries—there is occurring a liberation of the human spirit. New generations are growing up which are steadfast in their struggle with evil; which are not willing to accept unprincipled compromises; which prefer to lose everything—salary, conditions of existence and life itself—but are not willing to sacrifice conscience; not willing to make deals with evil.

This process has now gone so far that in the Soviet Union today, Marxism has fallen so low that it has become an anecdote, it's simply an object of contempt. No serious person in our country today, not even university and high school students, can talk about Marxism without smiling, without laughing. But this whole process of our liberation, which obviously will entail social transformations, is slower than the first one—the process of concessions. Over there, when we see these concessions, we are frightened. Why so quickly? Why so precipitously? Why yield several countries a year?

I started by saying that you are the allies of our liberation movement in the communist countries. And I call upon you: let us think together and try to see how we can adjust the relationship between these two processes. Whenever you help the persons persecuted in the Soviet Union, you not only display magnanimity and nobility, you're defending not only them but yourselves as well. You're defending your own future.

So let us try and see how far we can go to stop this senseless and immoral process of endless concessions to the aggressor—these clever legal arguments for why we should give up one country after another. Why must we hand over to communist totalitarianism more and more technology—complex, delicate, developed technology which it needs for armaments and for crushing its own citizens? If we can at least slow down that process of concessions, if not stop it altogether—and make it possible for the process of liberation to continue in communist countries—ultimately these two processes will yield us our future.

On our crowded planet there are no longer any internal affairs. The communist leaders say, "Don't interfere in our internal affairs. Let us strangle our citizens in peace and quiet." But I tell you: Interfere more and more. Interfere as much as you can. We beg you to come and interfere.

ABOUT THE AUTHOR

Russian exile and Noble Peace Prize recipient Aleksandr Solzhenitsyn is known throughout the world as the author of such monumental books as *The Gulag Archipelago,* (Harper & Row, 1974-78), *August 1914* (Farrar, Straus and Giroux, 1972) and *One Day in the Life of Ivan Denisovitch* (Praeger, 1963). The text here was originally presented in an address to the AFL-CIO in June of 1975.

IDEA FASHIONS OF THE EIGHTIES:
AFTER MARX, WHAT?

Tom Wolfe
January 1984

hat I want to talk about is something that my confreres in the world of literature and journalism resist: the notion that ideas can become articles of fashion which are adopted with no more foundation than styles in clothing. I see this as the key to the intellectual history of the United States in the twentieth century. Just in the last decade we have seen a tremendous change in styles of ideas.

The 1960s' fashion I have called "radical chic" actually continued well into the 1970s; it didn't die with the end of the war in Vietnam. In 1974, I attended a conference at a university in the Great Plains, a conference called "America in the Year 2000." It was held in a typical student activity center, one of those great butter-almond-colored buildings with expando-flex interior walls like accordions that are pulled back and forth by a night watchman in green balloon-seat twill pants. Here come the students in for the conference on "America in the Year 2000." They seem to me very lively, they are laughing, they are chattering to one another. Their veins are pumping with Shasta and Seven-Up. They are wearing bluejeans and bursting out of their down-filled Squaw Valley ski jackets. And no sooner do they settle down into their seats than the keynote speaker of the conference, a young historian in a calfskin jacket and hair like Felix Mendelssohn's, looks down, and he says: "America is a leaden, life-denying society."

Well, it was one of the few perfect keynote addresses that I have ever heard, because it set the tone for the next 36 hours as few such keynote addresses ever do. We were treated to a parade of speakers, each of whom filled in more dreadful details about American society. We were told that America is a country run by 60 families and 180 corporations, who control 95 percent of American wealth. We were told that every important decision is made by a small cabal of men who avoid publicity the way the werewolf avoids the dawn. We were told that due to the precipitous drop in the Gross National Product, the American veneer of freedom was no longer possible—that shortly the citizenry would be cowering in fear, awaiting that knock on the door in the dead of the night and that descent of the knout on the nape of the neck.

After 36 hours of this, it was all that I could do to bring myself to the last symposium in the conference, entitled, "The American Environment in the Year 2000." The prognosis was, as you might imagine, not altogether salutary. The first speaker was a young ecologist, who rose up and said, "Ladies and gentlemen, I am not sure that I want to be alive in America in the year 2000." He looked pretty lively at the time. He was about 37, he had on a magenta turtleneck disco jersey and a Madras jacket and a lot of other marvelous gear. The explanation of his dour prognosis was that due to the rape of the upper atmosphere by aerosol can users, a certain ion would no longer be able to come through the atmosphere to the earth, and this particular ion was indispensable for bone formation.

No more bone formation! Suddenly I had a vision that was worse than any that had come to me in the preceding 36 hours. I could see these marvelous women that I enjoyed watching walk down Lexington Avenue near where I live in New York City with their five-inch, pyramid-heel, three-color, patent-leather, platform-soled shoes, and their bluejeans smartly cleaving the declivities fore and aft, and I could suddenly picture them dissolving into blobs of patent leather and denim on the sidewalk, inching and suppurating along like amoebae. I could see the blind news dealer down at the corner of Lexington and Sixty-First Street trying to give change to a notions buyer from Bloomingdale's, and their hands run together like fettuccine over a stack of *New York Posts*. It was worse than anything I had ever imagined in my life.

CANDIDE IN REVERSE

At this point, for the first time in the whole conference, a student spoke up. "I don't know if I should interrupt," he said, "but I just thought there is one thing I should tell you. I am a senior here at the university now, and for four years my professors have been telling me pretty much the same thing that you ladies and gentlemen have been saying all during this conference, namely that the end is near, everything is going down the chute, there is not much to hope for. But in all honesty I must tell you that the biggest problem we have run into here at the university in my four years is finding a parking place near the campus."

The ecologist looked at him to see if this was a wise guy, a troublemaker; but you couldn't really tell, so he decided to play it straight. He says, "Well, you have to understand that a university such as this is a middle-class institution, and middle-class institutions are set up precisely so as to... "

The student broke in and said, "I know that, I know that, they have told me that. But what I want to know is, how old are you usually when it all hits you?" And then you could see that he was not a troublemaker. He was not a wise guy. He was someone who had planned to go back to Omaha or wherever and take a perfectly normal job, and he was afraid that one day he would be walking down the street and, as if they were ten-pin balls rolling off the roof, he would suddenly be wiped out by war, repression, pestilence, and the rest of the apocalyptic horsemen. He just wondered how that all came about. I could see that I was in the presence of a Candide in reverse. The original Candide was always told by Dr. Pangloss that he lived in the best of all possible worlds, and then everything went wrong. This young man had been told, and he believed it, that everything was going wrong—and yet he seemed to be living in the best of all possible worlds, and he couldn't explain it.

CONFRONTING THE GULAG

As late as 1974, this was intellectual fashion in the United States. Yet by 1976, instead of staging what I thought might be a cynical Bicentennial, writers and artists brought an almost positive spirit to the Bicentennial. They did not stage a riotous celebration, but there was a fairly good spirit. Something had happened. I think the thing that did it was the publication in 1973 of the first volume of Aleksandr Solzhenitsyn's *The Gulag Archipelago*.

That book had an impact on intellectual life in the United States and throughout the West of a sort that is difficult to measure this early in the game, but which I have no doubt whatsoever was quite profound. What that book did was to establish the fact once and for all that there was in the Soviet Union a network of concentration camps. This was not the first book to say the camps existed. Robert Conquest in England had documented the existence of this network of concentration camps; but he did so mainly by using the testimony of refugees, and we happen to live in a time when people do not believe the testimony of refugees in most cases.

But Solzhenitsyn came from within the Soviet Union, and he came with the blessing of Nikita Khrushchev himself. Khrushchev had made a grave tactical error in the matter of Aleksandr Solzhenitsyn. He had, in effect, for his own internal political purposes, put his arms around Solzhenitsyn at the time of the publication of *One Day in the Life of Ivan Denisovich.* He had said, first, yes, this book can be published; and second, it can be published because it's true that these things happened. (The implication, of course, was that they would not happen again since Khrushchev was now there instead of Stalin.) This gave an authenticity to Solzhenitsyn's words which could not then be withdrawn.

Solzhenitsyn's series of books on the gulag not only established the existence of a network of concentration camps in the Soviet Union but also proved that the concentration camps were not the product of the madman Stalin. That had always been the excuse: any time appalling things happened in Russia, Czechoslovakia or Hungary, it was always, "This is the legacy of the madman Stalin, who took socialism on a wrong turn." But Solzhenitsyn was saying that it didn't start with Stalin. It could easily be traced back as far as Lenin. Lenin, it turns out, is the man who *invented* the term concentration camps–not Hitler, but Lenin. His first act was to destroy all student political opposition within the Soviet Union by putting people into places you and I would call prisons, but which Lenin preferred to call "concentrations" of people being detained for their own good and the good of the society.

Solzhenitsyn went further, however. He said you cannot blame it on Lenin, you cannot even blame it on Marx; you have to trace it back to its root cause. And the root cause in his estimation was any system of *a priori* morality in which a group of men decide, "Morality starts here. We sweep away the moral basis of the past, morality starts here. We start morality from zero." Solzhenitsyn showed that you cannot start morality from zero, because such a course inevitably leads straight to the concentration camps. Since 1973, since *The Gulag Archipelago,* Marxism has been through as a spiritual force in the world. Marxism has never been a very powerful ideology in the United States. We have not been very good ideologues. Somehow we don't seem to be able to sit still for the Flemish bonding of the dialectic. Even people on the Left in America seem to be unable or unwilling to go through that tight logical process which has come to have such a hold on intellectuals in Europe. Instead, we have had a Marxist mist. There was always a Marxist mist over the next hill, a fuzzy glow by the light of which one could judge every solution that was tried in our particular form of democracy. But *The Gulag Archipelago,* with dramatic effectiveness, began to dispel that mist as the environment in which attacks on American democracy, particularly attacks from within the United States itself, could originate.

The arrival of Solzhenitsyn in this country in 1975 was quite an event as well. No one was prepared to see him. He was like an invisible man leading an invisible funeral through the United States. He came here on the arm of George Meany of the AFL-CIO. No one in the American literary establishment then or now had anything to do with Solzhenitsyn. He lives in this country, up in Vermont; yet no overture is ever made. The *New York Times* would not cover his two major speeches until they were humiliated into doing so by one of their reporters, Hilton Kramer–a man I have made fun of in matters of art history, but to whom I have to take off my hat in the Solzhenitsyn affair.

But someone else who ignored Solzhenitsyn was the then President, Gerald Ford. He was invited by the AFL-CIO to Solzhenitsyn's speech in Washington, and he said that he had a prior engagement with one of his daughters. I think it is touching that there should still be such strong family bonds this late in the twentieth century, but I also think that this is one of the major mistakes the man ever made as president of the United States. It came, apparently, through an agreement reached under the spell of détente by Henry Kissinger with the Soviets, that our government would look the other way when Aleksandr Solzhenitsyn arrived, which our government did.

VACUUM OF FASHIONABLE IDEAS

Today Marxism still exists. Marxists still exist. The spiritual force however, has gone out of it. No one any longer looks to Marxism in a religious way, as was done for years even by people who were not Marxists. The tenacity of Marxism can still be seen all over college campuses, but in what are usually amusing and not very threatening ways.

In architecture, for example, there is the new theory of rationalism, which comes to us from Italy. This is Marxism that has gone beyond baroque, into its mannerist phase. It holds that architects must go back before the eighteenth century, back to the Renaissance, for their forms. In other words, back to an era that was not tainted by capitalism. So rationalist architects in Italy take Renaissance buildings and strip them of all ornament, so that they are no longer overtly upper class, and then use what is left. You end up with eerie-looking buildings which have great thick walls with square window openings, and they look a bit like fortresses or jails. You can ask these people, "Why do you go back to the Renaissance, back to a time when buildings were built by monarchs and noblemen, many of whom were tyrants, despots?" They'll say, "Ah—at least they weren't capitalists." That's one form of mannerist Marxism.

In college philosophy and literature departments, the reigning concepts are things like constructivism and deconstruction, both borrowed from France. The constructivists—in an age of collisions of the races, explosions of the metropoli, wars so big they are known as world wars—debate endlessly about the meaning of structure and the structure of meaning. The deconstructionists tear down the structure of meaning and the meaning of structure at night, the constructivists build it up the next day. The basic underpinning of it is their contention that words and language as they have evolved in the West have been developed to serve the economic masters. It is the goal of both the constructivists and the deconstructionists to unmask the language apparatus and expose it for what it is.

Why would academicians in America be so enamored of ideas such as constructivism or rationalism? I think it has nothing to do with any basic liking for Marxism. It has to do with our colonial complex in the realm of ideas. To this day Americans in the arts, in literature, and to some extent in journalism, believe that in Europe they do it better, with more elegance, more refinement, more sophistication. In every other sector of life we have written our declarations of independence. In the area of the arts and cultural life generally, we remain the last little obedient colonists passively worshipping European ideas. The Europeans haven't asked to be worshipped. People here have taken it upon themselves to bow down and accept these ideas.

Various efforts have been made to fill the post-Marxist vacuum. The Left in this country is pretty well exhausted, and it knows it. It keeps trying to coalesce around some new cause or grievance, but without much success. One good example was the American Writers' Congress at the Hotel Roosevelt in 1981—a reunion of nostalgic New Dealers bemoaning what they called "self-censorship" among novelists, poets, and playwrights in the United States, thanks to commercialism in publishing. Somehow self-censorship is not quite comparable to the other kind, however. It was so transparently silly to have a conference on the subject of self-censorship that almost all organs that covered the event ended up giving considerable space to the counter-manifesto distributed by the Committee for the Free World, Norman Podhoretz's organization, which sharply contrasted the state of censorship in Poland and censorship in the age of the conglomerates at the Hotel Roosevelt.

COUNTERVAILING FORCES

This episode indicates, I think, that it is no longer possible for the fashions that have known to hold sway. They just can't march into the vacuum and take over any more. There are now countervailing forces. It was interesting to me that the makers of the movie *Reds* felt obliged to point out toward the end of the picture that what had begun as the altogether hopeful Soviet revolution had ended up as an authoritarian regime. Pointing out that rather obvious fact would have been considered a form of right-wing gaucherie within the movie business a decade ago. One of the few pictures made about the New Left and the campus protests of the 1960s was a picture called *The Strawberry Statement,* which by and large was quite enthusiastic about the movement, but which did take some pains to show that many people had joined the movement for frivolous reasons—to have a good time, to smoke a little dope, to get drunk, to score a few points with a girlfriend. The makers of that film were vilified as people who were poisoning the revolution. Now things have changed. The fashion has changed very rapidly in the last decade, even in the last five years.

But now we come to the question: "What are the countervailing forces?" The Left is now attempting to form behind an anti-business, anti-science, anti-nuclear banner. Socialism remains the goal, of course, but this is not a time in which anyone can present a socialist program by that name. But as these old forces regroup, what are going to be the countervailing forces? I am not at all sure.

This country has always lacked professional philosophers who would take it upon themselves to articulate in some structured form the foundations of American democracy, this system of ours which a couple of hundred years ago was an extremely novel thing in the world. Unless there are treatises that I'm not giving due credit, or of which I am not aware, we haven't had a great deal since the Declaration of Independence and the Constitution—which are after all not philosophical documents either; they are platforms and rules.

When I was working on *The Right Stuff,* I realized that NASA had no philosophy of the exploration of space. We have never had a philosophy of why we are going into space, except to counter the Russians. At the beginning of the space program that was enough. All you had to say was, "We must make sure that we capture the high ground of space," and you didn't need to tell Congress or anyone else anything more. But when you reached 1969, 1970, and later, you could see what the lack of a philosophy has cost NASA.

NASA has nothing to say, for the most part, except: "Well, we brought you the Teflon frying pan, we brought you a ballpoint pen that writes in a weightless environment, we have a computerized system that makes it unnecessary for doctors to make housecalls." Just what we needed. NASA has been driven to this through the lack of a philosophy—reduced to coming up with all the practical reasons why we should explore space, whereas the philosophical reasons, which might be along the lines of opening up the rest of the universe, rather interesting ideas such as that, are never presented. The one philosopher that NASA had was Wernher von Braun, and since he had first risen to eminence in rocketry under the Nazis, he was not exactly the best man to bring forth and say, "Here's our philosopher." Operations at the Cape were run by another German, Kurt Debus, who happened to have an even deeper accent than von Braun, as well as what appeared to be a Heidelberg dueling scar on his cheek.

FOR WANT OF A PHILOSOPHY

And so finally, on the eve of the launch of Apollo 11, when Neil Armstrong, Buzz Aldrin and Mike Collins were going up to land on the moon, Ralph Abernathy's Poor People's March headed for the Cape. Abernathy & Co. had their arguments worked out, which were, "We have millions of poor people in America, and you're spending billions to send people to the moon for no purpose; how can you justify yourself?" And a wagon train with Abernathy at the lead finally reached the Cape the day before the launch. Now NASA was in a tremendous hole, because NASA had no philosophy. No one had the nineteenth-century preacher's zeal to march up to anyone confronting him and say, "I'll tell you what we stand for. We're going to explore the rest of the universe on behalf of all mankind." There was nobody who would dare make such a statement, even if it ever occurred to him. Beyond this, NASA, being a completely civilian enterprise, had no armed forces defending their installations, so down at Cape Canaveral they hired the Wackenhut organization. Wackenhut recruited its guards from Florida farm boys, and half of them looked like they had not made it in the shape-up for the movie, *In the Heat of the Night.*

But they eventually thought up a very adroit strategy instead. Thomas Paine, the administrator of NASA, and Julian Scheer, the public affairs officer, decided that they would have Paine—a rather inconspicuous looking (though very dynamic) old World War II submarine officer—stand out alone in a field in a business suit, a sack suit. And while the television cameras zeroed in, while the Poor People's March arrived with bullhorns, Ralph Abernathy began to deliver a speech to this poor man standing out there all alone in the middle of a field; and suddenly the tables were turned. You had this colossal army with wagon trains and bullhorns and legions of people, facing one man in a gray sack suit. It was as if it were an unequal contest, and that defused the whole thing, and the launch went off on schedule. Now this was a brilliant public relations maneuver, but it would have been unnecessary if NASA had been armed with a philosophy, because philosophies tend to give people strength and confidence.

There is a general lack of a philosophy for anyone now on the Right to enter the intellectual vacuum with. There are no counterparts in the United States to France's Bernard-Henri Levy and his confreres, the so-called "New Philosophers." They are formal philosophers who are able to put over abstract ideas in an exciting way. And they understand intellectual chic. They understand fashion. Bernard-Henri Levy looks like the young Vittorio Gassmann. He is about six-foot-four, with flowing black hair. He also has impeccable credentials. He was on the Left for a while; he was on the barricades during the 1968 uprising in Paris. Then his whole outlook was changed by *The Gulag Archipelago.* He is a remarkable public speaker. I saw him at NYU in New York when he arrived there for a lecture, and he is the greatest lectern smoker since Mark Twain. Twain used to do great things with cigars. Bernard-Henri Levy smokes Benson & Hedges 800s, tremendous long skinny cigarettes, and he can talk and punctuate his conversations with jet streams from the nose, from the mouth, from the ears, the eyes, and he has a way of punctuating his remarks by tapping the enormous ash of his cigarette into an ashtray. The night I saw him at NYU they had not provided him with an ashtray; all there was was the bare floor of the dais where he was standing. And it became a fascinating spectacle: This man speaking, blowing smoke through every aperture in the human head, and tapping these ashes which were now hitting the floor; but he was so good at it that every successive ash hit exactly on top of the other one and began forming a conical pyramid. And at the end of his talk everyone rose up and applauded. I never knew whether it was over the brilliance of his presentation—he was in a very hostile room, there at NYU—or whether it was the feat of making a whole Benson & Hedges 800 stack up into one cone.

ACTS OF INSPIRATION

Also, the man has confidence. We are in an age that belongs to monomaniacs. Confidence is everything. In an age when people's values are so unsettled, when their outlooks are so uncertain, when they all make imaginary snowballs day and night, "on the one hand and on the other hand," somebody who is absolutely sure of his position is apt to carry the day. Thus when Bernard-Henri Levy would be challenged from the audience, when somebody would say, "You don't seem to realize what Marx said in his letter concerning the Ukranian Communist Party...." Bernard-Henry Levy would interrupt and say, "Sir, *you* had better know *exactly* what Marx said, otherwise after your question you will not want to be in the same room with me much longer." You had the impression of a man with encyclopedic knowledge. But most of all he had confidence, and I submit that such confidence comes from philosophical certainty.

There is no way that anyone can just say, "Well, let's get a philosopher, and the problem is on the way to being solved." You just can't do that. The great philosophers have been like the great artists. Their formulations have been as much acts of passion as cerebration, as much acts of inspiration as rationalization, and such things cannot be custom ordered. But there are certain things that are not being done which could be done and would be very useful. For example, until Solzhenitsyn, it didn't dawn on anyone that we have no history of the Soviet Union since 1917. That history doesn't exist. Solzhenitsyn is trying to write it now, in nonfiction and in fictional form. We have no history of Eastern Europe since the Second World War. I think it is going to begin to dawn on people what the lack of that history means—a lack, incidentally, that was prophesied by George Orwell in his book *1984*. As a result, we don't have much artistic material, we don't have the dramas, we don't have the movies that portray these worlds.

But above all—and here I will stop—we do not have the philosophy and the confidence that goes with it. Once you have that, you will find that problems such as the attitude of television networks simply fall into place very rapidly. I know a lot of people in television and they are not ideologues. They have their fingers in the wind. In a way, television, being a new medium, is the intellectual slums; and the networks are full of people who yearn for a higher intellectual status. So if the leading intellectual lights of America say a certain thing about some national issue, this same view will naturally be echoed on television. These things happen in the realm of ideas, not in the realm of conventional politics. The philosophy and the confidence that goes with it—these are everything. The age belongs to the monomaniacs.

ABOUT THE AUTHOR

Tom Wolfe, America's leading social critic, is the author of such best-sellers as *The Bonfire of the Vanities* (Farrar, Straus and Giroux, 1987), *The Right Stuff* (Farrar, Straus and Giroux, 1979), *The Electric Kool-Aid Acid Test* (Farrar, Straus and Giroux, 1968), *Radical Chic,* and *Mau-Mauing the Flak Catchers,* (Farrar, Straus and Giroux, 1970). With a Ph.D. from Yale University, he has worked as a reporter and essayist for numerous newspapers and journals of opinion. He is also a Hillsdale College Life Associate.

EXIT COMMUNISM, COLD WAR AND THE STATUS QUO

Jeane J. Kirkpatrick
January 1991

t is exciting to be here at Hillsdale College. I was pleased and honored when Hillsdale presented me with the Freedom Leadership Award in 1984. As a speaker for the College's off-campus programs for some years, I was also happy to share some of my views about the importance of Hillsdale on the College's recently released FreedomQuest campaign video. But this is my first visit to campus and, like Charlton Heston, who preceded me during this program, I'm impressed with what I see. I'm impressed with the hundreds of loyal and interested supporters who are here too, who share the sense that what goes on here matters. Indeed, the very idea of this college is important to our country, our values and our culture. So I congratulate you, Hillsdale, and I thank you for inviting me.

HOW 1989 CHANGED THE WORLD

I'm here to talk a little bit about the world of the late 1980s and early 1990s. The year 1989, in particular, was one of the most extraordinary periods in modern history. The most important lessons this year has taught us are, first, that we must expect the unexpected, and second, that we must stand firm for what we believe. The old adage, that if we have patience and persist, things will get better, turned out to be true. There was a very direct relationship between the United States' patient and persistent policies of President Truman and President Reagan. With his rebuilding of American strength in the 1980s, and his unembarrassed defense of democratic ideals at home and abroad, Reagan encouraged the remarkable changes that have occurred in Eastern Europe and in the Soviet Union and are indeed still occurring.

In truth, 1989 changed the world. At the beginning of that year, the world was much as it had been for the previous four decades. It was the post-World War II status quo: Europe was divided by a cold war created by a real Soviet threat, as evidenced by the brutal occupation of Eastern Europe and by continuing Soviet expansion into five continents. Soviet dominance extended into our own hemisphere, not only in Nicaragua, but by its attempted expansion into El Salvador, Guatemala, Colombia, Peru, Grenada, and Jamaica. It is difficult today even to recall the situation of the world in 1980, though it remained nearly unchanged up until 1989, when rather suddenly there occurred what the Soviets call a "change in the world correlation of forces." This change had been brought about by the resurgence and renaissance of American strength, and by the continuing decline of the Soviet Union. The Soviet Union was and still is the only industrial power in the world whose living standards are declining rather than increasing, and whose average life expectancy is declining (from 74 years for Soviet males to 71 years over a period of about five years in the last decade) while infant mortality rates are rising.

A "CRISIS OF THE SOUL"

By 1989, it was undeniable that the Soviet Union was in a decline severe by any standards. It was equally evident that such a decline had created a kind of "crisis of consciousness," or, perhaps, that the crisis of consciousness had created the decline. We don't usually talk about consciousness when we talk about Soviet leaders and Soviet policy. I've been discovering of late some fascinating facets of Soviet politics while reading the speeches of some of Mikhail Gorbachev's principal advisors. Let me share with you a few words from the text of Aleksandr Yakovlev, for example. Yakovlev is the man whom everyone believes to have been Mikhail Gorbachev's closest advisor in the late 1980s through 1990. Yakovlev has emphasized intellectual and spiritual factors in Soviet changes: "We have suffered not only a crisis in economics but a crisis of the soul," he said. This is Aleksandr Yakovlev on July 2, 1990:

"I am convinced that the time has come for truth. To speak of nobility, charity, honor, and conscience, even at a Congress of Communists, shaking from our feet the mud of enmity and suspicion that has built up over the decades. It is the very time for the party to take the initiative in the moral cleansing of our existence and our consciousness. This is why I am convinced of the historic correctness of the choice that was made in 1985 to establish perestroika."

He went on to remark on his activities in the years since 1985, specifically assigned to him by Mikhail Gorbachev:

"A special sphere of my work in recent years has been the Commission study of materials relating to the repressions visited on our country in the past. I will tell you honestly; it is heavy, spiritually exhausting work when the ashes of millions of people constantly haunt you. The good names of almost a million people have been returned. But there has been falsification of such a scale. Repressions could not have been a matter of chance and could not have been the consequence of an evil will alone. [By] whom and how is the mechanism of repression created and set in motion? How did it function? Why did nothing stand in its path?"

Yakovlev also discussed the Stalinist period. He paused over the collectivization in the Ukraine, that horror about which Robert Conquest has written so movingly and accurately in books like *The Great Terror* and *The Genocide of the*

Ukraine, in which a manmade famine was imposed upon the people of the Ukraine, and starving men, women and children were driven off their land, scattered, and killed. Yakovlev says, "In my view that was the most monstrous crime when hundreds of thousands of peasant families were driven out of the villages, not understanding why such a fate befell them. They were driven out by the authorities they themselves had established. The dead cannot be brought back but their good names may be restored in history." And then he added a line that has since become famous among his countrymen: "Let us remember not the empty shelves but the empty souls who have brought a change to our country which demands revolutionary change."

The reaction of Yakovlev, one of the most well-known public figures in the Soviet Union, is worth our serious attention. Unfortunately, his comments and those of others like him are being largely ignored or discounted in the West. Yakovlev quoted Kant in early September: "Long ago, the great philosopher Kant wrote that there are two prejudices: 'to believe everything and to believe nothing.' But then again, he wrote there are also mysteries, the scarlet sky above us, and the moral law within us." Imagine the second most powerful man in the Soviet Union–as he was at the time–talking about the moral law within us–and then imagine virtually all the major media outlets in the West ignoring his extraordinary pronouncement! Both are remarkable.

Yakovlev added, "According to the moral law, our society that is transforming itself into a free society has yet...in the process of transforming itself to overcome the obstructions of falsehood." He went on to charge that the confidence of the people had been abused in the old communist system, and that "the people wished us merely good and the State responded with the evil of prisons and camps." Yakovlev ends this comment with an extraordinary appeal, "Preserve me, Almighty, from calls for vengeance, from a new round of intolerance, that our society must know the names of the people who committed these deeds in order to assess them according to moral criteria."

SOVIET REPRISALS: THE DOG THAT DIDN'T BARK

I share these words of Aleksandr Yakovlev with you that I've been reading with growing surprise myself. I also want to share with you a sense of the depth of change that is taking place in the Soviet Union today. That change has, of course, already transformed the post-World War II world in which we had lived for over forty years. It was an uncomfortable world, because we were faced by continuous challenges, and because it imposed very heavy burdens on our country. Yet it was comfortable, because we knew it and were accustomed to it, and we knew what we should do—help defend the frontiers of freedom.

The most remarkable event of 1989 was something that didn't happen—like the dog that didn't bark in Sherlock Holmes's famous mystery tale. What didn't happen was that Soviet troops did not intervene to crush the liberation movements in Hungary, Poland, Czechoslovakia and East Germany. I was in Poland in late August of that year. The first elected government since World War II had been installed. It was, naturally, largely a Solidarity government, although you will recall that it included two communist ministers (who have only recently been fired). Those two communist ministers were in charge of the Defense and Interior ministries. The newly-elected Polish Solidarity government had agreed to give the communists, who had been clobbered in the elections, control over the armed forces and the police. Why? Because they thought they had to; because they feared that Soviet troops would crush their democratic movement.

At the time I was there last August, Solidarity's victory was still uncertain. No one knew what to expect; every step toward independence was taken courageously enough, but was attended by great misgivings. Two Solidarity leaders, ministers in the new government, confessed privately to me: "None of us forgets our years in prison." After all, they had been in prison fewer than five years before this time, when Poland was under martial law and no one's rights were protected. And it had been less than a decade since Father Popieluszko had been beaten to death for daring to speak about independence for his country.

The uncertainty existed for all Eastern Europe. No one knew what was going to happen in Hungary when its citizens announced that they were going to change the national constitution and open the border with Austria. Even though it was rumored that they had the approval of Mikhail Gorbachev, no one, not even Gorbachev, could predict the results of such unprecedented reform. We know now that when the border was opened, East Germans began to surge through in a kind of human tidal wave. We also know that this mass exodus began the process of the reunification of Germany. No one knew what would happen when the citizens of Czechoslovakia went into the streets for the first time since 1968. Miraculously, they did not encounter tanks—just each other—and there, too, freedom was realizable at last.

THE CHALLENGE OF NORMAL TIMES

The most important event of 1989 was really a non-event: the tanks that did not roll and the Soviet troops that stayed in their barracks. This was the end of the Soviet empire, and it disintegrated faster than any other empire in modern history. Obviously, the danger is not yet over—there are still Soviet tanks and troops in Eastern Europe, and there are tens of thousands of Soviet missiles. But the "will to empire" has disappeared. We can say of the year 1989 that it was the year in which history's most bold, daring and ruthless experiment in social engineering was effectively abandoned by the heirs of the men who began it.

Now, the question is, what will replace that experiment? Some Soviets like Yakovlev, who lived in the West for nearly a decade, talk of building a free society. Gorbachev often says the same thing, and although I am not sure that he understands what such freedom really means, he is a very pragmatic man who understands that reform is in his and the Soviet Union's best interest. In the last few years he has begun to ask questions that the Soviet people were, to say the least, unaccustomed to hearing. For example, he asked if it were true old Bolsheviks were guilty of the crimes they had been executed for, and even went to the trouble of establishing two investigative commissions to confirm that the victims of Stalin's purges were wrongly accused.

"Is it true?"—that is not a Bolshevik question, as anyone knows who recalls the infamous Moscow show trials of the 1930s. And Gorbachev followed up with another uncharacteristic question about the Soviet economy. He asked, simply, "Does it work?" When Bolsheviks before Gorbachev asked if the economy worked, what they really meant was, "Does it serve the Revolution?" To his credit, Gorbachev meant something quite different. He pointed to Soviet agriculture as an unworkable system and advocated following the practice of Hungary and China in leasing land to farmers. This system leaves the state in control, but starts the move toward private ownership.

Watching Soviet leaders like Gorbachev let go of power is a fascinating experience. The stops and starts, the infighting with other Soviet hardliners like Yegor Ligachev, the retrenchments and advances—these are all part of a great historical drama. There has never been a totalitarian state like the Soviet Union. There has never been one dismantled without great violence. Yet, so far, we seem to be witnessing a largely peaceful transformation to a more democratic political structure and perhaps to a market economy as well. It is not easy. No one knows how to do it.

Ironically enough, our libraries are filled with books on the transformation from capitalism to socialism, but almost nothing has been written about how to bring about the reverse. There are only one or two like that of the brilliant Peruvian Hernando de Soto, called *The Other Path*. They desperately need such books in Eastern Europe and the Soviet Union.

In the West, we also need books that will remind us that it was the West and democratic capitalism, not socialism, that won the Cold War. The totalitarian's conception of man as an object to be remade led to the long tragedy that culminated in the collapse of communism.

Communism collapsed because it was wrong about everything; about human nature, religion, economics, politics, and history. It espoused doctrines that were not true and did not work, but caused instead inhumanity unparalleled in the modern age.

ABOUT THE AUTHOR

Jeane J. Kirkpatrick served for more than four years as the U.S. Ambassador to the United Nations and was a member of the presidential cabinet. Resigning her post in 1985, she returned to Georgetown University as Leavey Professor and to the American Enterprise Institute as Senior Fellow. In 1985 President Reagan awarded her the Medal of Freedom. Her most recent book is *The Withering Away of the Totalitarian State...and Other Surprises* (AEI Press, 1991).

A NEW WORLD ORDER...
OF FREEDOM

Malcolm S. Forbes, Jr.
August 1991

At the turn of the century, there was considerable optimism that the 1900s would be the most enlightened period the world had ever seen. There was the seemingly unlimited promise of science, of compound financial growth, of industrialization, of international peace...and then came the Great Depression and two world wars that brought untold human suffering. Yet in the last decade of the 20th century we have a real chance to make good on that earlier optimism and achieve material and moral gains for millions of people.

THE NEW WORLD ORDER: WHAT IT WILL AND WON'T BE

We have a chance, in short, to build a "new world order," but *one that is very different than the term popularly implies.** It *will not* be some supranational government. It will not be a new ideology sprung from the ashes of fascism, socialism or communism. It will not give rise to collective institutions designed to control the masses or to remake the world. It will not be brought about by political decrees or fancy crusades. The new world order *will* be one that leaves individuals freer than ever before. It will be the product of evolution, rather than revolution. And its growth will be spurred by some very simple events that are already in progress.

The U.S. Leads the Free World

The first event is the United States' decisive rejection of the isolationism that dominated its policymaking in the 1930s and 1970s. The Persian Gulf War sent an unmistakable message: we won't tolerate aggression that threatens our national interests. On paper, Iraq was a formidable foe. It had oil, billions of dollars of revenue, heavy industry, stockpiled armaments, and a massive, experienced conscript army. But Iraq's might, built as it was upon dictatorial power, proved to be illusory.

In peacetime, we can't abandon our resolve. If the U.S. withdraws from the world, evil wins. Our responsibility isn't, of course, to be the world's policeman; it is to be the *leader* of the free world. We must fulfill that responsibility by encouraging other nations to adopt freer political and economic institutions and by resisting encroachments upon our own liberty—at home and abroad.

* For the record, we received several angry letters from readers who inferred from the title here that Mr. Forbes was pro-"new world order," i.e., in favor of global government. Even a casual reading of his remarks reveals otherwise, we are happy to report.

Technology Liberates

The second event that is helping to create a new world order is the high tech revolution. Now, most people regard technology as an enemy of individual freedom—the word conjures up huge, impersonal corporations, 1984-style totalitarian governments, and, according to Hollywood lore, berserk computers that want to take over the world. Nothing could be further from the truth. Technology is in reality the mortal enemy of tyrants and bureaucrats; it doesn't suppress ordinary people—it frees them from centralized control and gives them unprecedented power over their own destinies.

As George Gilder, Warren Brookes and others have pointed out, the computer chip is the symbol of the new liberating technology of the late 20th century. This tiny invention, made of "worthless" sand, is extending the reach of the human brain the way machines extended the reach of human muscle 150 years ago. Superficially, we still think of wealth as land, as piles of gold, as material goods, and, not so long ago, as slaves and serfs. But wealth is intangible. What is oil, for instance? It is simply black ooze. You can't even feed it to camels. What makes oil valuable is human ingenuity. Similarly, it is not the pieces per se of the computer chip but the uses to which you can put them that make for real wealth. Two hundred years ago, the Scottish moral philosopher Adam Smith introduced this notion, and the world is finally beginning to acknowledge his wisdom.

Totalitarian Governments Lose Control

The third event is the failure of centralized government. Everywhere, communist and other totalitarian governments are losing control. As their citizens get a little taste of freedom, they want more. Even in the most closed societies a person can fax written documents, receive satellite communications, and transfer billions of dollars in an instant via computer—in such an environment, how can repressive regimes do more than postpone their own inevitable collapse?

It comes down to a simple choice: nations can, as I said before, imitate the U.S. and adopt freer political and economic institutions, or they can continue, for a limited time, down the old path of slavery and dictatorship. Some nations will blindly choose the latter course. After decades of brutal war, North Vietnam conquered South Vietnam in the 1970s. The Viet Cong leadership immediately instituted the traditional kind of totalitarian tyranny in the South and, as a consequence, the best, most productive citizens sought (and still seek) escape, many losing their lives in the attempt. What has been achieved? Only more brutality. In the 1990s, it is poverty and economic devastation that are conquering the conquerors in this Marxist "paradise."

By contrast, look at what happened to Western Europe and Japan after World War II. These regions were in complete ruin. Experts thought it would be decades, indeed, generations, before they would recover. But within eight years their economic output *exceeded* their prewar record levels. Why were they able to make such a rapid comeback after near-total physical destruction? Because they had the political, economic and cultural skills to rebuild quickly. They had the "know-how" and the freedom to exploit and expand that knowledge.

Economic vs. Political Integration

Another thing to remember about the new world order is that it will not bring about political unity; it is quite likely, in fact, that we will see political disintegration at the same time that we see more economic integration. Let me give you a hypothetical example. Canada is a nation torn by strife between so-called Anglophones and Francophones. French-dominated Quebec has even threatened secession. What would be the consequences of such a serious political rupture? Quebec would still have a free trade agreement with the United States. It could still prosper and maintain strong economic ties with the rest of Canada. Different political systems don't preclude economic integration.

The same is true for Western Europe, where economic integration is imminent, but where political integration is as unrealistic as it is undesirable. While in office, Britain's former prime minister Margaret Thatcher fought against the kind of political unification and bureaucratization that they had in mind in Brussels, and her firm stance appears to be paying off now that her successor, Mr. Major, has appeared on stage making polite, soothing noises but essentially carrying on the same policies. Even in the Soviet Union there are signs that meaningful economic integration is on the way. The Baltic states, the Ukraine and other regions of the USSR may follow the example Finland set back in 1917 when it successfully broke away from the old czar's Russian empire and managed to stay independent. Today, Finland, a tiny nation with fewer than six million people, is one of the more prosperous countries in the West. In the new world order, any country—no matter how small or downtrodden—can achieve prosperity.

REQUIREMENTS FOR PROSPERITY

Whether it is Eastern or Western Europe, Latin America, the Soviet Union, Asia, or anywhere, there are four basic requirements that must be met if that prosperity is to be achieved in the new world order. They are amazingly simple, but all too often the experts, from policymakers to Ph.D. economists, ignore them:

Sound Currency

The first requirement is that a country must have real money, meaning a sound currency. The Soviet Union's desperate attempt to implement perestroika proves that a sound currency isn't merely an option; virtually every Soviet economic reform has failed. Why? Because rubles are worthless. The defeated and demoralized Axis powers—Germany, Japan and Italy—were in just such a state of collapse after World War II, but their miraculous economic recoveries were all preceded by currency reform. Unfortunately, how this postwar miracle was achieved has been all but forgotten. Today, centralized organizations like the International Monetary Fund and the World Bank typically encourage currency devaluations (and hence, inflation) and disastrous fiscal policies.

Low Taxes and Tariffs

The second requirement is low taxes and tariffs. Germany and Japan reduced their tax rates in the late 1940s and early 1950s and Korea did so in the 1960s—all saw their GNP rise dramatically. Hong Kong is also an outstanding example of what such incentives can do to create new wealth and a booming economy. High taxes and high tariffs don't create wealth—they destroy it.

Property Rights

The third requirement is legally protected property rights. What could be easier to understand than this basic freedom? The right to buy, hold and sell property lies at the heart of all economic activity. But what about a poor debt-ridden country like Mexico that is sitting upon vast reserves of oil? Why isn't Mexico prospering? Because nationalized and semi-nationalized companies control oil production, just as they control most of Mexico's abundant natural resources. Who wants to drill for oil when it will be seized by the state?

Minimal Barriers for Businesses

The fourth requirement is minimal bureaucratic barriers for setting up and operating businesses. Several years ago Peruvian economist Hernando de Soto published a monumental study, *The Other Path,* documenting the difficulty of setting up a business in Peru. He estimated that if you followed all the legal rules and regulations—dotted the i's and crossed the t's, and the illegal ones—paying numerous bribes at every step of the way—it would take a minimum waiting period of nine months before you received permission to open a tailor shop, sell retail merchandise, or establish virtually any kind of small business.

Peru is not alone; many countries penalize the would-be entrepreneurs that are the backbone of any prosperous economy. Some, like the United States, which is gradually tightening the noose around the neck of its small businessmen, need to de-regulate; some, like the Soviet Union, need to completely restructure their economy in order to allow any degree of meaningful market activity.

THE THIRD WORLD: CRISIS AND OPPORTUNITY

Nowhere is the need to implement these basic requirements greater, however, than in the Third World. It is not capitalism but their governments' refusal to adopt a sound currency, low taxes and tariffs, property rights, and minimum bureaucratic interference that condemns Third World nations to poverty, debt and stagnation. If you look at the debt burdens of Brazil and Mexico, for example, it is not their level of indebtedness that is the real problem. They are, in fact, no worse off than the United States, Australia or Canada at the turn of the century. What makes the difference is that they are over-bureaucratized, over-taxed and over-regulated.

Just a few years ago, Argentina and South Korea had equal levels of debt. Pick up any financial journal today and you will read about South Korea's steel manufacturing, its ship building and its computer chip sales. Argentina is more likely to make headlines for whatever is latest in a series of central planning disasters. But that does not mean that Argentina ought to try to clone South Korea's success. Not all prosperous Third World nations are identical, and not all have as much political and economic freedom as exists in the U.S. Just look at the so-called "tigers" of the Pacific Rim–Hong Kong, Taiwan, South Korea and Singapore–they operate in very different ways even though they share a general commitment to free market policies.

Economic Predictions

What gains has the emerging new world order brought for the Third World thus far? Let's turn again to Latin America. For over three centuries, Latin America has suffered under the yoke of economic feudalism–you also see it in Africa, the Middle East and the Soviet Union where it goes by a different name: socialism. But in Mexico the Salinas government is reducing trade barriers and economic regulations and is reforming the tax code. That's why Mexico is now growing at a rate it hasn't seen in 10 years, and that's not counting the informal signs of the economy's tremendous growth. One such index is the electricity industry–it is expanding three to four times faster than the Mexican economy as a whole. When the U.S./Mexico free trade agreement is signed, other countries will undoubtedly seek to join the new free trade zone and there's no reason why Latin America couldn't be experiencing growth rates comparable to the Pacific Rim by the end of the decade.

A number of Latin American countries are readying themselves for just such an economic miracle. Through free market reforms and increased exports, Chile has seen its economy skyrocket in a way that seemed impossible a few years ago. Venezuela, which was nationalizing industries in the 1970s, is preparing to embark upon an impressive privatization program in the 1990s. Brazil's government recently fired its socialist minister of finance and replaced her with a public champion of low taxation and free trade—perhaps the first to hold such a post in 400 years. In Argentina, the current minister of finance (at least he was still in office as of this writing) has actually tied his nation's currency to the U.S. dollar. Overnight, interest rates dropped from 200 percent to under 20 percent.

Peru's story has been even more dramatic. The mass media is filled with reports about terrorism, guerilla wars, and the tragic cholera epidemic in this small, beleaguered nation. Yet behind the scenes the foundation is being laid for a prosperous future. The newly elected Fujimori government is reforming the tax code and business licensing, reducing tariffs, and, most important of all, it is instituting genuine land reform. As a result, Peru's thriving underground economy is also being brought into the fold.

The Third World is not the only place where the winds of change are blowing. In France, leftism is all but dead—it is not only intellectually respectable to be anti-communist, it is to be a part of the mainstream. Since Paris, for good or for ill, has always set the intellectual fashions for the rest of the world, we can place great significance upon this fact. There are signs that the fashion has spread even to the previously impenetrable radical left wing of the Catholic church. The same priests and bishops who championed liberation theology in the 1970s are gradually realizing that poverty can only be cured by less state intervention, not more.

LESSONS FOR THE U.S.

While the new world order continues to develop abroad, it has had some setbacks in the United States. Yet there's no reason why the United States shouldn't, despite a very poor start in the beginning of this decade, enjoy one of the most productive periods in its economic history.

The Unnecessary Recession

The recent recession was one of the most *unnecessary* downturns of the post-war era. It was not preceded by inflation or by a rapid rise in inventories, and it wasn't brought on merely by the Persian Gulf War. Three major mistakes are to blame. First, the Federal Reserve kept interest rates too high too long. When the economy was booming several years ago, the Fed decided to raise interest rates with the express purpose of slowing it down. That's the proper way, according to the collective wisdom of all central bankers, to fight inflation.

Compounding that error was a second one: a regulatory reign of terror unleashed by politicians and lawyers in the aftermath of the S&L and junk bond scandals. As a result, many institutions were suddenly unable or unwilling to lend to otherwise creditworthy customers. And then the U.S. Treasury Department went on one of its periodic binges trying to knock the value of the dollar down. Not surprisingly, the dollar fell, unable to recover until the bureaucrats backed off earlier this year.

The third mistake was even more damaging. With an exquisite sense of timing, our leaders in Washington, D.C. decided just as we were slipping into a recession to call for a big tax increase. States and municipalities have been doing the same thing, thus contributing to an entirely avoidable economic downturn. Congress also failed to pass a meaningful cut in the capital gains tax. The rate that we have now—one of the highest in the world—keeps money locked into old investments, stalls innovation and new technology, and kills off thousands of potentially successful small businesses.

One of the biggest canards ever foisted upon the American public is that capital gains cuts exploit the poor and shield the rich—the truth is that they benefit everyone. By the same reasoning, high capital gains taxes hurt everyone, regardless of their tax bracket. If you take a one dollar bill and double it each year, after 20 years, it will have compounded to a total sum of one million dollars. But if you take that same one dollar bill, double it each year and then subtract 35 percent in taxes, after 20 years it will have generated only about $24,000. Let's look at it in another way. In the mid-1960s, the U.S. Dow Jones reached 1,000 points. Japan's Dow Jones was a little over 1,000. Since then the U.S. capital gains tax (depending on state and local taxes) has averaged between 28 and 35 percent. In Japan, the figure has been zero to five percent. Recently, we cheered when the U.S. Dow Jones touched the 3000 mark. In Japan, despite a severe stock market crash last year, the Nikkei Dow Jones is over 22,000. The truth is that taxes are not merely a means of collecting revenue; they are a price and if the price on innovation, productivity, success, and earning good incomes is too high, we are simply going to get less of them.

Practicing What We Preach About Free Markets

We need to practice what we preach about free markets and pay more attention to the four basic requirements for prosperity in the new world order. That's where we as individuals can have an important impact by reminding our families, our friends, our local communities and our state and national representatives that freedom, not more state control, is the key to the future. Here are just two examples of realizable reforms that we can start pushing for right now. Let me stress that these are random examples—we can substitute many others: (1) Congressmen should be forced to obey the laws that they pass for the rest of us. Right now they are exempt from some very basic ones. (2) We can help limit government spending by pressuring the states to adopt privatization programs that return basic services to the private sector.

These are flanking movements rather than trench warfare. And they are far more likely to succeed than, say, trying to slash Social Security or the entire domestic budget. You spend a lot of capital on such crusades and get very little return for it. Yet they do affect larger issues. Look at spiralling health care costs, for instance. A reform that ought to be considered is giving tax incentives to individuals to buy their own insurance instead of mandating that corporations offer expensive health plans that, in the end, are paid for by the consumer through higher prices on goods and services. Health IRAs would certainly be a popular solution to what threatens to be one of the thorniest domestic problems of the decade.

What about another big issue—the "underclass" in America? It is largely concentrated in the inner city and, depending on whose numbers you believe, ranges from 5 to 12 percent of the population. Jack Kemp argues that while we have a free market economy for about 90 percent of the population, we have a Soviet-style economy for this underclass. The economic incentives for getting out of it are few. You lose a lot of benefits. The effective tax rate if you start to earn an independent living can be 90 or 100 percent. And the rules about what you can do with your own money are severely restrictive, as one Milwaukee mother learned. She had saved several thousand dollars to send her child to college and when the welfare bureau found out about it, she was sentenced to 15 years for fraud. Worse yet, welfare rules by their very nature encourage illegitimacy and the breakup of families.

Beyond Economics: Encouraging a Moral Revival

Just as the destructive effect of 19th-century England's gin mills led to the rise of Methodism, the problems of the underclass and of our secular, often nihilistic culture may encourage a moral revival in the 1990s. History records that in 1830 the U.S. suffered from a per capita drinking rate nearly five times higher than it is today. Then came the first broad-based public health reform in this country. It was called Temperance, and, unlike Prohibition, it was a voluntary, religiously-inspired movement. Ten years after it began, the per capita drinking rate was halved.

Clearly, people do respond to moral messages. Today it's no longer an "in" thing in most circles to smoke pot or shoot up. The exception is in the inner cities where heavy drug use can be linked to economic deprivation and, most importantly, to the lack of moral instruction that families and churches can provide.

At the very least in any moral revival, you can give people responsibility— most of them eventually respond to it. For those who claim that the underclass, largely made up of minorities, can't accept much responsibility because they can't compete in a world where there is so much social injustice or because of cultural/racial barriers, there is plenty of evidence to suggest otherwise.

A hundred and fifty years ago, the Catholic church sought to help improve the deplorable condition of Irish immigrants in the cities. The acknowledged experts claimed that the Irish were too backward, too ignorant, and "very poor human material." The experts were wrong. When people want to get ahead, it's amazing the skills they can acquire. In the Persian Gulf, American enlisted men and women, many of them 18-20 year-old kids, learned to handle sophisticated equipment and pull off complex, demanding military maneuvers—and 23 percent of them were black.

There are hundreds of other examples that prove the same point in the U.S. and around the globe. A restoration of moral values is possible for all people, not just for the privileged, not just for members of one racial or ethnic group or of one nation. Of everything the real "new world order" offers, this is perhaps the most important blessing of all.

ABOUT THE AUTHOR

Malcolm S. Forbes, Jr. is the president and chief executive officer of Forbes, Inc., and editor-in-chief of *Forbes*, which, with a paid circulation of nearly 750,000, is the world's largest business journal. He is the regular editor of its popular "Fact and Comment" section, chairman of Forbes Newspapers, Inc. and serves on the board of numerous civic, business and educational organizations, including the Board for International Broadcasting, which he chairs and which oversees Radio Free Europe and Radio Liberty, the Ronald Reagan Presidential Foundation, and the Foundation for Student Communication.

CAPITALISM AND
THE FUTURE OF AMERICA

George Roche
(Special Edition) 1988

he brilliant young economist George Gilder has written that the most important event in recent history is "the demise of the socialist dream." However, he also notes "the failure of capitalism to win a corresponding triumph."

Why is this so, when capitalism has so obviously provided more material benefits for every individual, regardless of economic or social condition, than any other system in the history of the world? Why, when capitalism's intellectual defense has been so ably undertaken by some of the greatest minds of our time, is socialism, thinly disguised, still taught in our schools and promoted by our politicians? And why, when capitalism's results are so demonstrably humanitarian, is it still seen as a symbol for greed and exploitation?

The perplexing answers to these questions share a common root: They all lie in the realm of ideas. Ideas, I find myself often saying, rule the world—not armies, not economics, not politics, not any of the things to which we usually give our allegiance, but ideas. "Ideas have consequences"—in just three words Richard Weaver encapsulated an entire philosophy of life that is also a challenge, a call to action for all of us.

Throughout history there have been formative moments in which particular ideas and particular leaders have exerted a profound impact on the character and events of a nation. These special epochs, marked by the emergence of a new consensus, can readily be found in American history. The first great sea-change in American society occurred fully 150 years before the American Revolution when our colonial ancestors enjoyed a large measure of self-government. From the first, the American colonial experience had drawn heavily upon the traditional liberties of British subjects, and upon their rich heritage of individual freedom guaranteed by the Magna Charta.

By the eighteenth century, however, the British were pursuing a different goal. A new economic idea, mercantilism, dominated British thinking. Government planning and control regulated society and manipulated individuals. Eventually, the American colonists ran out of patience with this growing governmental interference in their affairs. During the summer of 1776, Thomas Jefferson wrote the Declaration of Independence, a revolutionary document destined to represent liberty for the American republic as long as it should endure.

Ironically, during that same summer in 1776, a little book was published thousands of miles away from the American colonies, a book destined to have a profound effect on the real American Revolution. The author, Adam Smith, was a professor of moral philosophy at the University of Glasgow, and the book was *The Wealth of Nations*. As a moral philosopher, Smith contended that men must be free to make their own decisions because, if they are not, a moral paralysis soon sets in. From this basic truth, he examined mercantilism and discovered that this early form of the planned economy was denying men freedom of choice and thus distorting British society. Eleven years later, fifty-five men met in Philadelphia to draft our Constitution. Motivated in part by the ideas articulated by Jefferson and Smith, our founding fathers charted our national path toward limited government, the dignity of free men, and the marvelous prosperity we have enjoyed in this country.

T he next great sea-change in our nation's history occurred around the turn of the twentieth century. Unfortunately, these new ideas favored the collective over the individual, redirecting America on an increasingly hazardous path as the century progressed. The setting was ripe. For years, as America's industries boomed, immigrants poured in, and cities mushroomed, it began to seem to some that the scale of life itself had become so magnified that the common man no longer had a fair chance to get ahead in the world. Far from what one might expect, the momentum for collectivism was imparted not by public figures but by little known men of ideas whose names not one in a hundred Americans would recognize.

In certain elite circles, some wondered whether the answers for America's growing pains might not lie elsewhere than in the common sense of the founding fathers and the tested traditions of our Judeo-Christian heritage–and whether those answers might not instead be found in the work of certain "daring" European thinkers like Marx, Darwin, and Freud whose ideas had rocked the Old World during the 1800s.

So a relative handful of professors and intellectuals, writing in the first years of this century and drawing on iconoclastic theories already well advanced in Europe, brought those ideas to America and began a process that remade the face of American society within thirty years, roughly between 1900 and 1930. These collectivist ideas spread from a few seminal thinkers, to the second- and third-hand purveyors of ideas–teachers, ministers, the working press–the word wielders. The collective mentality continued to spread, reaching the professions, the business community, the courts, the novelists, the artists, the general public and last–always last–the politicians. Of the first seminal thinkers of the new era, John Dewey has had a lasting impact on our philosophy, our education, our culture, and, ultimately, our government. From his "progressive school" experiment of the mid-1890s at the University of Chicago, Dewey advocated a system of education which would produce a new generation of Americans with a preference for group and social activity and who viewed themselves not as individuals but as members of a "total democratic society." He emphasized the unfinished nature of society and the universe, and called for "a new kind of religion" to be derived from human experience and relationships.

Dewey's intellectual colleagues were themselves busy on other fronts. At Columbia, anthropologist Ruth Benedict and her mentor Franz Boas were developing the idea that man could be understood only as a social animal, since his character was the exclusive creation of his society and environment. Charles Beard's *An Economic Interpretation of the Constitution* was another key turning point. He set aside the traditional ideas of American society in favor of an essentially Marxian philosophy of history in which the founding fathers were portrayed as having placed the economic welfare of a few ahead of the total social welfare of all.

The flamboyant Thorstein Veblen poured out his bitter frustration on the business community in shrill anticapitalist diatribes like *The Theory of the Leisure Class*. Meanwhile, Veblen's fellow economists John R. Commons and Richard Ely pioneered in charting a vastly expanded role for organized labor in the new collectivity. Sociologist Lester Frank Ward, one of the true patron saints of the modern American collectivist ideal, saw politics as a manipulating device designed to control all society, stating: "Modern society is suffering from the very opposite of paternalism—from under-government." In Ward, all those years ago, we thus find the original germ of an idea which has been central to the social planner's rhetoric from the New Deal era to the present.

By 1932, the year the arch-collectivist and political pragmatist Franklin D. Roosevelt was elected president, the intellectual revolutionaries had already done their work, and they rapidly became the new political establishment. Under FDR, the new generation of intellectuals managed to use the Depression as a pretext for a massive collectivization of American society throughout the decade of the 1930s. They failed to cure the Depression, but a "fortunate" circumstance—World War II—did it for them. After the war, the social engineers stood ready with further collectivist gimmicks such as the Full Employment Act of 1946.

There was steady pressure throughout the Truman years for major expansion of the federal role in health, in education, and in welfare—pressure that finally resulted in new government programs under the succeeding Republican president, Dwight D. Eisenhower. Thus Eisenhower proved once again that Republican administrations usually ratify rather than reverse the collectivist inroads of their Democratic predecessors. The same pattern of ratification and acceleration was repeated two decades later when the Nixon and Ford administrations helped consolidate most of Lyndon Johnson's Great Society programs, exacerbated the oil crisis and other economic woes through an unprecedented program of peace-time wage-and-price controls, and presided over the regulatory explosion of the early 1970s.

In the last months of the Reagan presidency, we were already wondering if the pattern had been repeated. Many saw Reagan's election in 1980 and his subsequent reelection in 1984 as genuine evidence of Americans' disenchantment with government, a disenchantment which cuts across ideological lines and is an inevitable reaction to the love affair with statism which has been carried on for so long. But whatever one thought of Reagan's actual accomplishments, it was uncertain whether much had changed. His critics crowed over the end of the Reagan era, convinced that it was the end of conservatism's brief resurgence.

U ndeniably the idea of capitalism, a central tenet of conservatism, remains under constant assault, and its detractors comprise a majority in our schools, our media and perhaps even our political and cultural leadership communities. One faction we may dub the "anti-capitalists," those who regard the redistribution of wealth in the name of "economic justice" as the proper goal of all economic activity. They claim that modern capitalism began with the Industrial Revolution and heralded child labor, wage slavery, urban squalor and a Hobbesian existence for the working class. The late 20th century, they insist, is still an era of exploitation.

A second group, however, focuses less on capitalism's evils than its alleged inadequacies. It is all right to defend free enterprise, so the reasoning goes, but today there are simply too many demands on the system—too many poor, too many problems, too many inequities—for individuals or the free market to handle. Government must, therefore, step in and act as the problem-solver. Far more people, I suspect, belong to this group than the first. They have accepted the need for intervention even though they may harbor no hostility to capitalism.

Both groups are obsessively results-oriented. They begin with the premise that the world is perfectible and that man possesses the means to perfect it through his own reason and through man-made institutions. Capitalism simply cannot fulfill their expectations. Yet no amount of intellect and no economic system, no man-made system at all for that matter, can cure every ill the world produces; it probably can't even cure half of them. Sadly, the false notion persists that some other system, some other grand vision, can achieve the impossible.

The central idea of capitalism does not lie in the miracle of the market or even the ingenuity of the entrepreneur. It rests, rather, on the fundamental principle of freedom. One of the great sources of strength for America has been our commitment to economic, political and religious freedom. Within our open society, individuals are free to provide for themselves and their families, to compete with others and to join with them in voluntary associations. We have been free to support those professions, businesses, schools, hospitals, churches, and cultural institutions which best meet our individual needs and preferences. In other words, we have prospered with competition and voluntary association in the private sector. We have done so, moreover, not because of any abstract ideology, but because we found it to be a system that works well. In the words of George Santayana, "The American people have made a philosophy out of not having a philosophy." The American economy, despite its ups and downs and the serious threats it faces from overregulation, the deficit, and the other problems of our times, has worked beautifully beyond the wildest dreams of the utopian social planners. But it has worked precisely because we have allowed individuals to act freely on their own.

Self-transcendence is the ability to rise above the merely animal, merely physical self, and freely choose the conditions and terms of our own existence, to decide what is of ultimate importance and act upon it whether or not other people understand, whether or not it is dangerous, whether or not it makes us rich or poor. Only human beings have that capacity. Only you and I do. We have the capacity to rise above our merely physical selves.

Self-transcendence, based on individual choice, touches every aspect of our lives. If economic transactions were based on the immediate cave man rip-off—the idea that I want to grab all I can get, and I want to get it right now, and I will not honor any obligation that interferes with this—no long-term economic planning, no economic contract would be possible. No investment, nothing of what we call a capital structure, could ever come into existence, unless legal contracts are honored. That necessitates self-transcending people, people willing to honor long-term commitments. That is also the leadership commitment we are discussing. All civilization is based upon the integrity of the self-responsible individual, directed by a view of justice, of restraint, and of responsibility.

There was a time when this country of ours valued such an idea. It placed its faith in the responsible individual and the institutional structure giving form to our lives. And it is the erosion of that faith which today destroys us from within. I submit to you that unless we recover it, all the methods in the world to do something better economically, technologically, or socially are just so much spitting in the wind. We must insist upon a return to a hierarchy of values which gives primacy to the dignity of the individual and to the institutional forms which guarantee that dignity. It is here that the free market, private property, private institutions—that whole private sector idea—has special validity, because it does leave people free to build their own voluntary associations, to be uniquely self-transcending, to get on with the dignity of leading their own lives.

Remember, then, when we as leaders are talking about the private sector, that we are committed to this not because it works, though it works very well. All kinds of economic arguments demonstrate that the free market provides prosperity. It solves social problems. It works. But that is not the argument that we should advance. People are not inspired by the promise that they will have more refrigerators if they are free men. Our message must not be that the free market is good because it works, but rather that it works because it is good—because it has the fundamentally proper view of human nature.

This is what capitalism offers for our American future. Together we can invest our resources and energies in a system which provides a level of prosperity and personal dignity unheralded in the history of the world. Its legacy of freedom, passed from one generation to the next, is now ours to defend for our children, and for all who will follow.

ABOUT THE AUTHOR

George Roche has served as president of Hillsdale College since 1971. "Firing Line," the "MacNeil-Lehrer News Hour," "Today," *Newsweek, Time, Reader's Digest* and the *Wall Street Journal* have chronicled his efforts to keep the College free from federal intrusion. Formerly the presidentially appointed chairman of the National Council on Educational Research, the director of seminars at the Foundation for Economic Education, a professor of history at the Colorado School of Mines, and a U.S. Marine, Dr. Roche is the author of ten books, including five Conservative Book Club selections, among them: *America by the Throat: The Stranglehold of Federal Bureaucracy* (Devin-Adair, 1985), *A World Without Heroes: The Modern Tragedy* (Hillsdale College Press, 1987), *Going Home* (Jameson Books, 1986), and *A Reason for Living* (Hillsdale College Press, 1989). His most recent book is *One by One: Preserving Freedom and Values in Heartland America* (Hillsdale College Press, 1990).